Miracles & Other Realities

*To Dave Todd
With Best Wishes
Lee Pulos*

Lee Pulos and Gary Richman

Miracles & Other Realities

Published in association with Robert Briggs

OMEGA PRESS
Vancouver and San Francisco

Distributed by **Gordon Soules Book
Publishers Ltd.** ● 1359 Ambleside Lane,
West Vancouver, BC, Canada V7T 2Y9
● PMB 620, 1916 Pike Place #12,
Seattle, WA 98101-1097 US
E-mail: books@gordonsoules.com
Web site: http://www.gordonsoules.com
(604) 922 6588 Fax: (604) 688 5442

Omega Press, San Francisco

© 1990 by Lee Pulos and Gary Richman
All rights reserved. Published 1990
Printed in the United States of America

First Edition

Designed by Side by Side Studios, San Francisco

Library of Congress Catalog Card Number 90-060922
ISBN 0-929-110-18-8
ISBN 0-929-110-20-X pbk.

All photos are by the author

Contents

	Foreword by Lyall Watson	vii
	Introduction	xi
1.	Glimpses of the Future	1
2.	Cultural Climate and the Early Years	15
3.	Struck by Lightning	29
4.	Mandrake Is Alive and Well and Living in Brazil	42
5.	Geller Comes to Brazil	58
6.	Scientists and the Psychic	79
7.	First Contact	102
8.	The General and the Psychic	125
9.	Divine Inspiration	142

10.	Transmutations and Transformations	161
11.	Perspectives	189
12.	Conceptualizations and Implications	216
	Epilogue	239
	References	249

Foreword

I have never met Thomaz, but I feel that I know him.

This account of his abilities by Lee Pulos and Gary Richman makes it quite clear that Thomaz Morais Coutinho is one of the most exciting discoveries in the history of the paranormal—as important in his own way as Daniel Douglas Home, Tony Agpaoa, or Uri Geller.

Everything about Thomaz rings true. His exuberance, his childlike enthusiasm, and his wayward ways are characteristic of many of those who stand at the center of strange experience. They share an ability to suspend disbelief, to treat the world in an unselfconscious and playful way.

They also share an ability to disturb, to leave those who work with them in a state of considerable confusion. I know the feeling well and, like the authors, have yet to find a way of dealing with it successfully.

When someone breaks all the rules right in front of your eyes, what can you do about it? Who do you tell? And why on earth should anyone believe you?

For some of us this is not an academic problem. It is a very real personal dilemma.

I believe that parapsychology matters, that it is asking some important questions. I feel certain that if it is to make any real progress, it must break out of the scientific straitjacket imposed by a perceived need to produce evidence in the form of a repeatable experiment. Anomalous experience is not like that. It is elusive, whimsical, and capricious, dependent on its context, and by its very nature unrepeatable. But nonetheless real for all that.

I see the need to develop an ethnography of the paranormal, a field technique that uses unobtrusive methods to explore paranormal experience without, as far as possible, disturbing it in any way. This is not easy, but it is at least possible with subjects such as Thomaz, who may be unpredictable but do perform often enough to reward a patient observer.

Lee Pulos and Gary Richman give a fascinating account of Thomaz's talents, which seem to range from clairvoyance to psychokinesis to whole carnivals of metal-bending. Thomaz has enough abilities to keep a convention of parapsychologists busy for years, but, as always, the mysterious is governed by its own Catch-22. Nobody is going to believe any of it without proof, which in our culture means seeing it for oneself, either in person or on camera. Moreover, a culture that also recognizes and marvels at skilled illusionists adept in both live deception at close quarters and in the creation of special cinematic effects will find Thomaz's feats hard to believe anyway.

The evidence for all paranormal experience is unsatisfactory in any event. It consists not of experiments, but of reports of experiments that are essentially unverifiable. All we have is someone else's word for what they believe took place.

Evidence, even in the hardest sciences, is not very different. It all boils down in the end to trust. I believe in the electron, for instance, even though I have never seen one for myself. I accept someone else's word for it. I have to. I am forced to base my belief, not on scientific evidence, but on social and political judgments. The only freedom I have is to choose my experts, my sources of information, as carefully as I can.

In the case of Thomaz, I am inclined to accept the account offered here, not just because I know and trust Lee Pulos, but because it feels right. It fits with what I know of similar experience elsewhere.

I am impressed also by the authors' willingness to deal with even the most outrageous experience as psychological fact, as a part of a belief system with a direct influence on those involved. I look forward to a time when we can turn anthropological parapsychology into a proper discipline with its own accepted methodology. Until then, I suggest that we can profit by offering a conditional, but warm welcome to honest attempts of this kind.

I hope to hear more of Thomaz.

Lyall Watson
London, England

Introduction

The only road to a fuller grasp of reality is the exploration of "super-natural" perception.
Albert Schweitzer

In Pouso Alegre, a small town two hundred kilometers from São Paulo, Brazil, six persons sit down at a table to observe a young pharmacist named Thomaz Green Morton. He has been described as "very ordinary" yet, with increasing frequency, he is creating deep shudders among scientists and the cherished laws of physics. In addition to the two authors are Tom Gorman, the marketing manager of Kodak of Brazil; his wife Eloise, a psychologist; Jim Jensen, president of a large successful American corporation; and Thomaz, in his usual attire—stripped to the waist.

Thomaz explains that his forearms are becoming "tingly," a signal that his "personal energy" is building up. He identifies the energy as a "transmutational force." On Thomaz's instructions, Jim pulls a silver dollar from his pocket and holds it in his tightly closed fist. No one else touches the coin; Thomaz sits six feet away, directly across the table, and asks each of us to hold something metallic in our hands to act as "conductors" of energy. A number of bent spoons and forks are lying around, the results of Thomaz's psychic work, and each of us chooses one.

Thomaz closes his eyes; his whole body becomes taut. Just as he is about to release the energy, he asks Jim for his astrological birth sign. When Jim replies "Pisces," Thomaz requests that we all invoke the sign by chanting "feesh-feesh" over and over. After a minute or so, Jim says that nothing has happened; he has experienced no sensations in his closed fist. Then he opens his hand.

The silver dollar has disappeared, presumably forever. In its place is a beautiful medallion—half again as large as the original coin. On one side of the medallion, two porpoises dance along the edge and the word *peixes* (Portuguese for Pisces) is imprinted along the bottom; on the other side, the twelve astrological signs are beautifully etched in the metal.

In the days ahead, this medallion would come to symbolize for us experiences that mock the laws of physics and presumptions about what we cherished as reality. Our lives and our way of perceiving time, space, and causality were never to be the same again. Once we had been touched by *authentic* magic—a state of being one with nature, not the sleight-of-hand of stage magicians—we realized the vast reservoir of human energies and resources. It raised old questions in a new way. It illuminated the possibility that answers to questions about the countless dimensions of human consciousness lie in the subtleties and shadows of the paranormal rather than the scientific versions of reality. Science, with its annihilating skepticism, tends to scale down the dimensions of human existence to that of a dreary mechanistic ghetto, destitute of any pathways of personal enlightenment or hope about our destiny.

What about Thomaz? What sort of person can so easily and quickly make shambles of our order of the universe? Is he a once-in-a-lifetime "freak" to be rationalized away? Or is he a window through which to see the future—an omen of laws of nature yet undiscovered?

One gets neither of these impressions in meeting Thomaz for

the first time. Born March 16, 1947, he has either worked in or owned pharmacies since he was seventeen. An early marriage produced a daughter, and he is the doting father of a son from his second marriage. Of average build and height, Thomaz has a shock of curly dark hair; he is almost always smiling and his eyes have a sparkle that complements his restless nature. His most characteristic feature is his spontaneity, his total immersion in life—he thrives on being with people and enjoys drinking and carousing with friends. Thomaz loves to sit over extended dinners and tell warm, humorous stories about his friends. On the other hand, he is also very unreliable about time and appointments. To the frustration of almost everyone, he regulates his life by an internal clock totally "out of sync" with any outer reality. While he recognizes that his powers are strange and exceptional, Thomaz is perhaps no closer to understanding their origins than any of his friends or the scientists who have spent hundreds of hours observing and analyzing him.

One of the guiding themes of this book is best illustrated by an old Sufi tale. A drunken oaf who searches for his lost keys under a lamppost is joined by a good samaritan. After a period of unsuccessful searching, the drunk is asked if he is certain that the lost keys are indeed under the light. "No," he replies, "I lost them in the bushes but it is too difficult to search where there is no illumination."

That story in many ways represents the dilemma of science today. It is much easier to do research under the bright surgical lights of a scientific laboratory, where one can carefully follow the choreographed rules of a mechanistic reality than to do field research—with all its uncertainties and lack of controls. If we are to illuminate the edges of our ignorance, the keys or answers to anomalies lie in the bushes. I like the term "psychic naturalist," which Roberts (1981) has used to distinguish field researchers from laboratory scientists. That naturalistic attitude has characterized our approach to Thomaz.

This book is about Thomaz—the man, his phenomena, and the impact of his "miracles" on the people who have been exposed to him. It is also an attempt to explore levels of explanation and a conceptual framework for those "miracles." After spending long periods carefully observing Thomaz, we began to see him as a metaphor for personal transformation, a living allegory, if you will, of the deep connection in each of us with the magical elements of our nature.

Physicist David Bohm (1983) pointed out that ever since Galileo, science has filtered and objectified nature by peering at it through lenses. This has applied to both the macroscopic universes of astronomers and the electron microscopic worlds-within-worlds of the small-particle physicist. Astrophysicist Michael Ovendon (1984) extends this analogy even further. Everyone looks at the world through his own personal lenses; these allow us to perceive reality in a certain way and to filter out what is incompatible with our belief system. Thus, the philosophical filter of many scientists allows them to view the world as a machine and human beings are reduced to biological machines, assembled from the building blocks of cells, tissues, and organs. The permanence of consciousness, however, does not fit in with a machine metaphor.

More recently, the Pribham-Bohm (1986) holographic model has animated the lenses and perception of the world by bringing the material and nonmaterial worlds together. The two scientists postulate an underlying energy field of consciousness beyond space and time. This field becomes "real" as the brain "lifts" and interprets frequencies, translating them into a three-dimensional everyday world. Again, flaws and distortions in the lenses filter out part of the total picture.

The philosophical lenses of a spiritualist also reduce and limit the categories of reality by perceiving everyday earthly transactions as partly influenced by benign or malevolent spirits. Then, of course, there are the Shiite elements of Christian Fundamentalism whose lenses filter in the "devil" as a causal force when alternate realities are suggested. Physicists use mathematical and visual analogies to describe unseen realities; shamans resort to symbolism and rituals for the same purpose. Stage magicians prescribe further limits on the nature of inquiry by suggesting that all paranormal phenomena can be replicated by sleight-of-hand. They ignore, of course, that hocus-pocus trickery does not disprove the reality of the event; they only prove that it can be reproduced by trickery.

Our physical senses sometimes block more aspects of reality than they allow us to perceive. For example, over four hundred years ago, Magellan's ships anchored at Tierra del Fuego for supplies. Because the Fuegans were essentially an isolated canoe culture, the ships were so far beyond their experience that the ships were "invisible" to them despite their bulk. They could see the smaller boats coming ashore, as these craft were similar to their own canoes; but the larger ships were outside their realm of possibility. Magellan's diaries and later expeditions describe how the village shaman helped the natives "see" what they thought was preposterous and beyond belief. The shaman's experience contained possibilities far greater than the villagers' and the impossible soon became obvious to all.

In a sense, Thomaz represents a symbolic mast on our cultural horizon. He is creating widening rifts in the topmost surface of our consciousness and helping us realize the confines of our physical reality. It is perhaps both a difficulty and a blessing that no prescription lenses can be worn to translate the displays of consciousness that accompany paranormal phenomena. It has been said that the most powerful state of consciousness known to humans is an open mind. Perhaps that might be a starting point for deciphering Thomaz.

The possibilities of what we can become are in themselves real evolutionary influences, and evolution is now moving fast enough to be visible. We can participate in changing the world by changing our beliefs about the world. As we replace the usual set of lenses through which we view the world, our image of ourselves changes and new opportunities come into focus, bringing with them new energies and new resources. While there is good reason for the celebration of the emerging power of consciousness, this optimism is balanced by dilemmas and conceptual impasses in the scientific laboratories of logic. Many proponents of the mechanistic world view feel duty-bound to display skepticism as if it were a badge of honor proclaiming their intellectual superiority.

The authors consider their research and investigative methods to be as rigorous as possible under the circumstances, but due to the controversial nature of the subject, we would like to share some of the research background with the reader.

Richman conducted personal interviews with two hundred persons, ninety percent of whom witnessed Thomaz's phenomena firsthand; the other ten percent included childhood friends, schoolteachers and administrators, physicians, and others who could verify dates and places. All of these interviews were transcribed from cassette tapes, and the tapes have been preserved. Richman also kept a meticulous personal log while he was with Thomaz, noting phenomena, persons present, time sequences, locations, and even his own subjective moods, as well as those of Thomaz and others.

Richman also inspected Thomaz's home and other locations where the phenomena were observed and scrutinized the surroundings for alternative causal mechanisms, such as hidden lights. He also lived with Thomaz and his family for varying periods totalling over eight months. He traveled with the Thomaz entourage and even participated in family squabbles and arguments. "The only sore spot," Richman says, "is that the Fasqueira incident (see Chapter Three) could never be totally verified, although townspeople knew of it almost as a legend or myth."

Richman also had the cooperation of, and access to, the records of Professor Mario Amaral Machado and his wife, Dr. Gloria Machado; Helena Cunha Bueno, an independent cinematographer who filmed more than sixty hours of Thomaz phenomena and interviews; and Lada, Thomaz's cousin, who has more than four hundred audio- and videotapes made at various times of Thomaz's psychic manifestations.

Our basic guideline for selecting phenomena to include here

Introduction

was that the feat must have been witnessed by at least five persons or by persons whose reputations and testimony were unimpeachable. Priority was given to phenomena witnessed by both authors, second priority to phenomena witnessed by Richman. At all times preference was given to situations in which either military, physicians, clergy, or business executives (in short, professional persons) were involved.

Finally, Richman collected many notarized affidavits from witnesses shortly after the events described in the affidavit. These documents were made by witnesses without suggestions or provocation, as a result of individual choice, and are signed and registered.

The authors would like to acknowledge the following, without whose genial cooperation and interest the present work would not have been possible: Monsignor Arlindo Mombach, Helena Cunha Bueno, Eloise Gorman, Tom Hatch, Robert Hunter, Fred Lichota, Professor Mario Amaral Machado, Dr. Gloria Machado, Dr. Elson Montagno, Theresa Esmeralde Souza, General Moacyr Uchoa, and Jana White.

Lee Pulos, Ph.D., and Gary Richman

CHAPTER ONE

Glimpses of the Future

Skepticism taken to an extreme becomes its own form of gullibility.

Joseph Wood Krutch

Our experience with Thomaz's universe began in a distinctly Brazilian fashion—over morning coffee. Thomaz's enthusiasm about life is infectious. His speech is animated, humorous and, despite a veneer of barely controlled restlessness in social situations, he immerses himself intensely into conversations. We were fortunate to share rare reflective intervals during isolated periods with him. In the hundreds of experiences that we participated in together he never once spoke unkindly, nor did he gossip even benignly about any of his friends.

Thomaz is also a very earthy, robust man with undeniable shortcomings. There are baffling inconsistencies between his professed spiritual yearnings and undisguised materialistic preoccupations. His insensitivity to people's needs and simple social necessities sometimes pushed us to the edge of bursting into a rage. He seems to sense when the "dam is cracking," however, and very quickly and sensitively he would do something very tender and affectionate to offset his callousness. Inevitably, our resentment would quickly melt away. This first morning, however, was intended to be light and exploratory. After we sat down, Thomaz picked up a teaspoon to stir his coffee. As he was stirring, we observed the spoon curl up in a complete 360-degree "loop-the-loop" fashion.

A second spoon also bent spontaneously as Thomaz lowered it into the cup. We took the spoons and could not straighten them without exerting considerable force. Comparing the two spoons, we found that they were almost exact duplicates of each other—both twisted in an identical fashion.

This was to become a common occurrence. Spontaneous metal-bending, like some sort of periodic psychic eruption, would occur in his presence whether he was touching or not touching the metal objects. Sometimes metal objects bent before our eyes when he was in the house but not in the same room as the phenomena. Thomaz's reaction to the metal-bending was one of excitement and enthusiasm. We were astounded by his childlike wonder every time a phenomenon occurred. Even though he had probably bent metal or transmuted and materialized objects thousands of times, he celebrated each occasion as if it were the first occurrence.

We agreed to travel with Thomaz from São Paulo to his home in Pouso Alegre. In this way we could observe him naturally and spontaneously in his everyday environment. Driving with Thomaz proved to be as disconcerting as the bending spoons. He literally catapults along the highway, apparently relying on some sixth sense to serve as an antenna while he passes traffic on a curve. The Brazilians have an expression, *"fique frio"* ("keep cool"), that Thomaz used frequently during the drive, both to reassure and to admonish us.

Our anxiety about his disquieting driving habits was quickly extinguished about midway during the trip when the car's interior was suddenly pervaded with a strong jasmine/eucalyptus fragrance. At that point, Thomaz announced the presence of an "extraterrestrial entity" that he identified as "Xils." At his urging, we rolled down the windows; the pleasing scent seemed to be coming from outside and wafting into the car. The odor became stronger with all the windows open. There were five of us in the vehicle (Jim Jensen, Lada, Thomaz, Gary, and myself), and we were travelling at one hundred forty kilometers per hour. We rolled up the windows. Shortly thereafter, there was a very bright blue-white flash of light inside the car, rather like that of a camera flashbulb going off but of longer duration. This was followed by a mini-explosion of red light, which Thomaz excitedly identified as "Bios." It was an astonishing experience for us, and our immediate reactions were to consider skeptical, logical "left brain" explanations for the lights. Thomaz urged us to hold onto something metallic, which would act as a "ground" and facilitate the flow of energies. The lights flashed forty or fifty times over the next hour and twice exploded outside the moving vehicle.

During the following week we were to see these lights, or energies, in a wide variety of locales and circumstances. Sometimes they would appear fifty yards away, over the lake adjacent to Thomaz's clinic. Other times they would burst and flash in front of people, even if Thomaz was twenty yards away or perhaps in another room. Twice, Jim Jensen and I were able to mentally evoke the flashing of the energies in a closed room without the presence of Thomaz. What was even more perplexing was that the lights somehow displayed an element of consciousness, as if they were an intelligent energy. In response to questions, for example, they would flash once for "Yes" and not flash at all for "No." The accuracy of these responses varied considerably, however, and did not seem to have any consistent design in the pattern of hits and misses.

The exploding lights have been seen by hundreds of people, ranging from visiting scientists and curious Brazilian generals to the casual passersby on the street. Helena da Cunha Bueno, a São Paulo freelance cinematographer who has spent dozens of hours patiently filming Thomaz has managed to capture "Kryptos," a different "light energy," in an extraordinary sequence of videotape.

At the end of every day, the authors met alone to review tape and to record all the events of that day. We were especially alert for inconsistencies in our perceptions, the possibilities of fraud, and of course, the implications of what we had witnessed. Besides discussing Thomaz's interpretation of the lights as extraterrestrial, we also considered the possibility that the lights were a kind of "psychoenergetic" force or volatile manifestation from his subconscious.

Though these speculations will be explored more extensively in Chapter Twelve, we discovered very early that the rules of science and logical inquiry had little relevance to, or simply did not fit with, the experiences we were having. For example, Thomaz sometimes refers to the above-mentioned fragrances as a kind of "psychic sweat." He hugged a friend and the "sweat" permeated her blouse; the scent remains despite frequent washings. We were careful to note that Thomaz was not wearing cologne that day. On another occasion, he put his finger to his tongue and transferred a touch of saliva to his friend's shirt in order to demonstrate the staying quality of the "perspiration." The spot he touched turned yellow; even more amazingly both the discoloration and fragrance remain on the shirt. That doesn't make sense! Ordinary perfume or cologne dissipates over time. We soon discovered that there was a perplexity and elusiveness about psychic phenomena that moderated our speculative hunches. Just when one of our theories seemed to be borne out, Thomaz would beguile us and produce another phenomena that was totally antagonistic to our earlier line of reasoning.

During dinner in Pouso Alegre one evening, Thomaz began pouring enormous quantities of salt in his beer. As he stirred it with a dinner knife, the knife twisted into an "S" shape. He then began to stir with a fork and the prongs of the fork twirled and curled around themselves ending up like some abstract sculpture.

Thomaz seemed strangely silly and agitated that evening. He kept pouring large portions of the salt onto everything he was eating. He picked up another fork, speared a piece of lettuce, and held it for his wife Lygia to eat. Within seconds, as we all watched, the fork appeared to perform a midair ballet, twisting and coiling into a twin of the first fork. There was the usual excitement, gaiety, and screams of delight that commonly accompany Thomaz phenomena, and everyone at our table was impervious to the gaping and incredulous faces from nearby tables.

We were joined during dinner by a young honeymooning couple. (Strangers attracted by the commotion around Thomaz will frequently invite themselves to be his guests and within minutes they become "dear friends.") The groom's father, it turned out, was an acquaintance of Thomaz. Thomaz became very sentimental and felt the occasion should be honored with a special gift. He took a piece of soft foil-covered paper from a cigarette pack and very quietly shifted into a deep concentration as he began tearing pieces of foil and folding the largest piece over itself several times. There was both an air of mindlessness and total absorption about him as he took a toothpick and began probing the foil as if he were examining an insect. Thomaz stopped suddenly and exclaimed, "No energy—I can't work," and suggested we continue eating. The piece of tinfoil, the size of a small egg, lay on the table before us. About two minutes later Thomaz excitedly exclaimed that the "energy was arriving," as he began to experience energy rising from the base of his spine, followed by "goosebumps" on his forearms. These are the signs usually presaging a buildup of psychic energy. He pierced the tinfoil with the toothpick, holding it about one foot above the table as he tried to mentally sculpt what the material would transmute into or become.

There was an incandescent light above us over the table and the shadow beneath the foil slowly took the shape of a bird with extended wings. The preposterous inconsistency seemed totally senseless until Thomaz shouted, "I know what it is going to be." He cried, "Ra!" and the tinfoil suddenly transmuted into a hard, metal phoenix bird with extended wings and fell to the table with a sharp clang. It was one-and-a-half inches by two inches in dimension with very fine detail in its wings, head, and tail feathers.

The observers were Jim Jensen, the honeymooners, Gary, four others including Thomaz's wife, and me. We all agreed that we could see the transmutation taking place from tinfoil to a hard silver metal. Even more staggering and difficult to comprehend was the appearance of the shadow—a kind of ethereal blueprint. The rules of transmutation of matter and causality were being violated before our very eyes, not to mention what this experience was doing to our comfortable and untroubled world view of time and space. In a sense, the "future" had presented itself before the present, until the substance was able to "catch up" with its shadow. The honeymooners interrupted their gentle embracing and sometimes awkward gaping at each other to spend the next four days wide-eyed with Thomaz. They acknowledged later, with typical rural understatement, that it was certainly a "different" way to celebrate a honeymoon.

The following day at lunch, Thomaz very excitedly began rubbing his forearms and said that a "levitating energy" was building up. We placed a fork on the edge of a plate; with great effort Thomaz tried to levitate it, but without success. After a minute or so, he experienced the telltale "goosebumps" on his forearms, announcing that the energy had changed to a "reconstituting energy." Thomaz asked Jim Jensen to take the thighbone of a chicken from his plate, scrape it clean, and snap it in two. A dentist from an adjacent table, who knew of Thomaz only by reputation, joined us to observe. Patrons from a nearby table also moved closer. Jim was asked by Thomaz to fit the two jagged edges of the bone together and hold them in place. He was further instructed to "mentalize" the edges of the bone fusing together. Thomaz then slipped into a very deep trance state and placed each of his index fingers on the back of Jim's hands, apparently to beam energy into Jim. At no point did Thomaz touch the chicken bone. As we all gazed at the point where the two broken pieces fitted loosely together, we were startled to see a bluish haze around the perimeter of the bone. The energy "envelope" then concentrated, like a miniature intense blue cloud, at the focal point of the two edges and stayed there for about ten seconds until Thomaz punctuated the experience with his guttural signature of "Ra!" The broken bone had fused together. Unlike the welding of metal, there was no telltale scar. We scrutinized it closely in bright sunlight. It appeared just as it was originally.

This experience added to our increasing repertoire of fascinating but intellectually troublesome issues. Thomaz was again being totally irreverent with the models of everyday science. It was as if a different order of the universe were bubbling up through the fountain of his mind, and we didn't quite know how to make sense of what we were experiencing. Did Thomaz play a game with time and somehow cause it to flow backwards to the point before the chicken bone was originally snapped in two? Or did he indeed somehow mobilize a psychokinetic energy to "heal" the fracture by accelerating time in some fashion?

Thomaz became very philosophical at this point and spoke movingly and meaningfully about the healing capabilities that we all possess. He declared that "electrical energy is the basis of all healing," adding that all matter, including inanimate substances, are infused with an "intelligent energy" at a very basic level. He is not certain of the mechanics of the process but feels that he somehow communicates through "visualization and my mind thoughts with the information fields that surround all matter in the world." This he attributes as the starting point for his metal-bending, transmutations, "healing," and telepathy.

The "mending" demonstration had taken place in the restaurant on the fourth floor of our hotel. Just as we were preparing to leave, two red flashes of light exploded in midair about fifteen feet away from our table and were seen by several of the patrons. Thomaz excitedly remarked that "Xils" was present. We then became aware of the now-familiar fragrance of jasmine and eucalyptus throughout the whole restaurant—a very large, open room. As we walked down the stairs to our rooms on the first floor, the fragrance was everywhere. Curious, we walked up and down the halls of each floor. The scent seemed to get stronger. We encountered a chambermaid on the second floor who had been checking several of the rooms to see if anyone had spilled a bottle of perfume or scented cleaning fluid. The delicate fragrance continued permeating every floor and every room for the rest of the week we were in the hotel with Thomaz.

The authors had been wondering about Thomaz's telepathic abilities since we had heard numerous reports about his so-called "X-ray vision." Thomaz joined Gary, Jim Jensen, and me in our room shortly after our conversation, without hearing or knowing what we had discussed. He began to ask many questions about Uri Geller and acknowledged that his own metal-bending powers did not begin until he heard about Uri's performance on Brazilian television in 1976.

He also inquired about Uri's clairvoyant faculties and defended Geller's abilities as genuine. Thomaz indicated that he now felt "inspired" and would demonstrate telepathy for us. We looked at each other in wonder. Were Thomaz's remarks mere coincidence or was this conversation in itself partial confirmation of his telepathic abilities?

Thomaz asked me where I kept my passport and identification cards. I reached into a small sealed pouch beneath the main chamber of my camera case. (It should be noted that, because of the value of the documents and cameras, the case never left my side; I took it with me even when I went to the washroom.) I held out the closed pocketbook. Thomaz placed one hand over his eyes and lightly touched my leather pouch with the other. Thomaz then turned, joked about the number of credit cards that North Americans carry with them, and went into the bathroom. Thomaz left the door open and faced the wall; Gary positioned himself between Thomaz and Jim and me, sitting on a sofa at the far end of the room.

Before I could get my credit cards out of the slots in the pocketbook, Thomaz began reciting the credit card numbers to Gary like a high-speed computer printout. There were twelve credit cards, bank cards, and medical and dental insurance cards. He rattled off the eight to twelve-digit numbers on each card without a single error. He then mentally "penetrated" a hidden fold where I kept my birth certificate and in a very puzzled tone declared "Lecourgos Peter Pulos" (my name in Greek on the certificate) and accurately furnished the certificate's ten-digit registration number, registration date, and date issued. Another card in the hidden fold that I forgot I had was my NAUI Scuba Diver card with seventeen digits. Thomaz had difficulty pronouncing NAUI, but, like a machine gun, he spat out the numbers as if he were reading them in his mind. It was the most dazzling demonstration of clairvoyance we had ever witnessed or read about or even imagined possible. But was it clairvoyance? Thomaz referred to it as "X-ray vision" in that he sees a kind of computer screen in his mind's eye that he simply "reads."

On another occasion, Gary was with an airline pilot friend of his. Thomaz was introduced to the pilot for the first time. Following the usual introductions, Thomaz "mentally X-rayed" the pilot's wallet and then very quickly read out the telexed meteorological and weather codes and flight conditions on a folded paper inside the billfold. The detailed numbers, letters, and codes were one hundred percent accurate!

These experiences not only began to shatter our dogmas about consciousness and brain function but also directed us to pay more attention to some of Thomaz's explanations. He stated that there is a universal pool, or fund, of all known information. He simply opened himself up and "absorbed the knowledge from within." This sounded very reminiscent of the Pribham model of holographic memory (Pribham, 1969), which suggests that the entire information field of the universe is contained in each of its parts—in this case each human being.

Thomaz's rather simple explanation about collective memory and information storage was vividly and dramatically displayed in his "note-burning" demonstration, one of his identifying trademarks.

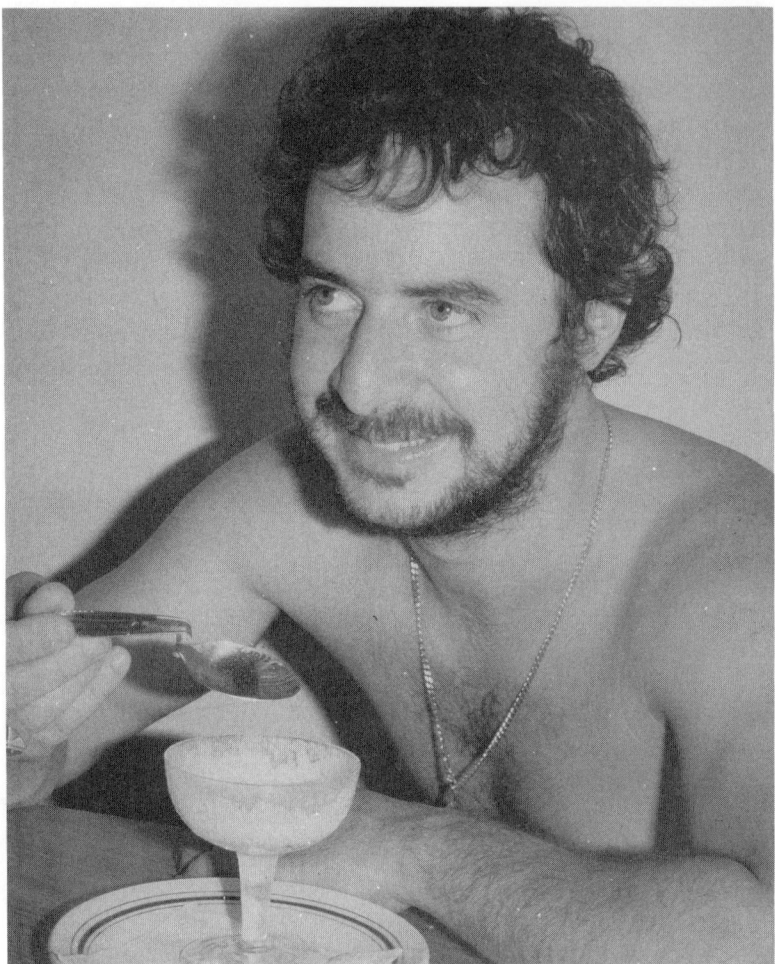

Figure 1-1

During one of our somber discussions about universal intelligence, we took a break and room service brought us refreshments, including a dish of ice cream and a saltshaker for Thomaz. As he was about to eat the first teaspoon of ice cream, the spoon curled into a 360-degree loop-the-loop (Figure 1-1) and the ice cream plopped into Thomaz's lap, changing the mood from philosophical conjectures to levity. He laughed at the unplanned "psychic joke," picked up another spoon, and it too bent and flopped ice cream onto his trousers. As he finished eating the ice cream with the curlicued spoon, the metal cup containing the ice cream suddenly folded so that the two edges came together and touched. We all tried to pull it apart but were unable to budge the metal lips. Thomaz presented the cup to Gary, who had earlier talked of losing weight, the implication being that he could never retrieve food from an almost-sealed container.

Five minutes later, the prefatory chills along both of Thomaz's forearms indicated that energy was again building up but he remarked that "this energy was different." He asked me to produce an American dollar bill and then to write my signature twice on the face of the bill. Thomaz never touched the bill at any time and he was sitting on the other side of the table in his usual attire, stripped to the waist. I folded the dollar bill three times so that it was about one-inch square and held it tightly in my closed fist. Thomaz said he was going to "invoke all the forces of spiritual and universal wisdom" and "scorch" my birth date someplace on the bill. Despite all we had experienced, I silently questioned this prediction—my cerebral divisions of logic versus intuitive knowing were bubbling inside. Thomaz held a lit cigarette and burned the back of my clenched hand as a symbolic gesture and underscored the moment with his explosive "Ra!" A few moments later, I opened my hand, unfolded the dollar bill, and made certain it was the one with both my signatures on it. To my astonishment, charred along the edge was my birth date, "06-01-1928" (Figure 1-2). Thomaz repeated the procedure with Jim Jensen, burning his Social Security number along the edge of the bill.

On a subsequent trip to Brazil, Jim brought his eleven-year-old daughter Julie, and Thomaz became very fond and protective of her. Once he asked her to go through the same procedure, except asked what she would like burned on the bill. She responded, "Thomaz this way (horizontally), Julie this way (vertically), the word 'love' in between, and February 24, 1970" (Julie's birth

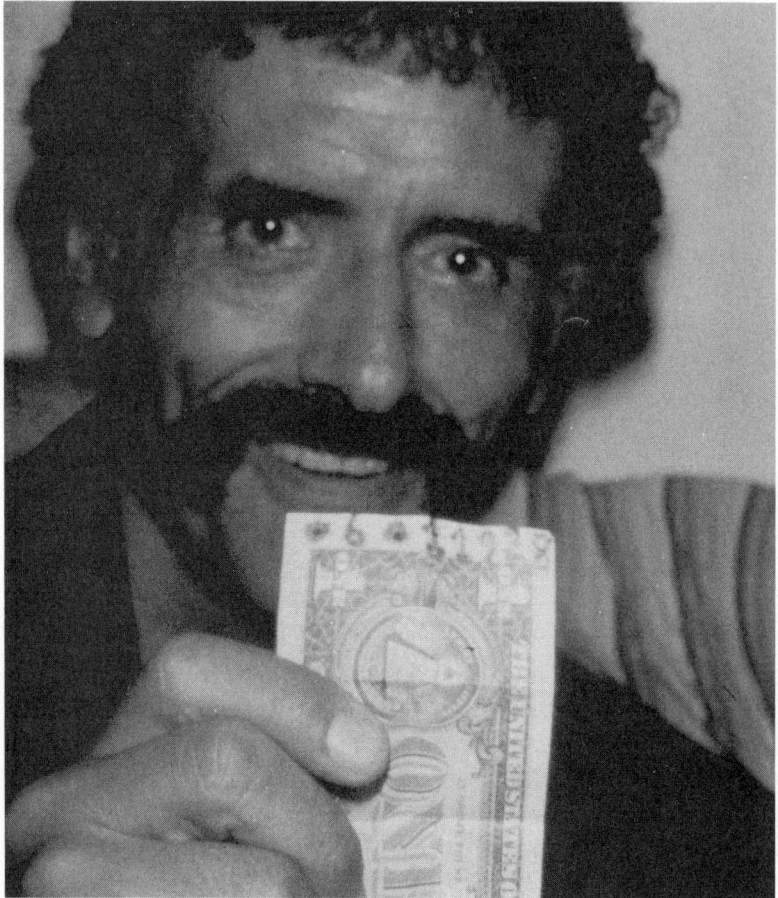

Figure 1-2

date). Thomaz mobilized the energy in his usual fashion, and burned the back of Julie's hand with a cigarette. After she flinched, she unclenched her fist and unfolded the bill. It was burned with the words and date just as she had requested. The impressions left in the paper appear as if someone had taken a cigarette and very patiently burned a series of small perforations to form the letters and numbers.

These experiences enlarged the area of our own psychological cauterization; very subtly, we were experiencing a purging and cleansing of the lenses that reflect such a limited vision of the human condition. Travelling with Thomaz involved long periods of waiting and tolerating his wanderings and richocheting around the countryside. He seemed to have no consideration for rules of social conduct and etiquette for keeping appointments. In these quiet and reflective moments, we saw ourselves as latter-day Rip Van Winkles—asleep under a cloud of cultural anesthesia. We realized we had lost touch with many ancient and primitive beliefs, that mind totally permeates the universe, and that magic—the real magic of consciousness—underlies our relationship with nature. Perhaps the veneer of civilization, with its initiatory rites of passing into reason and technology, had obscured and debased the mysteries that could govern a more wholesome spiritual renewal.

The most recurring, unpredictable, and spontaneous psychic whirlpool around Thomaz was the carnival of metal-bending. It happened so often that we became increasingly more blasé and accepted it as a normal occurrence. In December 1981, we went to a large, open, and fluorescent-illuminated restaurant for dinner. Several people were ahead of us in the line for the salad bar, and they took food from the bowls in a normal way. Thomaz waited impatiently, then walked by without stopping or touching anything at the salad counter. He proceeded to a special Brazilian preparation at the far end of the line. I was immediately behind him, but as I reached under the sneeze guard for the large ladles in the salad bowls, all five metal spoons (fourteen to eighteen inches in length) were bent in the now familiar curlicue.

Shortly thereafter, Thomaz sat on a metal folding chair at our dinner table and within five minutes, the bottom portion of chair "melted" as if it were made of butter and collapsed Thomaz onto the floor. I went to a different part of the dining room and selected another chair. Five minutes later, the inverted U-shaped metal legs slowly crumpled and we helped pick Thomaz up from the floor once more. Two waiters then brought in a very large, heavy, metal backless piece of furniture, fortunately padded with leather. Thomaz finished dinner sitting cross-legged, grinning and snickering over the humor of it all.

Andy Pulos, my brother, had been sitting next to Thomaz throughout this episode. Andy is a highly successful businessman, developer, and builder and has had over twenty-five years of experience working with a wide range of construction materials, including steel beams and infrastructures. He carefully examined and photographed both chairs and declared that due to the nature of the twisting and compression of the legs, a blow torch would have been necessary to achieve that kind of pliability and plasticity. There were no tell-tale signs of scorching or pressure indentations. In later conversations with the waiters and management of the restaurant, they acknowledged that spontaneous metal-bending was common when Thomaz was present. On occasions, the phenomena would occur at other tables or locations in the room and the circumstances would have to be brought to his attention. No wonder the waiters seemed blasé by all these highly irregular incidents. They had all seen Thomaz so often, they accepted these paranormal occurrences as quite normal.

In the following chapters we will explore Thomaz's life—the context and heritage that gave birth to these kind of phenomena. Is Thomaz some sort of capricious mutant, who, like a shooting star, will quickly blaze and extinguish himself, leaving behind only bent spoons and tales of aberrant power? Why Brazil and not North America? Do special geophysical, genetic, or psychological ingredients need to be "simmered" before turning into a magical psychic bouillabaisse? What sociological impact does the release of unconscious forces on small, religious Brazilian communities have on its people? A healthy and natural skepticism must certainly inspire the response "I won't believe it until I see it." As Lyall Watson (1979) states, the other side of the same coin is equally true—*"I wouldn't have seen it—unless I believed it."*

CHAPTER TWO

Cultural Climate and the Early Years

The most beautiful thing we can experience is the mysterious. It is the source of all true art and science.
Albert Einstein

Brazilian Spiritism

Behind the glittering veneer of Rio de Janeiro lies one of the world's most mystical countries. Almost seventy percent of Brazil's one hundred twenty million people admit to varying degrees of belief in spiritism. Stories of the miraculous and paranormal are reported almost daily in the newspapers. The convictions of millions of Brazilians about the validity of such phenomena as poltergeists, spirit possession, psychic healing, mediumistic writing, and reincarnation all strengthen the *espiritista* movement and its foundations.

Brazil is also a very modern, highly industrial society with sophisticated cities and culture. São Paulo is one of the largest cities in the world, supporting a population of thirteen million. Boasting well over half of Brazil's gross national product, it is the headquarters of dozens of multinational corporations.

Though Brazil is the largest Catholic country in the world, its consciousness has also been profoundly influenced by the various forms of spiritism practiced by its people. Christian spiritism was founded by Allan Kardec, a French educator, in 1857. Besides ascribing to a very basic Christian tenet, Kardecists also believe that one can communicate and interact with spirits from other dimensions.

Like the United States, Brazil is a melting pot of many nationalities, with a large black population that dates from the seventeenth century when Portuguese explorers brought over thousands of African slaves. The black community has become an integrated component of the country's mental climate. This early heritage led to the formation of *Umbanda*, which is a mingling of traditional African customs and sacraments of the Catholic church. *Candomble*, an older and purer African mode of spiritism, is predominant in the state of Bahia and its capital Salvador. There is also what is loosely referred to as *Macumba* or *Quimbanda*, which signifies "black" as opposed to "white" magic.

However, it is Kardecian spiritism and its many centers that sustain the constituency of the middle and upper classes. Playfair (1976) has written extensively on paranormal phenomena in Brazil and described his involvement with two spiritist centers. The adherents of Kardecist spiritism and *Umbanda* are of all races, including a large oriental population; the full range of socioeconomic classes is represented.

It would not be unusual for a Brazilian shopkeeper to go to one of Rio's glittering beaches at night, light a candle, and leave a two-layer cake and a gift of whiskey on the sand. This would be his offering to *Iemenjá*, the mermaid goddess of the sea, in return for the promise of increased business or the improvement of a relationship. Should a Brazilian experience a heart murmur, he would just as likely go to a spiritist center for diagnosis and treatment as he would to seek out a heart specialist. When ill, many Brazilians seek counsel from both *espiritista* sources and modern medicine.

Holistic health practitioners in North America are rediscovering what Brazilian native and traditional healers have known for centuries. One's attitudes and beliefs—positive or negative—will usually manifest in that person's body as a state of wellness or disease. In downtown São Paulo, a three-story building functions as the healing and training center for the *espiritista* foundation. Each month, sixty thousand persons are treated in this setting at no cost either to the patient or to the government. The center is staffed by trained *espirita* volunteers who come from all walks of life. On any given day, a Varig airline pilot, assistant deputy minister of health, housewife, or typewriter repairperson may work side by side, their common goal being to serve the ill. All volunteers undergo a four-year training period. During the first year, everyone takes basic courses in psychology, nutrition, philosophy, and physiology. Either by expressed interest or by assignment, the next three years are spent specializing in becoming counselors, mediums, or "laying-on-of-hands" healers. At the end of the rigorous training, the successful volunteers are granted the privilege of working with patients. The authors spent considerable time interviewing staff and patients as well as in personal treatment at the center. We were deeply impressed by the care and concern given to the wide variety of cases. The admonition to "treat each patient as if they were your first" was heard frequently.

In contrast to the North American model of client passivity and "being done to," spiritist philosophy teaches active client participation and preventive measures. The role of mind as "creator and destroyer" is constantly emphasized. Related to the religious aspects of spiritism are the concepts of karma and reincarnation. Following death, spiritists believe, one's soul or core energy transcends to another realm not unlike life on earth. In the interim period between reincarnations, a person's deeds are reviewed, and in view of previous errors, a future existence, including cultural and family context, is carefully planned. Accordingly, spiritist doctrine emphasizes free will, but there are cause-and-effect relationships believed to be present in all events. For example, a woman who had unjustly beat her children in one life might choose to reincarnate as the offspring of a cruel and malicious parent. This would provide her with the opportunity to learn and grow through experiences, in order to develop the *espirita* characteristics of purity, humility, and charity.

This, briefly, is the cultural and metaphysical matrix for a large number of Brazilians. Afterlife, recurring reincarnations, communication with spirits through mediums, are topics as common as football pools and good restaurants. A refreshing quality of *espirita* philosophy is that one never charges a fee for healing or psychic counseling or the medium's channels will be severely restricted. Today, a schism has developed between the older, more doctrinaire *espiritas*, who view Kardec's teachings as immutable dogma, and the more "liberated" supporters who want to infuse new discoveries with cosmologies from physics and psychology. This division is reminiscent of the earlier evolution-creationist controversy and of recent attempts to modernize Catholic doctrine. Despite the growing schism, the Brazilian government honored Kardec by issuing a special postage stamp commemorating the one hundredth anniversary of his birth.

Francisco Candido Xavier, known fondly as "Chico," best exemplifies spiritist ideals. Born in 1910, he began having psychic and mediumistic experiences at a very early age. Raised in poverty and the recipient of only a limited education, Chico worked most of his life as an underpaid government employee. At the age of twenty-two he began entering trances and while in this altered state would serve as a medium or channel for "higher energies" doing automatic writing through him. Purportedly, a number of discarnate authors have collaborated with him; since 1932, he has produced more than three hundred books. The scope and profundity of his works range from scientific monographs and philosophical treatises to books on mathematics, poetry, novels, and even children's literature. He has also written about afterlife, the mechanics of mediumship, and the entire cartography of the spirit world. The rich imagery, complex metaphors, and mystical wisdom in his writings are hardly what one would expect from a man who is half-blind, has a fourth-grade education, and cannot read.

Chico represents a personal ideal to millions of Brazilians and his photograph is frequently found hanging on newsstand kiosks alongside those of current race drivers and football heroes. However, it is Chico's humanitarian and charitable nature that led Freitas Nobre, a federal congressman from São Paulo, to collect tens of thousands of signatures on a petition that he submitted personally in Stockholm nominating Chico for a Nobel Peace Prize. Chico receives no money for his readings or from his books. All royalties go to a charity bearing his name that distributes food and clothing for the needy. His rare appearances on television attract millions of spectators. A 1981 program, produced by Brazil's TV Globo, illustrated clearly what he means to millions of households: The title of the special was "Chico Xavier, A Man Called Love."

Chico has also willingly submitted to scientific study. In one case, electroencephalographic electrodes were attached to his scalp as he went into trance. He places one hand over his eyes while the other writes so quickly it seems as if his writing arm is in a frenzy. According to Guy Playfair (1980), the "electrical language" of Chico's brain during automatic writing displays the abnormal stutter usually manifested in epileptic brainwave patterns. Yet there is no history of epilepsy in his medical record, and Chico is adamant that mediumship is a normal ability available to everyone who chooses to develop it. Perhaps equally as important as his loving nature and spiritual qualities is the continuing impact of Chico's writings on increasing the average Brazilian's awareness of the probability of other realities and forces in the universe.

Psychic Healers

While Thomaz was growing up, another simple, uneducated man, also from the state of Minas Gerais, began to capture the nation's imagination. In 1956, Jose Pedro de Freitas, who lived in the small town of Congonhas, extracted a tumor from the stomach of an old woman. He performed his surgery in the presence of several witnesses using an old kitchen paring knife, with no anesthetic, no antiseptic, and no antibiotics. The patient felt no pain and recovered in a remarkably short time. Freitas, a Catholic, claimed that it was the spirit of a deceased German physician, "Dr. Fritz," who conducted the actual surgery. Freitas, or Arigo as he was later known, converted from Catholicism to spiritism and subsequently performed thousands of operations very quickly and without any sterilization procedures.

In May 1968, Andrija Puharich, M.D., led a team of North American doctors and surgeons to assess, film, and document Arigo's surgeries and cures, described as miracles by observers. The team witnessed this simple, untrained peasant treat more than three hundred patients a day. Cases included as many as one hundred "kitchen knife surgeries." He never tied off blood vessels, yet there was no major bleeding. Ninety-five percent of the thousands of diagnoses he made agreed with those of the medical team, who had the benefit of laboratory studies. Arigo would sometimes bark out orders in German, even though out of trance he had no knowledge of that language. He also wrote thousands of pharmacologically accurate prescriptions. On occasion, he prescribed a medication that had been developed but not yet released from Swiss research laboratories.

Following the team's visit, Arigo was openly acknowledged, both by the North American physicians and the *New York Times*, as "the eighth wonder of the world." The Minas Gerais Medical Association, however, contested that Arigo was practicing medicine without a license, and he was sentenced to a jail term in 1958. Arigo never accepted money for his healings, and he continued to see patients in prison during recreation periods. Brazilian President Juscelino Kubitschek, himself a physician, pardoned Arigo and he returned to Conghonas to continue his mission. In 1971, Arigo had a vision of his "leaving this plane" in an automobile accident. In typical *espiritista* fashion he accepted his fate. The pain never felt by patients was experienced by an entire nation as his death made headlines in all the Brazilian newspapers. John Fuller (1974) has superbly told the story of

Cultural Climate and the Early Years

Arigo and Puharich's investigations in *The Surgeon of the Rusty Knife*.

While the heritage of Arigo still lingers in the consciousness of many Brazilians, other similarly gifted healers have continued to work with various segments of the population. During 1978 and 1979, I spent several weeks in the village of Christianopolis, in the northeastern state of Sergipe. Our team included a cinematographer and we filmed dozens of surgical operations performed by a functionally illiterate twenty-eight-year-old woman known simply as "Maria," or sometimes more formally as Dona Cicera. Maria did all her diagnoses psychically. She functioned much in the fashion of a general practitioner, prescribing herbs, medication, and counseling about life-style and nutrition.

Several times a day, however, she would motion a patient to her "operation room" and with little ado and no preparation, would create a surgical opening with a pair of scissors. Like Arigo, she used no anesthetic or sterilization, but patients felt no pain. Dust wafted in from passing trucks and sometimes a stray dog would wander in and curl up under the table. Maria would leave the patient to hold her instruments in a gaping abdominal opening while she ministered to an outpatient. To close the wound, Maria would shift into a deeper trance, run the handle of a knife slowly over the opening, and bring the edges of the skin together. She never sutured; the operation site was simply covered with a bandage.

We observed her expertise in orthopedic, thoracic, general, and opthalmological surgical procedures. All of the cases we followed and interviewed responded without any ill effects. Six weeks after our first visit, Beverly Morgan, M.D., an opthalmological surgeon from California, spent two weeks as Maria's "assistant." Dr. Morgan (1982) acknowledged that "Dona Cicera had a special gift for healing and that most of her surgeries had paranormal features."

Not all psychic surgeons are illiterate and poor. Jose Guedes, a middle management textile manufacturer, goes twice a week to an outlying area of São Paulo, and changes into a white surgical smock. With the assistance of eleven mediums, he enters trance, his facial expression, demeanor, and accent taking on a harsh Teutonic quality. I have seen him perform a cataract operation with the patient calmly sitting on the edge of an examining table. Once we observed him take what looked like a fourteen-inch knitting needle made of surgical steel and slowly penetrate the cartoid artery. Its trajectory was downward and toward the heart. After it had been thrust eight inches or so into the thoracic cavity, he peered at the patient's chest as if he were doing a fluoroscopy. No pain, no discomfort, and again, the patient sat on the edge of a table gazing and smiling at friends around the room. This served as a diagnostic procedure for even more dramatic surgeries that took place toward the end of the same day.

Gary spent many hours over a two-week period working with a research team that investigated another spectacular healer who is also from Minas Gerais. During the week, forty-seven-year-old Odilon Silva is a state court judge, but on weekends, he is known simply as "Odilon the healer." Judge Odilon's specialty is the treatment of cancer and he sees hundreds of persons every month. Sometimes he cups and squeezes the afflicted area with his hands and the tumor simply disintegrates. Other times, he extirpates the mass with a scalpel. More often, he beams "energy and light" into the ailing area.

Odilon's healing sessions are always attended by one or more local physicians, sometimes as observers, sometimes as patients themselves. One physician filmed a series of spectacular cures with before-and-after X-rays and laboratory studies. Odilon insists on pre- and post-X-ray documentation in all cases he treats. Like Arigo, Maria, and Jose Guedes, the judge does not charge for his services and gives all credit for the healings to a "spirit energy" that works through him.

Cultural Climate

In addition to the *espiritista* philosophy gently permeating their consciousness, Brazilians also possess a sense of spontaneity and openness that creates an atmosphere receptive to psychic phenomena. They are a friendly, robust, and unrestrained people and feel that as a nation they are guided by the firm hand of destiny. A common expression in Brazilian Portuguese is Se Deus Quiser—"if God wishes it to be." This phrase is used as a rejoinder to a variety of situations, ranging from a teenager speculating about marriage with his girlfriend to a businessman asking his stockbroker if market conditions will improve. The acknowledgement of destiny also extends into political realms. The majority of Brazilians agreed that then-president Juscelino Kubitshek was acting as an "instrument of God" when he decided to move the capital of the country from Rio de Janeiro to Brasília, a futuristically architectured city in the flatlands and marshes of central Brazil.

In contrast to Brazil's beauty and spiritual qualities, this bewildering country is also characterized by large-scale poverty, unemployment, and economic misery among the low-income groups. Even though the economic barriers separating the classes are wider than in most countries, the people mingle easily and do not hesitate to embrace or display emotion openly with each other on the street. Hatred and resentment are basically alien to the Brazilian character. Rather, Brazilians prefer to share a common optimistic vision that their country is the nation of the future and one day will be a global power.

Thomaz's Boyhood

Such is the cultural mosaic into which Thomaz was born on March 16, 1947. His father, Glycerio Morais Coutinho, a third-year medical student, and Gessy, his wife, were praying for a son as they already had two daughters. Glycerio, however, knew it would be a boy and had already selected a name to honor one of his scientific idols, William Thomas Green Morton, an American dentist who was credited with the discovery of the anesthetic properties and application of ether in general and dental surgery. Thomaz was thereby christened Thomaz Green Morton Souza Coutinho.

Thomaz was born in Conservatoria in the municipality of Valenca, a small agricultural town eighty kilometers from Rio. As was the rural custom, he was delivered by a midwife who was also retained as a nanny for the next several years. Young Thomaz suffered from intestinal problems so he was kept on a special diet of mashed avocado for five years. A late developer, he was slow to walk and talk. Gessy prayed daily that her sickly son would not die.

Glycerio, strong-willed, disciplined, and studious, went on to earn degrees in both medicine and pharmacy. "Dr. Morais," as he preferred to be addressed, was a very strict disciplinarian and frequently used his thick leather belt on Thomaz and his sisters to uphold his demanding standards of obedience.

Dr. Morais described himself as "having a streak of the gypsy in me," and the family moved frequently. When Thomaz was one year old the household moved from Conservatoria to Pouso Alegre, where Dr. Morais opened his first pharmacy. The family lived in a comfortable two-story house in the center of town. Dr. Morais managed a busy medical practice as well as a pharmacy in his typical sixteen hour-a-day schedule. Introduced to the work ethic early, Thomaz waited on customers and was taught by his father to give injections. When he was seven, he stood on an orange crate and administered his first injection by throwing a syringe like a dart at a fat woman's arm. He practiced and improved his technique by injecting syringes into various kinds of fruit. By the time he was eight, Thomaz was sufficiently skilled to administer intravenous injections.

Pharmacies maintain a very unique status in Brazil. Although it is illegal for any nonlicensed person to give injections or fill prescriptions without medical authorization, most people prefer to consult with a pharmacist rather than a doctor about minor illnesses. The Brazilian Ministry of Health has recently attempted to regulate the administration of potent and potentially detrimental remedies, but it is still possible to purchase a range of drugs, from birth control pills to tetracycline, without a prescription.

Cultural Climate and the Early Years

Most pharmacists are skilled clinicians; by listening to a patient's litany of symptoms, the pharmacist can dispense an array of appropriate pharmaceuticals. Most pharmacies also have "treatment rooms" where injections can be given and cuts, bruises, and minor accidents involving toxins can be treated. Perhaps most importantly, the pharmacy also serves as a community social center, similar to a turn-of-the-century American barbershop. People go there simply to mingle, gossip, and carry on with the usual neighborly diversions.

While a pharmacy in Brazil might compare to a physician's small clinic in Europe or rural America, Dr. Morais' pharmacy was particularly hectic; he was also a doctor. A more enchanting feature of these therapeutic and medicinal centers was an unusual romantic connection to the past. All pharmacies offer traditional alchemical and homeopathic nostrums in addition to the modern pharmaceutical armamentarium. Dr. Morais, of course, was well acquainted with these old-world remedies and his wife's father and brothers were also pharmacists; they all pooled their wonder-working formulas, which had been handed down for generations.

Dr. Morais trained Thomaz rigorously in this ancient art. By the age of twelve he was thoroughly knowledgeable about a vast array of plants, roots, "old wives'" remedies, herbal poultices, and other extraordinary homeopathic potions. Thomaz was also taught early that the most important ingredient of all in these remedies was the personal energy of the alchemist, and he instinctively employed this concept in working with patients. His father's formulas were extremely successful, and the many patients who traveled from other townships believed that most of the curative power came from Dr. Morais' individual "vibrations" and vitality.

Pouso Alegre has not changed much over the past twenty-five years. Most traffic tie-ups are caused by stubborn horses that draw wagons and carry supplies. Typical of small towns, Pouso Alegre has a soap opera quality. Everyone in Pouso Alegre knew that Dr. Morais was a strict disciplinarian and that his children had formed a closer bond and shielding alliance with each other in self-defense. The family were devout Catholics and attended mass regularly. Although Dr. Morais was very religious, his personal library contained what the Church would have branded as "subversive literature"—books on hypnosis, mind power, and occult sciences. So Thomaz was raised with a range of differing beliefs.

Until he was fourteen, Thomaz was fairly introverted, physically delicate, but quite mischievous. His teachers saw him as a truant and below-average student. He loved to mimic and he would go to one cowboy film after another so he could "become" Hopalong Cassidy or the Lone Ranger. He also imitated his father, and in elaborate scenarios in which his sisters appeared as nurses and patients, Thomaz would become "Dr. Quicura" (doctor who cures). Neighborhood playmates would come to have their temperatures and pulses taken, and he would administer prescriptions such as a small vial of water—"three drops a day for ten days."

Thomaz also acquired a reputation for his less amusing pranks. Once when the whole family was fishing, Thomaz (who had a cast on his right arm at the time) pretended to fall in the water from the boat. He stayed under the surface, breathing through a hollow reed. Dr. Morais panicked and jumped in, fully clothed in his white three-piece suit and straw topper, to "save" his son. Thomaz's punishment became even more severe when Mrs. Morais burnt the seat of her husband's soaked trousers and all the money in the back pocket, as it was hanging over a log oven to dry.

When he was ten, Thomaz experienced a tragedy that he claims still resonates in his subconscious. He and a nine-year-old friend nicknamed "Little Frog" went to a nearby lake, the town's swimming hole. According to newspaper accounts, "Little Frog" was struck on the head by a windmill and knocked into the water while Thomaz was undressing in the bushes. Thomaz, an excellent swimmer, tried to save his friend but lacked the physical strength to haul him up from the bottom. Little Frog drowned.

Despite his rescue efforts, Thomaz was held responsible by some of the townspeople. Fearing that his son would be scarred from the unjust accusations, Dr. Morais decided to leave Pouso Alegre and relocate in another town for a short time until the whispers and gossip were forgotten.

Aside from childhood whimsies and that one haunting trauma, growing up in Pouso Alegre was, for Thomaz, comfortable, healthy, and permeated by an earthy contact with the forces of nature.

Power Spots of the World

Minas Gerais, the name of the state that Pouso Alegre is located in, literally means "general mines" because of the pervasive content of iron ore in the soil. The iron oxide gives the countryside a rust hue, a distinctive feature of the state. While mining is an important source of revenue, Minas Gerais relies more on its dairy industry and agriculture for general livelihood. However, since Chico Xavier, Arigo, Judge Odilon Silva, and Maria, among many other gifted mediums and healers, all come from the same area, many people speculate that the state is one of the "power spots" of the world. These charged areas, whether because of the high iron content in the soil or other earth forces, seem to provide a fertile spawning ground for psychic energies. Almost all the psychic healers in the Philippines, for example, come from a small radius in the province of Pangasinan. Most of the renowned curanderas of Mexico are from Vera Cruz. Stonehenge, England, and Standing Rock, South Dakota, are recognized as focal points for powerful healing earth energies. Colin Wilson (1978) provides compelling evidence that the earth is crisscrossed by ley lines similar to magnetic force fields. Just as the human body has sensitive acupuncture points and meridians, the earth has these sensitive power centers. Of course, it is possible that these energies can also have adverse effects, such as poltergeist activity. Dowsers (water diviners) have also complained that when they tune in to "strange electricity" in different patches of the earth, the contact often results in dizziness and disorientation.

It is unlikely that Dr. Morais was aware of, or even interested in, the intriguing hypothesis of "strange forces in the ground." However, he had heard of Chico Xavier and Arigo, and like most Brazilians he found it easy to accept the notion of "inexplicable phenomena." So, in addition to providing his children with a proper Catholic upbringing, Dr. Morais also expanded his readings and family discussions to consider the possibility of the supernatural as an integral part of human existence. It wouldn't be long before the horizons of human possibilities would be dramatically challenged by his very own meek, mischievous twelve-year-old son.

CHAPTER THREE

Struck by Lightning

It's a riddle wrapped in a mystery inside an enigma.
Winston Churchill

Fasqueira Incident

It was Thomaz's twelfth birthday. Dr. Morais did not believe in commemorating such occasions and acknowledged holidays only under rare circumstances. He was a studious, hard-working man who believed that everyone should share his regimen of long hours. The youngster, however, had other ideas. Dr. Morais had purchased a small farm in the district of Fasqueira, near Pouso Alegre. Fasqueira literally translates as "a place where lightning strikes." The region has unusually frequent thunderstorms, and a nearby grove of eucalyptus trees poking into the sky often attracts the accompanying discharges of lightning. In the center of Fasqueira is a small lake that provides excellent fishing. Thomaz felt drawn to that spot to celebrate his birthday privately.

He had been working in the pharmacy all day, and when his

father denied his request to be allowed to go fishing at five o'clock, the youngster struck back, threatening to shoot marbles with his friends. He knew that his father resented the "pint-size undesirables" who might contaminate him with notions of shirking work or studying. Dr. Morais opted for the lesser of two evils. He allowed Thomaz to go fishing, instructing him to remain overnight at the farmhand's shack; he would come by for him in the morning.

Thomaz streaked out of the pharmacy, walked six kilometers to a fork in the road, and was picked up by an ox cart, which carried him the final four kilometers to his destination. As he lay on his back in the cart looking at the rapidly accumulating dark clouds, he had a strange thought. "A strange force was drawing me there," he recalled. "It felt as if I could not resist it." He also thought it odd that "a big cloud seemed to be following us." His absorption was broken by the rumblings of thunder and the sprinkling of rain. He jumped off the ox cart and ran to the caretaker's shack, where he found his bamboo fishing pole. Quickly digging up several worms, Thomaz headed for the lake.

Dr. Morais' farm is located two hundred meters east of the lake. A path leads from the lake to a small grotto below. Water flows through the grotto, where a statue of Our Lady of Lourdes stands on an elevated ledge. At this local shrine Thomaz received his first communion. On a nearby hill overlooking the area is an old church with a bell tower and steeple.

Thomaz bolted to the edge of the water, where he left his fishing pole and can of worms. Making his way down to the grotto and shrine, he recited the Lord's Prayer and cupped cool water into his mouth. Fulfilling this customary ritual for anyone fishing at the Fasqueira, Thomaz returned to his lakeside spot to fish. As he lay there in shorts, bare feet dangling in the water, the fishing line stretched into the water, his drowsy reverie was broken by the chiming and echoing of the church bell. On the sixth and final gong, a bolt of lightning uncoiled from a peculiarly low dark cloud, struck the top of the bamboo pole, and sizzled down the pole as if it were a quick-burning fuse. Thunder exploded around him. Thomaz felt that he was being catapulted in two directions simultaneously. His physical body bounced upwards several feet in the air "like a Ping-Pong ball," and then jolted back. At the same time his mind floated eight or nine feet above the scene and could "see" all that was happening below.

Thomaz was bewildered and alarmed. "How can I be up here and down there at the same time?" he wondered. He could actually see his physical body, motionless and suspended in midair. He was still clutching the remains of the charred fishing pole in his hands. He tried to scream but had no voice.

Time seemed to melt; he could no longer use it as a reference. Fear gave way to terror when he saw a circular cloud descend and envelop his physical body, which began to emanate, or be bombarded with, multicolored sparks; he couldn't be sure. As if to escape from what was happening, he thought of himself as soaring upward. Suddenly, he found himself at a much higher altitude, but below he could still see the Fasqueira and his body.

He became aware of a profound calming silence, shattered by a loud booming blast, followed by more silence. Then, from the vicinity of the cloudy shroud around his physical being, Thomaz heard a voice that he recollects as sounding "neither masculine nor feminine." It had a "clear but echoing" quality and intoned a message.

"Tho—maz, Tho—maz," the voice called. "Today you are specially protected by varied forces . . . by natural forces . . . you will be our antenna . . . you will be able to help others and enact strange phenomena . . . but you will never be able to use this force for your own benefit . . . save the remains of your fishing pole, and when you need it, use it . . . you should give splinters of the pole to those in need and it will form a spiritual chain among them . . . you can effect this power every evening at six o'clock." Further, everyone who received a fragment of the pole was to be instructed to meditate and "mentalize" healing thoughts at 6:00 P.M. daily.

After this curious pronouncement, Thomaz could "see" the circular cloud lift and slowly dissipate. Suddenly, his out-of-body consciousness melded with his physical form. He experienced the sensation of defying gravity and his body floated to the earth as if in slow motion. Touching the ground, Thomaz felt a great sense of relief and thought to himself, "That was the most incredible dream I have ever had." He was puzzled by the fact that he began his dream at the edge of the water, yet awakened nine meters away. Even more baffling was the charred fishing rod which he still clenched in his hands. The boundaries of his reality at that moment were wobbly. He still tried to justify his experience as a dream. "Where is the rest of the fishing pole? How did I get here? Am I going crazy?" Looking up at the darkened sky and threatening rain, Thomaz took off, running as fast as he could.

He arrived at the farm and was surprised to find Jose, the hired hand, milking the cow. "What are you doing milking a cow at this time of the day?" the perplexed youngster inquired.

"Look, little Thomaz, at what time would you expect me to milk the cow? It is six o'clock in the morning," Jose retorted.

Thomaz suddenly realized that twelve hours had passed. He thought it had been less than an hour! He decided to confide in Jose. He placed his hand on Jose's shoulder and began, "But Jose...."

The sentence was never completed. The instant Thomaz's hand touched Jose's shoulder, a powerful jolt hurled the man backwards. The cow and its calf were also propelled several feet to one side. The metal milk pail under the cow crumpled, even though no one had touched it.

Jose looked at Thomaz dazedly and screamed, "Just look at you, boy—you're giving shocks! The devil has taken over your body!"

"No, Jose! It's not that! What happened was...." Thomaz was unable to complete the sentence; the terrified farmhand had run to his cottage, where he told his wife Maria to lock the door and board up the windows. The devil was loose at the Fasqueira!

Maria responded immediately. Thomaz was locked out and they pleaded with the youngster through a crack in the door not to touch them and to please go away. Thomaz, more frightened than ever, began to sob and begged them to open the door. He explained that the devil was not with him in any way and told them about the lightning, the floating experiences, and the strange voice. But this story only made matters worse for Jose. In his rural simplicity, he deduced that since Thomaz had been struck by lightning, he had to be a "walking dead." Thomaz began to cry even more loudly, screaming that he too was frightened. He begged for mercy. Jose and Maria took their Bible and began to read aloud and pray.

This medieval scenario lasted more than a half-hour. Then Jose came up with an inspired proposal. He ordered Thomaz away from the door, warning him not to touch anything. Cautiously, Jose opened the door, took a pick and shovel, and began digging a hole fifteen meters away. When he was finished, he ordered Thomaz to stand inside the excavation. The boy protested that he wasn't dead, but reluctantly lowered himself inside. Jose then covered the youngster with dirt, allowing just his head and extended arms to remain above the ground. Then he took a length of metal pipe and drove it into the ground. He wrapped a piece of barbed wire around it and ordered Thomaz to take hold of the loose end of the wire with both hands.

This curious ritual went on for twenty minutes. Jose then dug up the dirt and released the boy from his penitence. Maria had prepared some tea, which she left in an agate cup on the ground, as Thomaz was still not permitted to touch anyone.

At this moment, just after eight in the morning, Dr. Morais drove up in his carriage. He ran over to his son, embraced him warmly, and asked how he was feeling. Jose was still agitated and warned Dr. Morais not to touch his son, because he was "full of electricity and giving off painful shocks." "Not any more, Jose," Dr. Morais replied. "You managed to discharge Thomaz when you dug the hole and used the barbed wire as a ground—and there's more—I know everything that happened to my son. He was fishing, when a dark circular cloud descended on him. . . ." Dr. Morais then went on to describe in perfect detail and sequence the events of the preceding fourteen hours. He added that all of this information had come to him in a dream the night before. Taking the fishing pole from Thomaz, he said he would keep the pole for Thomaz as he was too young to understand the meaning of what had just happened to him.

Jose looked at Dr. Morais with wide-eyed distrust and skepticism, which soon gave way to his native superstition. If Dr. Morais' explanation was genuine, then the farm, the Fasqueira, and the entire family were cursed and hexed. By noon, Jose had packed his meager belongings onto his mule and departed with Maria, never to return.

The story of the incident soon spread throughout the town. Since the property was now believed to be haunted by the devil, Dr. Morais could not get anyone to work for him. Later that year, he sold the farm for half of its value.

What Thomaz experienced at the Fasqueira certainly provokes our tidy assumptions about reality. Other events that day disrupted even more "laws of nature." Though Thomaz clearly heard the church bell six times, the bell had no clapper and had not rung for years.

Twenty-one years later, to the day, on his thirty-third birthday, Thomaz visited the Fasqueira with two journalists who distinctly heard the church bell ring six times as Thomaz recounted the incidents for them. With an intuition that the "lightning experience" might happen again, Thomaz had brought another bamboo fishing pole with him; at six o'clock he sat by the lake holding the pole over the water. A startling explosion of thunder followed the six chimes and Thomaz was abruptly thrown back, but not upwards. He lost partial consciousness and blood began to flow from his nose and mouth. This time, however, the pole was not burned or charred. His recollection of this second event was hazy because of his altered consciousness at the time. Since Thomaz's powers were in full bloom during this period, one must consider the possibility that what transpired was caused by his own very intense psychokinetic abilities.

Upon regaining his senses, Thomaz carried on with his narration and showed the journalists the spot where he had been buried by Jose. New grass had grown over the small patch but it was still possible to see the scars of the shovel and turned-over earth.

The "legend" of that day is still very much in evidence in the memories of long-time residents. When Gary and I asked the town folk if they knew Thomaz, a typical response was "Oh, you mean that boy who was struck by lightning down by the lake. I remember everything that happened—everyone around here knows about that...."

Mobilizing Psychic Ability

For many observers, bent silverware and the psychic battle cry of "Ra!" have become associated with Thomaz's eruptions of psychokinetic energy. But of greater meaning and relevance to Thomaz is what happened to him on his twelfth birthday. He sometimes downplays his psychokinetic abilities but he never glosses over the story of the Fasqueira. Everyone who spends any time with him must listen to the complete chronicle of every single incident that day.

As Thomaz unfolds each event, he becomes totally absorbed in every detail. He speaks with his hands and eyes, with such compelling passion that you cannot help but be mesmerized by the reality of that twelve-year-old's awe and bewilderment. The sincerity of his gestures and tone of his voice convey the feeling that he is speaking directly from the heart.

On occasion, he wanders from the main theme of his narrative, becoming uncharacteristically pensive while examining the essence of psychic abilities. For Thomaz, feeling is the most important key to mobilizing psychic capabilities. To Thomaz "feeling" means the ability to actually enter or "become one" with the object on which he is going to work. If he is going to bend a spoon, for example, he disassociates from himself and projects inside—and fuses with—the essence of that particular spoon. He emphasizes that he is not *imagining* that he is inside the spoon; imagination is not enough. He must "cease to exist" as a person and "exist only as the spoon or object he is going to move or bend." This means transcending the five senses, which he feels are too limiting. Thus, his intensity is infused into every part of his existence. When he talks about lightning, he becomes "electric" himself and you can feel the energy crackling and popping throughout the room. When he shouts with enthusiasm and asks you to recall your first love or kiss, he expects you to be able to recapture and "become the eternity of that feeling which is forever pulsing on your lips." It is perhaps for these reasons that Thomaz enjoys having adolescents around him when he works. He ignites their animated eagerness and they fuel each other's excitement.

Thomaz's insistence upon total immersion into life's forces, particularly within psychic phenomena, has many referents in the mystical literature. Berman (1984), in discussing the practice of ceremonial magic, emphasizes that all nature is alive and a very personal presence. Mind is imbedded in every aspect of the cosmos, including "inanimate" objects such as stones or metal. By becoming one with all creation, a mystic or wizard can invite it to do certain things, or influence its energy or structure. The key is to celebrate the bond with nature by fusing with its essence as simply as possible. Roszak (1975) describes how "higher" religions like Judaism, Christianity, and Islam have weakened this link by elevating humans above nature. Many of the more mystical and occult traditions such as Kabbalism, Taoism, Hermeticism, and Tantrism have maintained their original archaic rituals, which underscore a magical vision of creation.

Winkelman (1982), in a scholarly review of the anthropological literature on magic, describes certain "laws of thought" common to many cultures that utilize *psi* and paranormal phenomena in their social order. One of the basic principles of magic is the law of similarity, or the belief that the shaman can produce a desired effect by imitating it. According to Frazer (1929), a practitioner of true magic "sees in the imagination the images of the wished-for results." He adds that central to the development of psychic powers is "complex visualization—desire—and intense concentration." For psychokinetic processes, many healers and "technicians of the sacred" emphasize the role of strong emotions associated with positive expectations. Practitioners are also emphatic that participants in a ceremony must believe it is going to work. It is frequently noted in the literature (Castaneda, 1968; David-Neel, 1931) that the presence of nonbelievers will render magical activities useless. Apache healers consider it impossible to cure someone who is skeptical (Opler, 1983). Mauss (1972) points out that certain Mexican *curanderas* feel that the effectiveness of healing practices is weakened if taught to incredulous people. Even parapsychologists such as Palmer (1971) have discovered a strong relationship between belief in ESP and high scores in ESP performance tests.

Thomaz does not read books anymore and his attention span for reading anything is limited. He does not claim to have any distinctive knowledge. In many hours of conversation with him he has never revealed any memorable appreciation of mystical or magical practices. However, without knowing that he knows, Thomaz practices and embodies many of the central characteristics of ancient principles of magic. When he first began to bend metal objects, he began by convincing himself that he was Uri Geller. We find it ironic that many parapsychologists, with their disciplined emphasis upon rationality, the "minimizing of effortful striving," and the employment of skeptical stage magicians as observers, apply such stringent experimental criteria that sometimes the very "emotional juices" necessary for psychic demonstrations are squeezed out of both the psychics and experimenters. From our observations of Thomaz, spontaneity and an emotional "detonation" are critical to paranormal phenomena.

Electricity and Psychic Ability

In addition to identifying the mental and emotional windows to Thomaz's inner world, one cannot overlook the impact of lightning on the youngster's consciousness and biological systems. Each cell in the human body is like a miniature magnet with a positive and negative charge, surrounded by a measurable field. There are twenty-seven trillion cells in the human body, and this enormous number of "minimagnets" creates a very discernible bioelectric sphere that surrounds a person like a huge cocoon. Burr (1972), Becker (1982), and others have described in a series of experiments how shifts in human consciousness can have a very profound effect on the voltage gradient of a person's body field. Changes in these electromagnetic fluxes are influenced by hypnosis, healing, ovulation, and external power lines that have strong electrical waves extending for a considerable distance.

Becker (1977), an orthopedic surgeon, has used low-voltage direct current stimulation to accelerate healing in broken bones and to regenerate amputated limbs in salamanders. Based on a series of over one hundred forty experiments, Becker believes that a second, much more subtle nervous system has gone unrecognized by science. This second system controls healing and possibly explains how hypnosis, acupuncture, and certain painkilling drugs work. Hypnosis is frequently cited in the parapsychology literature (Edmunds, 1961; Tart, 1964) as facilitating ESP and other *psi* processes.

While subtle shifts in the human electromagnetic "envelope" can be detected by altering consciousness through meditation and hypnosis, there is very little evidence supporting the effects of more extreme electrical insults to the body. Heard (1963), in an interesting review of the role of lightning in the evolution of human consciousness, refers to the intriguing frequency of telepathic and precognitive flashes of patients who have undergone electroconvulsive therapy. The electrical storms in the brains of certain epileptics throughout history are also related to visions and special gifts of knowing.

In more recent writings, Motoyama (1975) and Sannella (1976) describe experiments linking mysticism with science by focusing on the awakening of the Kundalini. While this process has been evident in the mystical literature for over four thousand years, psychologist Motoyama and physician Sannella describe complex physiological syndromes that relate to this powerful "electrical energy" in the base of the spine. As the Kundalini rises, a consciousness awakens that is related to the emergence of the whole spectrum of paranormal powers. Pearce (1981), an American educator and author, movingly compares his own Kundalini experience to the phenomenon of lightning.

What would happen if there were a sudden and dramatic electrical insult to the body instead of the subtle influence of hypnosis or low voltage direct-current stimulation? Like Thomaz, Uri Geller also received a powerful electrical shock as a youngster. Geller (1975) described how at the age of three and a half he was playing under his mother's sewing machine in Israel. Noticing a blue glow inside the machine, he touched it with his finger and received a very severe electrical shock. This incident did not receive much attention until Geller later startled the world with a series of mind-boggling phenomena, including metal-bending and telepathy. The series of controlled experiments on Geller in laboratories all over the world are reviewed by Panati (1976).

Mathew Manning of England also received a staggering electrical jolt as a youngster. Shortly after, his house became the center of a series of poltergeist phenomena, including objects flying across a room and massive pieces of furniture moving without being touched. Dr. A. R. G. Owen, a physicist, consulted with Manning's family and school. He advised the youngster to channel his undisciplined energy through automatic writing—an ability that stopped all poltergeist activity (Manning, 1974). In a series of later experiments, he demonstrated metal-bending and other psychokinetic phenomena. He has since channeled his energies into healing and is a very articulate spokesman for understanding and developing latent psychic abilities.

Dr. Pietro Cassoli of the Bologna, Italy, medical school is observing and working with Luciano Muti, a forty-four-year-old Italian psychic. At age twenty, Muti was in a coma for two days following a serious motorcycle accident. Since that episode, he manifested a wide spectrum of psychic abilities, particularly psychokinetic displacement of large objects using only his mind. Peter Hurkos, the internationally acclaimed Dutch psychic, attributes the onset of his telepathic and clairvoyant powers to falling off a ladder, striking his head, and losing consciousness (Browning, 1970).

For the past eight years, I have examined a number of children who have exhibited a wide array of paranormal abilities. The usual reason for the referral is that the youngster's psychic abilities presented disconcerting and bewildering challenges to both parents and teachers. One nine-year-old boy, for instance, experienced a series of precognitive "visions" just as he was drifting off to sleep. The accuracy of his predictions was so precise and disconcerting that his mother wanted to stop his dreamlike images so the family could go back to leading a normal life. The mother had received a strong electrical shock midway through the pregnancy with that son.

Of course, many individuals who have been struck by lightning or subjected to electrical jolts do not display any psychic abilities whatsoever. However, there is sufficient tantalizing correspondence between powerful "electrical trauma" and the ensuing reordering of brain/mind functions to inspire cause-and-effect speculation. Of course, the fine line between strong electrical insults and lethal dosages has minimized the number of cases in this area.

New Perspectives

As the result of personal changes, impelling pressure from his followers, or perhaps his own deep need to be accepted, Thomaz has reinterpreted the lightning as a "ray" from extraterrestrials and more recently, as a special energy from a divine source. His account about the out-of-body experience, the tolling of the bell at the Fasqueira, the message from the mysterious voice, and his reverse levitation have all been internally consistent in numerous retellings. We have heard the narration dozens of times and have also listened to his account on three different videotape recordings. At times, we felt like district attorneys looking for a slip or a flaw. The details remained faithfully honest and in accordance with Thomaz's first recounting of the events.

Despite the brief periods of coherence and consistency in working with Thomaz, we often experienced longer stretches of frustration and bewilderment. Nothing in our training or background had prepared us to systematize extraordinary or unnatural experiences. No conceptual categories for the paranormal make sense. Perhaps part of our problem was that we were trying to make sense of acausal and nonlogical phenomena. We kept urging each other to examine or experience Thomaz from a fresh, untutored perspective. Children, we observed, have no difficulty in accepting him for, in their world, everything is possible and plausible.

CHAPTER FOUR

Mandrake Is Alive and Well and Living in Brazil

> The skeptical scientist told the psychic that he would have to see a demonstration of psychokinesis to believe it. The psychic told him to move his little finger, which he did. "Did you believe it?" asked the psychic.
>
> Ingo Swann

Introduction to Hypnosis

Following the incident at Fasqueira, life went on as usual. Thomaz continued to work at the pharmacy and his father was busier than ever with patients. The only keepsake from that memorable day, the charred fishing pole, was kept on top of Dr. Morais' dresser. The doctor neither spoke to anyone else about the events nor did he go out of his way to discuss them with Thomaz.

A month after the Fasqueira affair, Thomaz and two friends, Vanderlei and Manoel, went to the circus, a typical big-top spectacle with clowns, acrobats, and wild animals. The headline attraction was Dr. Wu, an elderly, rotund Asian billed as a master hypnotist. Attracted by Dr. Wu's publicity, the boys decided to see his show. They became absorbed with the roll of the drums and his very slow dramatic entrance. The lights dimmed, and slowly, dramatically, his head swaying back and forth like a cobra's, Dr. Wu entered. Gradually, he engaged the eyes of everyone in the audience. Then suddenly he shouted, "Sleep!" Most of the audience and nearly all the children present slumped over into a deep trance. But not Thomaz! He remained alert throughout the show, and later teased his playmates for the ease with which they had been hypnotized.

On the way home, the boys stopped to play at a construction site. Even though Thomaz had no prior knowledge of hypnosis, he boasted to his friends that he could do everything that Dr. Wu demonstrated earlier. Thomaz was challenged and Vanderlei volunteered as a subject. Touching his friend's forehead with his index finger, Thomaz shouted, "Sleep!" Vanderlei slumped over like a Raggedy Ann doll. Thomaz pinched and prodded him, and the absence of any sensations suggested that he was in a deep somnambulistic trance. Manoel congratulated his new hero. But when Thomaz hollered, "Wake up!" just as Dr. Wu had, he received no response. He cried out again and despite all the clamoring and shaking, Vanderlei remained in trance.

By now, the afternoon twilight had faded to near darkness. In desperation, Thomaz began to pray and asked God for a sign or inspiration that would release his friend from this strange sleep. Suddenly, Thomaz's mind was flooded with the events of Fasqueira, and particularly with the image of his fishing rod. Leaving Manoel to stand guard over the deeply hypnotized Vanderlei, Thomaz ran home, climbed over a wall, crawled through a window, and tiptoed to his father's bedroom. Just as he was slipping out of the house with the fishing rod, his father caught him and challenged him to explain what he was doing. Thomaz replied that he had no time to talk and raced back to his two friends. As he was running, he felt the fishing pole pulsating in his hand. For the first time in his life, he was to say later, he "felt a strong faith" that if he really believed he could do something, he would.

Returning to the construction site, Thomaz approached Vanderlei cautiously, touched his forehead with the burnt end of the fishing pole and shouted, "Wake up!" Slowly, Vanderlei opened his eyes, but could remember nothing that had happened since leaving the circus. Relieved that nothing serious had happened to his friend, Thomaz headed home. His relief was short-lived, however, when he saw his father waiting for him with the dreaded leather strap. Thomaz confessed and to his surprise, received not a whipping but a warning about the dangers of "strange forces." Dr. Morais took a book from his library on practical hypnosis, told Thomaz to read it carefully, and sent him to bed.

Evolving Psychic Talents

After reading his father's book, Thomaz grew cautious, deciding to limit his experiments to animals. In a relatively short time, he was stroking cats, dogs, and chickens, touching them on the forehead and causing them to fall into a cataleptic stupor. Some of his experiences extended beyond the animal kingdom. One lazy afternoon at the pharmacy, a clerk named Toninho was sweeping the floor. Thomaz began to tell the clerk about the hypnosis experience, but Toninho cut him off—he refused to believe it. Thomaz declared that he would demonstrate his powers. Just then, an old man drove up in his wagon. Watching the man hitch his horse to the post outside, an odd expression appeared on Thomaz's face. After gazing at the old man for a moment, he went directly to a high shelf, pulled down a bottle of Elixir 914 and wrapped it up. When the man entered and asked for a bottle of Elixir 914, Thomaz handed it to him already packaged.

Thomaz explained to the skeptical clerk that he "knew" what the customer wanted before entering the store. Toninho scoffed that it was mere coincidence. Thomaz turned his back on him, took a bottle of Simatozan from the shelf, and wrapped it. Just then, the door opened and a heavy-set lady approached Thomaz and asked for a bottle of Simatozan. Thomaz continued this astonishing exhibition of precognition for the next ten customers who entered the pharmacy. For the eleventh customer, he wrapped a bottle of Exilir de Inhame. Surprisingly, the man forgot what he had come to purchase. Thomaz waited patiently. Suddenly, the man said, "I know now—Elixir de Inhame."

Not only was Thomaz accurate in his precognition of the type of medication the customer would want, he was also very precise as to strength and dosage. As closing time approached, Thomaz elatedly predicted that the last customer of the day would be an elderly lady who would purchase a bottle of Emulsao de Scotch. Toninho, despite everything he had witnessed, underscored his disbelief by betting the youngster that it would not happen. Just as they were locking the door for the night, an elderly woman appeared and asked for Fruit Salts. Disappointed, Thomaz asked if she wanted anything else. She said there was not. Thomaz shrugged and said, "Oh, well, at least I was right that it would be an elderly woman." Moments later, the woman returned, knocked on the door, apologized, and said that she had meant to buy Emulsao de Scotch instead of Fruit Salts. Thomaz was so excited he didn't charge her and triumphantly collected his wager from Toninho.

There was more to come. On the day after this sensational display, Thomaz administered his first painless injection. As he describes it, "It was a totally unconscious act—I was giving an injection as usual and the lady exclaimed that she felt no pain." This bewildered the youngster because he had neither willed nor "mentalized" that circumstance. Puzzled, but pleased, he continued to administer painless injections. His reputation spread and in short order customers were coming to Thomaz from other pharmacies and nearby towns. Even today, despite his hectic schedule, Thomaz will stop to administer shots to frightened children and old friends.

The phenomenon of natural analgesia is by no means unique to Thomaz. James Esdaile (1846), an English physician in the 1840s, was able to induce total body analgesia simply by passing his hands many times over a person's body. This would presumably reorganize the patient's bioelectrical field, resulting in numbness, so that Esdaile could perform major surgery without an anesthetic or antiseptic.

On many occasions, the authors witnessed Brazilian healers using crude surgical instruments to open up a person's body with no apparent pain or discomfort to the alert patient. However, we are still quite perplexed about this aspect of Thomaz's abilities. Are his pain-free injections paranormal, or is there an "x-factor" related to his own electrical fields? We cannot be sure. However, the electrical insult to Thomaz's body on his twelfth birthday began to establish itself and unfolded in increasingly strange and inexplicable ways.

Mandrake the Magician

Thomaz's psychic development seemed to be connected in some way to his exposure to circus performers and magicians, most of whom he saw on film. Fond of movie matinees, the young boy would marvel at magicians who could pull rabbits out of hats and coins out of ears. Displaying an intensity that has stayed with him into adulthood, Thomaz began to believe and become totally convinced that he could replicate everything the film magicians did. Other apparent shifts began to emerge in his personality since the lightning. Before the age of twelve, Thomaz was occasionally a "hell-raiser" but basically a quiet and introverted child. Following his twelfth birthday, he seemed to undergo a distinctive personality change. He became very outgoing and confident, and his personal energy became more emotionally charged and irrepressible. Thomaz became the ringmaster of his own circus with his sisters Sonia and Vera portraying everything from belly dancers to animal trainers. Thomaz's favorite role was Mandrake the Magician. He had seen Mandrake on the screen and read the comic book serialization of his exploits.

One day, Thomaz played Mandrake to an audience of some twenty neighborhood children. Wearing a makeshift costume, performing with exaggerated flourishes, he astounded his audience by pulling a rabbit out of a hat. Spurred on by the response, he invited one of the youngsters to come "on stage" and began pulling coins out of his ear. He also managed to pluck an egg out of a little girl's ear. His audience was most appreciative when Thomaz "transformed" coins into pieces of candy, which were gobbled up by the enthused members of the audience. The audience became totally captivated when a coin or egg would rise slowly towards the ceiling and then vanish completely.

In one of his Mandrake shows, Thomaz decided to demonstrate juggling. Somewhat clumsily, Thomaz began with two balls. In a flash (Thomaz claims now in recollection) there were not two but five balls in the air that quickly fell to the floor. Thomaz was unaware that he was exhibiting real magic, not the distorted version of stage magicians. In short, he didn't know what he was doing. He had never read a book on sleight-of-hand or the conjuring of illusions.

He didn't realize that stage magicians utilized tricks and optical illusions to elicit imagined phenomena in their audience. Like some of the so-called "Geller children," who are able to replicate Geller's mental metal-bending by simply being told they can do it, Thomaz believed he could manipulate reality by visualizing the changes in his mind.

Thomaz performed many times in his backyard circus. He soon acquired the nickname "Mandrake" and it remained with him through high school. During this period, Dr. Morais moved the family again, this time to Alfenas, one hundred kilometers from Pouso Alegre. The state biomedical school was located there and he wanted to complete his degree in pharmacy. Self-conscious over his frail, adolescent physique, Thomaz attached two rocks on the ends of a metal pole and spent hours in the backyard lifting weights. He continued to dazzle his friends and schoolmates with his magic. With his improved body image and ever-increasing confidence, Thomaz ventured into more creative expressions of his mischievousness.

Not wanting to risk again what happened to his friend Vanderlei, Thomaz restricted his hypnotic activities to animals. In one of his many truant episodes, he led two of his friends to a farmer's ranch. To their amazement, he hypnotized the watchdog, mesmerized two chickens so they wouldn't make any noise, and fled with the booty, which they cooked and ate. After several weeks of poaching, Thomaz and his friends were caught in the act by the farmer. As it turned out, the farmer, who had been looking for a thieving cougar "that made no noise and left no tracks," was relieved to find the poachers were human.

Thomaz's evolving psychic talents sometimes took on unpredictable and foolishly whimsical forms. At sixteen, during a boring chemistry class, he began to focus his energies on his ballpoint pen; in short order it was "writing by itself." He then caused the pen to levitate about a foot above his desk; understandably, this caught the attention of all of his classmates. The teacher marched over to Thomaz and, not having witnessed what was distracting the students, called him an irresponsible troublemaker. Upset because his concentration had been broken, Thomaz impulsively willed the teacher to have a bowel movement. According to the teacher's recollection, he covered his abdomen with his hands and said, "You don't have any power over me!" Moments later, he was forced to leave the classroom, embarrassed by a painful attack of acute diarrhea. The resulting uproar led to an angry confrontation involving Dr. Morais, Thomaz, and the school authorities. The boy was suspended and made to repeat chemistry the following term. Uncharacteristically, Thomaz spent the summer vacation plotting revenge—he wanted to levitate the teacher, and spent many hours unsuccessfully trying to levitate a log.

When fall classes resumed, Thomaz returned to chemistry class and persuaded the students to participate in a practical joke on the instructor, who had not yet arrived. Without telling his classmates they were about to be hypnotized, Thomaz drew a pair of concentric circles on the blackboard. The class was "counted down" and then thrown into a deep trance with the command "Sleep!" Thomaz took his seat and slumped over, feigning hypnosis. His revenge boomeranged when a new chemistry teacher entered the room. The instructor tried to rouse several of the students; when he could not, he ran with alarm to the principal's office. The principal inspected the class roster, marched into the classroom, and went directly to Thomaz. He tweaked his ear and Thomaz, frightened and unnerved, went to the front of the class where he brought all the students out of trance by counting backwards from ten to one. The teacher and principal were ignorant of the principles of hypnosis, but their mystification did not keep them from notifying Dr. Morais; Thomaz received a severe thrashing he still recalls vividly.

Six months later, Dr. Morais moved to Botelhos, a small town near Alfenas, where he established yet another pharmacy. Thomaz's sister Sonia had reached marriageable age and met her future husband, Noe, in the town. In accordance with the conservative customs of the region, unmarried women were never allowed to go out alone so Thomaz was assigned the role of chaperone to Sonia and Noe during their promenades, making certain Dr. Morais' early curfew was observed.

About this time Thomaz's relationship with his father began to decline steadily. The oppressive atmosphere and strict discipline demanded by Dr. Morais precipitated a deep depression in the teenager. He was barely passing his high school classes, excelling only in English. Thomaz gradually changed his unruly and mischievous ways. The class teacher came to trust him, so much that Thomaz was chosen as the substitute teacher and monitor whenever the instructor was absent from the classroom.

Becoming a Pharmacist

After their marriage, Noe and Sonia moved to a nearby town, Cambuquira, where Noe opened his own pharmacy. Cambuquira is one of the many "mineral water resorts" in the region. Tourists from all over Brazil and Argentina make the pilgrimage to this small town for the curative effects of its pure spring waters. Now eighteen, Thomaz had not yet finished his high school requirements. Six months after Noe launched his practice,

Thomaz began negotiating with his father to allow him to move to Cambuquira. Noe, who had become like an older brother and good friend, had promised Thomaz room and board in exchange for work at the pharmacy. Finally, Dr. Morais consented and his only son embarked on a new adventure—independence.

Thomaz proved to be an ideal employee. He would report for work early in the morning and was willing to work twelve-hour shifts without complaint. He loved to clean and organize the merchandise on the shelves. In reflecting about this period, Noe commented that Thomaz's most outstanding trait was the warmth and rapport that he established with customers. Shortly after his arrival, business increased more than three hundred percent. Patrons came to ask specifically for the personable Thomaz to prescribe their medication or administer "painless injections." At the end of his long day, Thomaz often fell asleep with his bedside lamp still on, a book on hypnosis in his hands.

During this period, Thomaz's growing popularity was nurtured by continuing reports of his healing powers. Nilza Borge, a middle-aged patient, was troubled with a severe stuttering problem for fifteen years. Following a hypnotic regressive treatment with Thomaz, she suddenly regained normal speech. Another middle-aged patient had suffered from violent seizures most of his life; twice he had to be restrained with a straightjacket. Thomaz worked with him for a full day combining hypnotic suggestions and "charging him with energy." The man was apparently cured and did not experience any further seizures.

It is difficult to determine if Thomaz's proficiency in hypnosis is a reflection of his extensive reading or a direct consequence of the lightning episode at age twelve. We suspect that his skill for inducing rapid hypnotic states is related somehow to the electrical disturbance of his body and mind fields at that time. His ongoing reading and studying were perhaps an attempt to refine his own understanding of hypnotic phenomena. He still has an interest in hypnotic phenomena. He frequently puts animals into "trance" and hypnotizes his cousin Lada. In the thousands of hours Lada spent with Thomaz from 1979 to 1984, he referred to hypnosis only offhandedly. His waning curiosity was gradually replaced with coming to grips with his extraordinary psychic gifts and a more mature outlook toward life in general.

During the next five years, Thomaz became somewhat of a nomad, establishing temporary residences in six nearby towns. More important, respected citizens became increasingly aware of Thomaz's abilities. He was openly encouraged to develop his paranormal talents. Subsequently, Thomaz left Cambuquira to open his own pharmacy in Conceicão do Rio Verde. Dr. Morais provided the initial financing for the purchase of stock and Noe continued to offer moral support.

Shortly after his arrival in Conceicão, Thomaz was approached by a young man from a small city seventy miles away who related the following story. This man's father had been an outstanding opera singer in São Paulo and Rio de Janeiro. After a successful premiere one evening, the singer received an anonymous phone call notifying him that his fifteen-year-old daughter had been struck by an automobile and killed. In shock, the man lost his voice. He rushed home and was relieved to discover that his daughter was in fact alive and had not even been out that evening. The cruel hoax took its toll, however, and the opera star developed an hysterical aphonia. He spent the next three years visiting psychiatrists, psychologists, speech therapists, and spiritist healers, but he never regained his voice. His only means of communication was writing messages with his gold-plated writing pen and pad. With this image, Thomaz experienced a "tingly goosebump" sensation in his forearms, feeling intuitively that it contained the solution to the problem, but did not know how or why.

Two days later, the son arrived alone for an initial consultation. Thomaz responded to a "strange inner intuition," and presented the son with two small fragments of the burnt fishing pole, and gave him instructions on their use. Daily at six o'clock, he and his father were to sit next to each other, holding the fragments in their hands, and pray. The son was also told to visualize his father speaking normally and to return in fifteen days, bringing his father. Precisely fifteen days later, both men walked into the pharmacy. Thomaz, aware of their entrance, was in the back of the shop but purposely made them wait for a period before they were ushered in by an employee. Pretending not to recognize the son, Thomaz asked him, "Are you the one who has come for a consultation?"

Bewildered, the young man responded, "No, it's my father."

Thomaz turned and stared at the older man.

"Oh, you're the one. What is your name?"

Thomaz had taken out a record card on which to enter the information. The son tried to interrupt, but Thomaz ignored him and continued gazing at the older man.

The former singer did not know what to do. Once more, Thomaz asked the singer for his name. The perplexed man brought out his unfailing gold pen and tablet and began to write. But Thomaz continued to pierce the patient with his eyes.

"I didn't tell you to write anything!" he said. He snatched the pen and paper, threw them down, and shouted, "What is your name?"

The singer, flushed with anger, retorted, "I can't talk, you son of a bitch!"

Realizing what had happened, he began to shout, cried, embraced, kissed Thomaz's hand and proclaimed that a miracle had just taken place. Thomaz tried to explain that it was not a miracle but simply a manifestation of the singer's faith. In exasperation, Thomaz told him that if they didn't return home immediately and resume a normal life, he would cause the man to lose his voice again.

The next morning a long line of people formed outside the pharmacy. Everyone had heard of the "miraculous cure" and had come for a personal miracle. Thomaz's response was to entrust the shop to a clerk and leave town for two weeks.

It was during his sojourn to Conceição do Rio Verde that Thomaz married a local girl, Rosangela. Shortly after the wedding, Rosangela gave birth to a daughter, Natalia. The marriage was somewhat unsteady from the beginning and was a continual source of irritation for Thomaz. Many evenings after his long day at the pharmacy, Thomaz would stop off at the home of his best friend, a district judge, instead of going home to his family. Rosangela was not happy in Conceicão do Rio Verde. Thomaz agreed to move and spent several weekends driving around the region to research different locales. Eventually, Thomaz and Rosangela decided to move to Carmo do Cachoeira, which had only one other pharmacy and a population of twenty thousand—small enough for their country style of living. Before moving, Thomaz took his family to São Paulo for several months. His daughter, born prematurely, was in need of specialized medical care that could only be provided by a metropolitan hospital.

Wherever he moved, Thomaz soon became the most popular and most talked about person in town. During the six months he lived in São Paulo, he worked for a large drug store. Even as a clerk, his personality drew in so many new customers that the pharmacy was rescued from impending bankruptcy. Other clerks who worked with Thomaz recall his "simplicity—down-to-earth manner" and his ability to "communicate with anyone regardless of class, race, or wealth."

A trait that became obvious during this period was Thomaz's total ineptness at managing money. He displayed no appreciation of cash flow or budgets, simply spent more than he earned and all his friends described him as having an "open hand." He will inevitably pick up the check at a restaurant, even for strangers at nearby tables. His constant journeys, new automobiles, purchasing of electronic gadgets, and overly generous birthday and Christmas gifts all contributed to a state of chronic indebtedness.

Developing Psychic Talents

Once settled and established in Carmo do Cachoeira, Thomaz developed a close friendship with Saul Villela, a banker and owner of the building in which Thomaz opened his pharmacy. The two men had lunch together almost every day, and on weekends Thomaz spent many hours at the ranch owned by Villela's father. The older Villela, a retired physician, quickly became intrigued with Thomaz's increasing displays of apparent magic. On one memorable evening, Mr. Villela had invited a group of friends to be entertained by the extraordinary mystifying wizardry of his young friend. A spectator was invited to pick a card from a deck, show it to all onlookers, and then reshuffle the card back into the deck. Thomaz never touched any of the cards at any time. By focusing his energy and concentration on the deck, Thomaz caused the target card to edge its way slowly out of the pack and onto the table.

This demonstration of psychokinesis was followed by one of Thomaz's unique transmutation displays. He asked six of the men to sit in a circle. One of them was asked to take a one cruzeiro note from his billfold and pass it from person to person. By the time the bill reached the fifth person's hands the cruzeiro had become a guarani, currency from Paraguay. Sometimes the note would transmute into an Argentine peso or an American dollar. By the time it had returned to its point of origin, it had been reconstituted to its original form, a one cruzeiro bill. Thomaz always stood well outside the circle and never touched any of the currency.

On another occasion, Thomaz, Saul Villela, and a group of friends were drinking beer in a small pub. Thomaz offered to pick up the tab, which totaled one hundred fifty cruzeiros. At Thomaz's invitation, Saul joined him as he approached the cashier. Thomaz handed her a five cruzeiro note and told her to "take the charges out of this five hundred cruzeiro bill." The note transmuted during the transaction and the cashier returned the "change"—three hundred fifty cruzeiros! Everyone at the table laughed in enjoyment at Thomaz's supernatural joke. Saul, being a banker, returned to the cashier and asked to see the bill Thomaz had given her. There in the compartment for the five hundred denominations was the original five cruzeiro note. It should be pointed out that these sorts of transmutations have happened many times with Thomaz, but he has never taken advantage of his powers, nor has he ever cheated anyone. He always scrupulously paid the proper amount of the tab.

Soccer Lottery

Another phenomena that evolved during this period was a psychic feat that became one of Thomaz's trademarks. Soccer is Brazil's national mania; the Brazilian national team has won the World Championship three times. Every Monday, the Federal Reserve Bank issues a soccer lottery ticket, covering thirteen games for the week. Bettors can wager varying amounts, depending on how many teams they elect to win, lose, or tie. Almost all Brazilians, soccer buffs or not, play the lottery with accompanying dreams of wealth and retirement. Many times Thomaz has invited a friend or customer to bring him a new lottery form. The person is asked to fold it and hold it tightly in his clenched fist. Taking a lighted cigarette Thomaz will then burn the back of the person's hand. After his energy releasing "Ra!", the ticket is unfolded.

Depending on the circumstances, as few as two games or as many as thirteen teams will be selected, each indicated by a small hole psychokinetically charred into the ticket. According to Thomaz, he does this by "collecting information," letting his unconscious tap into the universal knowledge pool. He then transfers the energy by "channeling" the heat through the hand and onto the paper. Sometimes the charred selections will "move" and transfer to different boxes before the observer's eyes. In other words, the "burn" will dematerialize and reconstitute in another section of the slip of paper. Thomaz's accuracy varies, but he has made several astounding predictions in this fashion. No one, however, has benefited substantially from the payoffs.

A Growing Legend

Literally hundreds of Brazilians have worked with Thomaz. When they meet and exchange "Thomaz stories," they almost always display the emblematic burn scar on their hands. This scar seems to serve as a private symbol and metaphor for a kind of knowledge that can only be acquired by indirect and mysterious means.

In discussing his personal experiences with Thomaz, Saul Villela is less awed by the miracles than with his dignity as a person. Once a pregnant woman fainted outside the pharmacy. Thomaz carried her inside, administered first aid, and spent time talking to her, calming her fears. He then closed the shop, drove the woman to the hospital, had her admitted, and assumed all financial responsibility for her treatment and care. Thomaz also seemed very sensitive to people's personal needs and would go out of his way to talk with upset or anxious clients. He would not necessarily entertain or display his wizardry every day. Nonetheless, he would touch or grace an herbal remedy or prescription, assuring the client that "special energy" had gone into its preparation.

Superstition and fabrications have added unfounded dimensions to the legend of Thomaz in the district. One of these stories told about Thomaz was that he had the ability to resuscitate the dead. It seems Thomaz had gone to the hospital to visit the mother of a friend and arrived to find a room of weeping relatives. Just five minutes before the patient had been pronounced clinically dead. Thomaz abruptly blew out the candles and said, "What do you mean she's dead? Don't grieve—that won't help her." Within a few moments the "corpse" twitched and then moaned. The ensuing pandemonium brought a rescue team of doctors and nurses, who revived the patient.

Thomaz insisted that he had absolutely no power over a lifeless form, but was unable to convince the adulatory relatives. The attending physician unwittingly played into their belief by refusing to admit that he had made a serious diagnostic error. Despite Thomaz's sincere denials, the least the family would concede was that it was a very "suspicious coincidence" that the woman revived at the very moment Thomaz leaned over her.

Rosangela, Natalia, and Thomaz lived in Carmo do Cachoeira for only two years, interrupted by brief intervals spent in nearby towns. Despite Thomaz's brief stay and the passage of time, the townspeople even today remember the psychic feats, transmutations, and miracle cures that Thomaz brought with him. Their most vivid recollections, however, were of his warmth, the attention he lavished on his customers, and the special care he gave to children.

CHAPTER FIVE

Geller Comes to Brazil

Faith is to believe what we do not see and the reward is to see what we believe.

St. Augustine

The interior of Minas Gerais is one of the most charming regions of Brazil. In contrast to the anxious excitement of the coastal cities, it has a calm and healing atmosphere. Many Brazilians visit the picturesque towns, but most tourists are drawn from Argentina, Paraguay, and Chile. The principal attractions are the rustic villages and mineral water springs that fan out through the countryside. Set among green rolling hills, each town features special parks abundant with natural springs. The mineral elements vary in their composition from town to town. Doctors frequently prescribe certain springs for their patients depending on the nature of the ailment.

Relocation to Trés Corações

When his marriage came to an end in 1974, Thomaz moved to the town of Trés Corações, just ten miles from Cambuquira where he had been living and working with his brother-in-law, Noe. Trés Corações translates as "three hearts," a name derived from the river that loops through the town, forming the shape of three hearts. The little town is held in very special esteem in Brazil; in 1941, it became the birthplace of Edson Arantes do Nascimento, later known as Pele, the legendary soccer wizard who led Brazil to three world championships. Voted the athlete of the decade by the European press, Pele is honored by a magnificent statue standing at the town's center.

Thomaz's relocation to Trés Corações was precipitated by the breakup of his marriage. His ex-wife, Rosangela, moved with their daughter to a nearby town and took up residence with her mother. Thomaz made the transition from marriage to bachelorhood gradually. He opened a pharmacy in Trés Corações while still maintaining the first pharmacy in Carmo do Cachoeira. Once again his father assisted with start-up costs. Thomaz, as usual, had little capital—he squandered a good deal of his money picking up restaurant tabs for his friends. To make matters worse, he also developed a mania for automobiles during this period, purchasing a new car every six months, and with casual recklessness destroying it by hot-rodding through the countryside.

During this difficult period of his life he also began drinking, showing preference for beer and imported Scotch whiskey. His favorite bar was a small nightclub owned by Paulo Costa, who went on to become Secretary of Tourism for the region. Thomaz always drank with friends and always paid for the rounds. In a country where an ounce of Chivas Regal can cost up to ten dollars, it is not surprising that Thomaz was chronically in debt.

Eventually, Thomaz sold the pharmacy in Carmo do Cachoeira and attempted to establish a whole new life for himself. Despite the lingering memories of a failed marriage, he began seeing a local girl, Lygia Goz, a tall, beautiful young woman of Turkish descent. She provided a simple, down-to-earth balance to Thomaz's chaotic and unruly life-style, which affected even the organization of his pharmacy. When supplies ran low, Thomaz "increased inventory" by placing empty boxes on the shelves. Former employees still chuckle at how he would spend hours carefully stacking and rearranging packages for medicine and pills, most of them empty. Days later, he would remove everything from the shelves, conscientiously dust the bottles and boxes, and reshelve them in a totally different order. Even today, Thomaz will wander into his pharmacy and without warning will go into what the staff calls a "reorganization frenzy."

Thomaz's move to Trés Corações in 1974 was an important milestone in the acceleration of his psychic abilities and in relating to those powers more maturely. No longer satisfied merely to entertain friends with astonishing displays of phenomena, he made an effort to understand the meaning of paranormal energies and what happened to him at Fasqueira. His search for meaning engaged the imagination of some of the local intellectuals. Finding him sincere, a number of prominent and well-educated townspeople stimulated and encouraged his psychic growth, and soon he won their trust and respect. An entourage of friends, fans, and "paranormal groupies" began to form.

One of Thomaz's most enduring friendships began in a seemingly innocuous fashion soon after he took up residence in Trés Corações. Seito Masahilo, a forty-eight-year-old mechanic, worked at an auto parts factory in São Paulo. The only son of Japanese immigrants, he had been promoted to a traveling sales position with a territory that included Trés Corações. While refueling his automobile at a truck stop one day, he suddenly doubled over in agonizing pain. The attendant told him of a local miraculous pharmacist who possessed unusual curative powers. By simply "touching" the medicine bottle, the attendant said, he was able to energize the contents, thereby adding to the potency of the medication.

Because of his discomfort, Seito needed little convincing; within a half-hour he had arrived at the pharmacy. Listening intently to Seito's complaints, Thomaz reached for a specifically prepared, homemade homeopathic remedy, added one more ingredient, and handed it to his customer. Seito immediately took a dose of the medicine and experienced almost instant relief. Instead of charging Seito for the remedy, Thomaz asked his new mechanic friend to examine his recently purchased jeep that was always stalling. In short order, Seito repaired the jeep and had it running smoothly. This seemed to cement the instant rapport of the two men, so much so that Seito left his job, moved to Trés Corações, and opened a garage. Their friendship soon became indispensable. Thomaz continued to treat Seito for several physical ailments, and in return Seito repaired Thomaz's exhausted, badly abused automobiles.

Thomaz continued to date Lygia, but he could not be described as devoted during this period. Some of his determined womanizing could be attributed to his ruined marriage, but Thomaz also attributes his behavior to the Brazilian-Latin "macho" mentality. He does exude a very powerful charisma many women find irresistible, and this appeal seems to transcend mere physical attractiveness. "I feel a strong, sexual, magnetlike pull in his direction . . . it is like the electricity you sometimes feel before an orgasm," one woman remarked. Lygia, who is very jealous, went through a trying series of episodes with Thomaz. They were married in 1980 and today Thomaz openly admires Lygia's nature and her tolerance of a husband "driven by impulses."

Thomaz is a gentle and indulgent person in most situations, but he also has a demanding and perfectionist streak. On Sunday, all pharmacies in town close down, with the exception of one, which is required by law to remain open. One Sunday, the rotation fell to Thomaz's drugstore. As it was a quiet day, the on-duty clerk was across the street chatting with a friend. Thomaz, driving by, saw his clerk and became furious. He fired the clerk and offered the job to a friend. During this period, Thomaz was punctual, organized, and conscientious, almost to a fault, in his efforts to serve the public; he expected the same dedication from everyone on his payroll. It is ironic that as he became better known as a psychic, his character traits of reliability, promptness, and compulsiveness faded like so many other aspects of his former life.

Geller's Visit

In 1976, Uri Geller, the internationally famous psychic, came to Brazil, accepting a joint invitation to be the opening speaker at a parapsychology congress and to appear on Brazil's Globo television network. Geller was readily accepted and openly welcomed in this naturally mystical country. His demonstration on television was watched by more Brazilians than any other program in the history of the country except for world soccer matches.

In his typical manner, Geller astounded the viewers by exhibiting clairvoyance, telepathy, and metal-bending under controlled circumstances. Scientists observing in the studio provided their own silverware; Geller bent, distorted, and, in two cases fractured the spoons and knives, using only his mind's energy. In some instances, he would lightly stroke the metal; in other cases someone else held the cutlery and Geller would not touch it at all.

As he had done in similar demonstrations in Europe, Asia, and North America, Geller invited the viewing audience to replicate what he had done in their own homes. Countless Brazilians held knives, spoons, broken watches, radios that had not worked in years, and keys of various sizes before Geller's image on the screen. Within minutes, telephone calls flooded the station switchboard; excited viewers were reporting the mind-boggling display of a new visual vocabulary. Bent spoons, twisted forks, flexed keys, and old broken watches were awakening from long slumbers—all expressing defiance of conventions on a national scale. Brazil was seeing the early editions of a new vision of reality.

Thomaz did not see Geller on television. He had been spending a few quiet days on the farm with his sister and brother-in-law. When he returned to Trés Corações, he stopped at the bus station luncheonette for a beer, where he happened upon his friend, Paulo Costa. Paulo was one of the few persons in this unsophisticated region who openly encouraged Thomaz to develop his paranormal powers. Thomaz, he thought, was becoming psychically "flabby." Most of his demonstrations were now taking place in the nightclub, late in the evening, sitting around a table with a group of friends. Paulo had seen Thomaz repeatedly "repair" cruzeiro notes that had been torn in two; he had witnessed pieces of a paper napkin transmuted into bills of varying denominations. Most of these absurdities of logic took place in a spontaneous or even whimsical fashion. Paulo began encouraging Thomaz to become more disciplined, to train on a regular basis.

First Metal-Bending Attempt

Paulo felt confident that Thomaz could replicate all of Geller's feats, and more. Excited, he gave Thomaz a detailed account of Geller's exhibition. "Thomaz, why can't you bend metal?" Paulo challenged. Thomaz replied that he neither knew how, nor had it ever occurred to him to even attempt such a thing. Four beers later, Thomaz decided to respond to his friend's invitation. He asked the waiter to bring him a soup spoon. He took the spoon and calmly raised it above his head. Closing his eyes, Thomaz concentrated intensely. In his own words, "I felt a streak of energy beginning at the base of my spine; it went all the way up to the top of my head . . . I heard the sound of this energy—it was like a million bees all buzzing at the same time . . . I had to open my eyes . . . I could see it . . . the energy was like sparks or rays of light coming out of my hands and fingertips . . . I then held the handle of the spoon in both of my hands. . . ." To the amazement of both Thomaz and Paulo, the spoon fractured into two pieces! Just like that! Gone forever was another member of Thomaz's shrinking family of limitations.

Thomaz was excited by his success but also annoyed with his

failure to *bend* the metal for that had been his intention. He possesses a childlike streak of stubbornness when he does not achieve what he has set out to do. For example, Thomaz became a psychic wild man in his solitary enthusiasm for making compass needles spin, particularly when told about Nina Kulagina, the noted Russian paranormal who could spin a compass arrow by psychic force alone. Thomaz became obsessed to the point of perversity. He would remove his shirt, sit hunched over a table, close his eyes, and begin to concentrate. After a few moments, he would extend his arms straight out over a large compass, and then his entire body would join the rhythmic back-and-forth movement of his hands. The hissing noise of his hyperventilation would usually be the signal for the compass needle to begin spinning, as if it were being twirled by an invisible hand. At such times, Thomaz seems to enter into a seamless unity in which his mind, body, and spirit fuse into a total synchrony with the compass. The needle often spins so fast that observers can only see a blurry whirl. But this never seems to satisfy Thomaz. His childlike temperament usually surfaces at this point and he stubbornly proclaims, "I am going to make this compass explode!" With continued hyperventilation, tensing of his muscles, and an increasing feverish crimson spreading over his body, Thomaz continues to push himself, sometimes losing consciousness and requiring resuscitation with lime juice and salt. He has been able to create total magnetic disarray, but he had not yet shattered a compass. Consequently, his physician has prohibited Thomaz from working with compasses again because he never knows when to stop.

So, on that lazy day in the bus station in 1976, Thomaz began to feel that same kind of nagging obstinacy as he had with compasses. He was haunted by questions. "Why did the spoon break instead of bending? Why can't I do it?" He later theorized to the authors that he could not bend metal because he was simply "green"—he could mobilize the right kind of energy but did not know how to control its intensity.

That night, he began to practice his newly discovered faculty.

With great intensity, he worked alone at his new mind-emancipating task. One piece of silverware followed another, but without success. Thomaz managed to fracture every single fork, spoon, and knife in the kitchen but was unable to bend them. At the end of the session he had an orange crate full of fractured cutlery that had been "psychically unglued."

Paulo, visiting Thomaz at his apartment the next day, suggested a practical alternative. "Try bending coins," he suggested. "They are smaller and perhaps easier to manage in directing energy." Taking Paulo's suggestion, Thomaz held a coin in his outstretched hand, closed his eyes, concentrated intensely, and "forced energy" into the palm of his hand. Opening his eyes, he saw that the coin was curved, almost at a ninety-degree angle. Success! Needless to say, Thomaz spent much of his spare time over the following days psychically bending coins until he got bored with it all.

Several days later, Paulo suggested that Thomaz had too much money invested in silverware to leave it laying about in an old orange crate. "Why don't you try to mend those pieces together?"

In Thomaz's words, "the hairs on my arms stood on end" when Paulo made his provocative suggestion. "The hairs on my arm act like an antenna," Thomaz explained. "When they go erect, I know that something is happening or will happen shortly—the hairs on my arms are like my personal public address system for anything out of the ordinary."

Picking up two pieces of broken spoon, Thomaz held them together, edge to edge. Focusing his consciousness, he saw a "flowing connectedness" and visualized the spoon in its original state. He could also see a very thin energy shower of "sparks" emanating from his thumbs and fingers and enveloping most of the spoon. The subtle energy cloud could not be seen by Paulo, but both men saw the spoon "restore itself" and shrieked at the same time—another triumph. Thomaz spent the next several days psychokinetically mending his silverware collection. At times, like an exacting artisan, he would physically fracture the spoon again and mend it with the welding arc of his consciousness. Thomaz was feeling good about what was happening. Inspired, he continued his pyschic flexing and apprenticeship in working with metal. It was only a matter of time before he would add to his control, increasing editions of reality.

It happened three nights later. Thomaz went to Paulo's nightclub and in the middle of a half-drunken conversation, asked for a soup spoon. Holding it above his head, he began twirling the spoon as if he were waving a flag at a soccer game. To his delighted astonishment, the spoon twirled into three distinct loops, just where the stem arches, before spreading into the bowl of the spoon. It did not break! Thomaz was congratulated and embraced by Paulo for his perseverance. One of the men with them picked up the spoon and looked at it incredulously. Using both hands and exerting considerable force, the man tried to straighten out the spoon, but it was made of strong metal and he could not change its capriciously acquired shape.

For the next several weeks, Thomaz went through a period of "metal-bending madness." At every meal, in every restaurant he would twirl spoons and forks in the air, as if he were a child brandishing an imaginary sword. If he rotated to the left, the metal would twist to the left. If he wanted the stem to rotate to the right he would twirl the spoon clockwise. Initially, Thomaz believed that the gyrations of his arm and direction of spin determined the final shape of the silverware. Through trial and error, however, he discovered that arm motion had nothing to do with metal-bending.

His experimentation during this early phase became very costly. Though restaurant managers were at first amused by the flamboyant presence and the intriguing absurdity of misshapen cutlery, this soon changed. In addition to the usual charges for food and drink, Thomaz was presented with a special tab for "damaged silverware." Even so, dozens of restaurants in the region have kept literally hundreds of bent knives, forks, and spoons. They serve as sculpted reminders of how Thomaz was continuing to rearrange our flawed visions of what is natural and possible.

Other Metal-Bending Feats

In the course of his psychic evolution over the next few years, Thomaz discovered that it was not necessary for him to touch the silverware. Simply passing his hands over a spoon or fork on the table was sufficient to kindle the metal-bending process. Many times cutlery would bend spontaneously at the end of the table opposite to where Thomaz was sitting. Frequently it would have to be drawn to his attention.

One of the most mystifying episodes of metal-bending took place in June 1980. Gary had gone to Trés Corações to spend a week with Thomaz. Following dinner one evening, several friends accompanied Thomaz home for a nightcap. After making drinks for his guests, Thomaz began to search frantically for something in the kitchen. He wanted to make a very special medicine chest for his son Raphael and discovered a beautiful cedar case. It contained a 160-piece silverware set given to Thomaz and Lygia as a wedding gift. He started to pick it up and Lygia put her foot down. She would not let him have the chest, and a short while later, she concealed the cedar box under a pile of old newspapers in the bottom shelf of the pantry. Thomaz found it but she abruptly stepped in and looked her husband squarely in the eye. He shrugged his shoulders, walked back to his guests, and an hour or so later, the guests left and Thomaz and Lygia went to bed.

Gary spent the night on a sofa located in a small room directly in front of the master bedroom. He woke up at 7:30 A.M., made coffee, and went into the living room to transcribe notes and bring his diary up to date. Thomaz, who rarely wakes up before midday, awoke at 11:30 and rushed excitedly to Gary. He said, "Gary, you know that silverware box . . . I think . . . let's go find it!"

As they walked into the pantry, he mumbled, "Oh my God! If it is true, Lygia will have a fit." Gary did not know what he was talking about. They reached under the pile of newspapers, pulled out the cedar chest, and Thomaz warily lifted the top. Every single one of the one hundred sixty pieces of cutlery was twisted, bent, or curled. Thomaz cried, "Oh no!" and then began to laugh. Gary, having vowed never to be surprised again by anything Thomaz did, was dumbfounded.

Thomaz explained that he had gone to bed the night before obsessed with wanting to do something with the cedar chest for their infant son and irritated with Lygia for interfering with his plans. Drifting off to sleep, he continued to mull things over. His preoccupation seemed to blend into a lucid dream. In the dream, he crept into the pantry and removed the cedar box. He was determined to make a medicine chest for Raphael. Continuing the dream, he went into the kitchen, removed the contents of the cedar box, and threw Lygia's precious cutlery inside an old drawer. He was unable to close the drawer so he visualized the knives and forks bending to fit the limited space. He was still unable to shut the drawer and left three or four forks hanging outside, their metal tongues extended in a symbolic gesture. "There," Thomaz said, "that was my dream."

Gary, a very light sleeper, heard no sounds in the house the entire night until he woke up. Thomaz could not provide an explanation of how all the cutlery had bent during his dreams. We were left with the unfashionable conclusion that there are indeed some elements of irrationality that serve as connective links between our everyday lives and our dreams. Needless to say, Lygia was furious, and Thomaz, in exchange for the cedar chest, had to replace the silverware set.

During our second visit in 1982, Thomaz agreed to demonstrate metal-bending so that we could document it on a video camera. Thomaz and I drove into town and I directed him to a large supermarket. Once inside, Thomaz went directly to the liquor department to purchase two bottles of Scotch. I wandered through the aisles until I came upon a large circular bin full of inexpensive silverware. Each package had three pieces of cutlery and was tightly wrapped and sealed on both ends with cellophane. I placed about eighteen of these packages into the shopping cart and went directly to the checkout station. Thomaz had preceded me in the same line, paying for his own Scotch. As I began to hand the clerk the packages, I noticed that three knives in one package were bent into a tight "S" shape. The cellophane paper was intact. I started to explain in broken Portuguese that the knives were bent or damaged and that I would take them back and replace them.

I froze in mid-sentence, realizing what had happened. Five of the packages contained bent cutlery. All of the forks were distorted in an identical fashion (Figure 5-1). The knives and spoons had their own distinctive misshapen personalities. What most startled and astounded me was that the tines of the forks were poking grotesquely in several directions. The cellophane wrapper, however, was not punctured and the price tag was glued on the same spot as the other packages. Thomaz was at first surprised and perplexed. Then he began a little dance of jubilation and chattered excitedly all the way back to the clinic. Upon my return to Canada, I had two of the packages framed. This unusual art display is now hanging in my office as a reminder of Thomaz's innocent defiance of scientific presumptions.

Metal-bending is no longer a challenge for Thomaz. He does not have to concentrate, visualize, or will the phenomenon into being. Spoons bend spontaneously as he is stirring his coffee, and metal coins and medallions frequently fracture into two pieces in his presence. One evening he went to bed at a friend's home and when she and her husband awoke to make coffee the next morning, the fireplace tools, including a shovel, poker, and metal stand, were all twisted and gracefully frozen in a midair pirouette. Thomaz was still asleep!

Aside from the lightning experience at Fasqueira, Thomaz claims that Uri Geller's visit to Brazil had the greatest impact on his psychic development. Even though Thomaz had demonstrated more powerful phenomena, metal-bending seemed easier for people to accept initially. Geller also seemed to serve as a role model for Thomaz—Uri had become a multimillionaire from his

Figure 5-1

public demonstrations and book sales. Slowly, Thomaz began to identify himself as a psychic. After all, his profligate lifestyle was difficult to support solely by his pharmacy.

Influence of Friends and Admirers

Four years had gone by between Thomaz's earlier awkward efforts at metal-bending and the 1980 incident where he seemed to physically materialize the events of a lucid dream. Thomaz's abilities were evolving! He had also gone from cautiously accepting his strange abilities to enjoying the satisfaction his powers provided for his friends. He was also experiencing an increasing sense of fulfillment and was seriously considering "being a psychic" as a profession, instead of treating it as a curious pastime. However, there were many false starts, frustrations, and welcome diversions along the way.

In 1977, while lunching at a restaurant, he picked up a fork, and twirled it in the air. Another restaurant patron, Colonel Vianna Peres, a military officer, bolted upright. He walked over to Thomaz's table, introduced himself, and picked up the fork, which now had a double loop in the stem. He was unable to bend it back into its normal shape. He reached over to another table, took an identical unbent fork, and, again, could not bend it without exerting great force.

This incident marked the beginning of another friendship, one that introduced Thomaz to a number of the colonel's friends, many of them intellectuals who developed a scholarly interest in this curly-haired, bright-eyed young man. Thomaz, after all, was a large rock in their now barely navigable scientific stream. The group, which included physicians, artists, and lawyers, met often, less for entertainment than for serious explorations—explorations that added a refreshing dimension to Thomaz's psychic growing pains. The young psychic was stimulated by their questions and hypotheses. They often asked about the source of his energy. Was he a channel for spirit entities? Extraterrestrials? Some other earthly force? Does the energy come from an intrapsychic source rather than external origins? Why is the availability of the energy unpredictable?

Unlike skilled stage magicians, who can imitate most psychic phenomena whenever they want to, Thomaz cannot always perform upon command. Several times he tried to produce phenomena for the colonel's friends and couldn't. Interestingly, phenomena would manifest only when Thomaz would lighten the situation with humor or playfulness. Thomaz openly acknowledges that this "special power" cannot be summoned in the same way as one forms a thought. It is "something else," and his interpretations have varied with time and influence of personal associations. Regardless, he must wait for the "click" and the alarm-arousal of the "hairs on my forearms standing up" before he can channel specific energy.

The colonel and his friends provided a much-needed leavening influence on Thomaz. The spreading network of Thomaz's admirers and supporters was soon widened to include someone very much beloved by him. Ovidio Loyola, chief of police in Trés Corações, married Thomaz's sister Vera. For Thomaz, Ovidio was not just a brother-in-law. He was a brother, a devoted friend, a "camarada." In turn, the warm-hearted chief of police became Thomaz's most avid enthusiast and supporter. During their many nights on the town together, Ovidio repeatedly encouraged Thomaz to go to the United States for "official" assessments and investigation by scientists. Intensely proud and protective of his brother-in-law, Ovidio always assigned at least one member of the police force to be present at Thomaz's demonstrations. One skeptical citizen who had never seen Thomaz's work in person, spent the night in jail because he suggested to Ovidio that Thomaz was "fraudulent."

Another important influence entered Thomaz's life at this time—Dr. Bernardino Dessimoni, a general practitioner and psychiatrist. Dr. Dessimoni cannot account for the "irresistible urge" that led him to abandon a lucrative practice at his own clinic and move to Trés Corações in 1978. He first met Thomaz at the town's military club where Thomaz was demonstrating

Figure 5-2

metal-bending. After an evening of cautious scrutiny, the doctor was convinced that Thomaz was genuine. Dr. Dessimoni pledged offhandedly to tear his medical diploma in two as a symbolic testimonial to the psychic powers that are eluding classical science. Later Thomaz requested that his physician friend honor that pledge. Reluctantly, Dr. Dessimoni tore the diploma in two as directed (Figure 5-2). He was then instructed to fold each half again, three times. Both halves were placed under his right hand, which rested on the table top. Thomaz closed his eyes, held his breath, and stretched both arms straight out over the doctor's hand. He said, "At this moment, I 'mentalize' with all the mental, spiritual, and universal forces that your medical degree become mended, but that a small tear remains as a memory of this day . . . at this moment . . . Ra!" Dr. Dessimoni lifted his hand and saw that his medical diploma was totally reconstituted—except for a two-inch tear at the top (Figure 5-3). A series of high-speed photographs were taken by two of the many observers during the "tearing-mending" session.

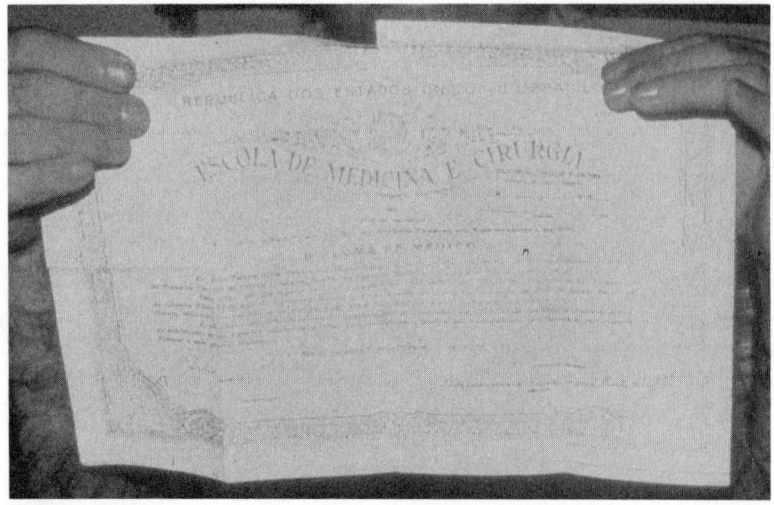

Figure 5-3

Dr. Dessimoni is now a close friend, supporter, and advocate of Thomaz's abilities to his medical colleagues. Thomaz has had relatively few problems with the medical community. As a nonlicensed layperson, he could be charged, fined, or even sent to prison because he openly diagnoses, treats, and prescribes medication for illnesses. The various Brazilian state medical associations have made several aborted efforts to prohibit "unorthodox" treatment. It would appear, however, that President Juscelino Kubitcheck's pardon of the legendary Arigo established a precedent. Practically all of Brazil's many laying-on-of-hands mediums, trance healers, and psychic surgeons have a special and tacit immunity from prosecution.

Influence of Cousin Lada

Thomaz's world often seems to be a series of enchanting synchronicities and meaningful relationships that align at just the right moment. On January 30, 1979, Teresa Esmeralda Souza,

Thomaz's cousin, moved from Rio de Janeiro to Trés Corações. Teresa, or "Lada" as she is affectionately called, is fifty-six and totally blind. She suffered a detached retina seven years before, and slowly lost her sight, first in one eye, then in the other. Lada, formerly a successful administrator in one of Brazil's largest multinational tobacco companies, had desperately tried all resources to save her failing vision—first Western medicine, ophthalmologists, and two visits to the United States for surgery at noted medical centers. Nonetheless, her eyesight blurred into gray, formless shadows. She turned next to more ancient traditions—acupuncture, nutrition, a rigid macrobiotic diet, healers, and even a trance-medium who specialized in former lives. She was given a "karmic explanation" for her blindness and was led through a hypnotic regression into a past life. Despite her wider spiritual perspectives on the origins of her blindness, her vision was not restored.

Lada's mother, Dr. Morais' sister, left Minas Gerais at an early age and rarely saw her relatives. Through family gossip, Lada had heard of her mischievous cousin but never met him. She was totally unaware of the incident at Fasqueira and knew nothing of Thomaz's rapidly developing powers. Then, during one of his visits to a homeopathic laboratory in Rio, Thomaz decided to pay a courtesy visit to his relatives. He was very much moved when he learned of his cousin's affliction and instantly decided to do everything in his power to restore her sight. Lada's interests had always been of an intellectual and literate nature, with little experience in the supernatural realms. That was soon to change. Thomaz had to return home but promised to come for her in ten days. Swept away by his enthusiasm, Lada couldn't wait. She packed her belongings and accompanied Thomaz to Trés Corações the next day. They have rarely been apart ever since.

A disciplined person, Lada brought a sense of order into her cousin's chaotic lifestyle. She moved into his apartment and sensed that it reflected an "excess of bachelorhood." The refrigerator contained only beer and all of Thomaz's friends had keys to the apartment. Slowly, given reasons to adjust to someone else's needs, Thomaz began to change his habits, allowing some routine into his life.

As his cousin learned the history of Fasqueira, of the "voices" that had told Thomaz to "mentalize" every evening at six o'clock, she encouraged him to follow their admonitions. As a result, regardless of where he is or what he is doing, Thomaz faithfully leads a group meditation daily at six and again at midnight. Though the content of his "mentalizations" varies slightly each time, he always includes a stirring passage on blindness along with the direction of healing energies to every illness imaginable, love for mankind, for God's beauty, and a special appreciation for animals.

One memorable evening, while meditating with Thomaz on the veranda of his clinic overlooking the lake, he led us through a series of concentration and healing visualizations. As he was concluding the "mentalizations" with special reference to the "birds created by our maker," there was a pause and a silent hush. From behind us a flock of almost one thousand birds flew over the house, dipped down in a respectful salute toward the lake in front of us, and then veered sharply to the right in tight squadron formation. Coincidence? Perhaps. Nonetheless, we felt that for a few exhilarating moments we had become a part of the ineffable synchronistic flow of the universe.

Lada also took charge of distributing splinters from Thomaz's charred fishing pole to needy recipients. Regardless of where they lived, recipients were advised on participating in the evening "mentalizations." These sessions have now become the rallying point for an evening with Thomaz.

In recent years, Thomaz has become increasingly less active in managing the pharmacy. He now makes occasional appearances, but the actual management is conducted by his staff. Rarely awake before midday, Thomaz will spend the afternoon inventing errands, visiting friends, and reorganizing his clinic. His reputation has grown enormously in the past several years. Many of his admirers will travel to Minas Gerais for the weekend just to be near him.

With her special dignity and grace, Lada has become an unofficial hostess and spokesperson for Thomaz. Perhaps most importantly she has quietly insisted on documenting in detail every single phenomenon. She has taped more than three hundred hours of extensive interviews that she herself meticulously conducted. Every person connected with Thomaz—friends, chance acquaintances, patients, scientists, and the authors—have been interviewed by Lada. Every Thomaz phenomena that has been observed by more than one person is recorded on tape. She has done a great deal of cross-referencing, as most sessions with Thomaz include several observers: All are interviewed to assure consistencies or inconsistencies in their perceptions and recall.

Lygia has also kept a very extensive "psychic diary" of her husband's extraordinary activities, recording the date, circumstances, and nature of the paranormal event. Names and addresses of witnesses are postscripted. Though much of the data for this book has been obtained firsthand or through reliable witnesses, we were fortunate in having access to these two interweaving but separate sources of information. Whenever we had any doubt about a particular incident, a detailed account was always available through Lada's or Lygia's records.

Other persons have also documented Thomaz's demonstrations. A professional cinematographer from São Paulo has filmed over one hundred hours of Thomaz's sessions. Paranormal phenomena are notoriously "shy," whimsical, and almost impossible to capture and reduce to a mere two-dimensional reality. There is a video record, however, of transmutations, metal-bending, transteleportation, and Thomaz spinning a compass in his uniquely magnetic fashion. In addition to filming phenomena, cinematographer Helena da Cunha Bueno has captured much of the "electricity" and overpowering emotions that affect observers during sessions. She has also conducted in-depth interviews of Thomaz describing his "energy rushes" rising from the base of his spine. More recently, he has added new information describing the subtleties and complexities of the energy, along with tantalizing references to his transteleportations to an alleged parallel universe called "Aphron-V." Early in 1981, Thomaz purchased a portable video recording unit. Lygia has mastered the equipment and now chronicles every paranormal event that Thomaz is involved in.

Despite many ministrations, remedies, and Thomaz's psychic surgery, Lada is still blind. He has referred to this keen disappointment as "a reason for always remembering the meaning of humility." Lada serves as a reminder of Thomaz's shortcomings, at the same time helping him to gain confidence enough to pursue a full-time mission as a psychic. In her wise and determined manner, she is helping her cousin expunge the word "impossible" from his vocabulary.

CHAPTER SIX

Scientists and the Psychic

> ... there exists an 'interconnectedness' of the human mind and matter ... which could have far-reaching social and political implications for this nation and the world ...
>
> *U.S. House of Representatives Science and Technology Committee, June 1981*

In North America, at least eight scientific publications currently report research activity on psychic phenomena. Despite a sparse allocation of $500,000 per year, a growing community of Western scholars is aggressively pursuing parapsychological investigations. Although Brazil is probably the most fertile and diverse focus of psychic activity in the world, no full-time *psi* researchers reside in that country. The government has not created agencies, nor provided any resources or research funds. It has failed to formally legitimize and explore what is one of the country's true natural resources.

Brazil's Practicing Parapsychologists

Most Brazilian researchers are employed full-time as psychologists or engineers; they are engaged in parapsychology as a hobby. In addition, the investigators are generally spiritists and frequently mediums themselves. One could easily challenge this very narrow and perhaps biased group as unscientific and lacking in rigor. Regardless, Brazilian parapsychologists have a pantheon of marvels in their files that would stagger even the most cautious of Western scientists.

Two scientists in Brazil stand out as leaders and innovators in the field of parapsychology. Gloria Lintz Machado, M.D., is a practicing physician and psychiatrist. As a concert pianist, she also holds an academic appointment at the Federal University of Music in Rio de Janeiro. Dr. Machado inherited an interest in "frontier sciences" from her physician father, who devoted his professional career to developing a form of medical treatment that uses the healing properties of water. Dr. Machado combines a healthy sense of skepticism and scholarly curiosity with a generous, warm, and energetic personality. Her husband, Professor Mario Amaral Machado, is an electrical engineer who abandoned a successful career with a petroleum corporation to pursue the paradoxes of psychic phenomena. He is an excellent administrator and thoughtful scientist who is able to see beyond our limiting philosophical filters.

Together, the Machados founded the Rio de Janeiro Institute of Parapsychology in 1967 and the Brazilian Association of Parapsychology in 1976. The Institute is housed in a two-story house one block away from the city's capacious Maracana soccer stadium. Mario Machado creates and assembles all the equipment used in the various tests and experiments with psychics. These range from interferometers to sophisticated Kirlian apparatus components. The Institute includes a small clinic in which alleged healers and psychic surgeons are investigated. Volunteer patients for healing experiments are given full medicals and thorough pre- and post-laboratory workups. The Institute is overseen by a board of directors representing a broad spectrum of the business and professional community and distinguished by their pursuit of excellence in Institute activities. Although both Machados are spiritists, their laboratory work is firmly grounded in scientific methodology and observation techniques.

The Brazilian Parapsychology Association commemorated its founding in 1976 by sponsoring Uri Geller for a series of demonstrations in Brazil. Since then, the Association has convened every two years with notable success. The format of the meetings is varied and unique. Scientists and parapsychologists present traditional papers and progress reports on their research, but the conferences also provide a forum for healers, deep-trance mediums, and materialization psychics to demonstrate their abilities in front of a critical yet receptive audience. The Association has also been successful in establishing a parapsychology degree program at the University of Parana.

Most of Brazil's better-known psychics live in the southeastern part of the country, but a number of outstanding mediums and psychic surgeons live in small villages and generally inaccessible regions throughout the country. Aside from the meetings of the Association, there is no formal communication network to inform interested researchers of paranormal occurrences. An unofficial "underground" notifies concerned individuals by telephone or by forwarding town newspaper clippings describing local psychic events. (Gary Richman, the Machados, Dr. Hernani Andrade of São Paulo, Monsignor Arlindo Mombach of Salvador, General Moacyr Uchoa of Brasília, and many others are all part of a loosely structured but purposeful collaboration to draw attention to the importance of capricious anomalies.) It was through this information network that the Machados first heard about a young pharmacist from Minas Gerais whose powers were even more baffling and "magical" than those of Uri Geller.

Thomaz and the Machados

In February 1979, Thomaz was invited for dinner at the Machados' home, which is located in one of Rio de Janeiro's luxuriant, hillside forests. Mario Machado, a seasoned *psi* researcher, is very careful to create the proper context in which psychic abilities can most easily be manifested. Western parapsychologists are just beginning to realize that paranormal capacities are substantially diminished by rigid constraints or by the presence of unemotional, indifferent observers. Thomaz, in particular, will never allow himself to be scrutinized in mechanical, "psychic-slave" fashion. He understands intuitively that the more science restricts its focus to order and predictability, the less meaning unfathomable events of the psyche will have. Mario and Gloria Machado also realize that the elusive process of psychic consciousness is much more important than the end product or magical event.

The evening began in a warm and hospitable fashion. Superb Brazilian food, an excellent wine cellar, and levity established the mood of the group. Thomaz knows that he cannot always mobilize his energy simply by willing it to be there; he has to have harmony with his observers, the surroundings must be consonant with his mood, and most important of all, he must be animated by the "psychic click" and flow of electrical energy up his spine.

Thomaz began describing to the Machados how Geller's 1976 television appearance affected him and his subsequent development as a metal-bender. Recollecting, he demonstrated how "I picked up a soup spoon and bent it . . . I then concentrated and commanded that everything on the table bend. Ra!" At that moment, all the silverware, a silver tray, and metal water pitcher on the table bent, twisted, and went into varying degrees of molecular collapse (Figure 6-1). The Machados' initial stupor over a ruined sterling silver dinner set was replaced with the electrifying realization of what they had just witnessed. And Thomaz hadn't even touched the silverware as most of it was outside his reach!

An important relationship had been born. Thomaz liked and trusted the Machados and agreed to further experiments in their laboratory. The next morning at the Institute he allowed himself to be stripped and was examined thoroughly, including mouth, ears, and hands for possible chemical tampering. All this was

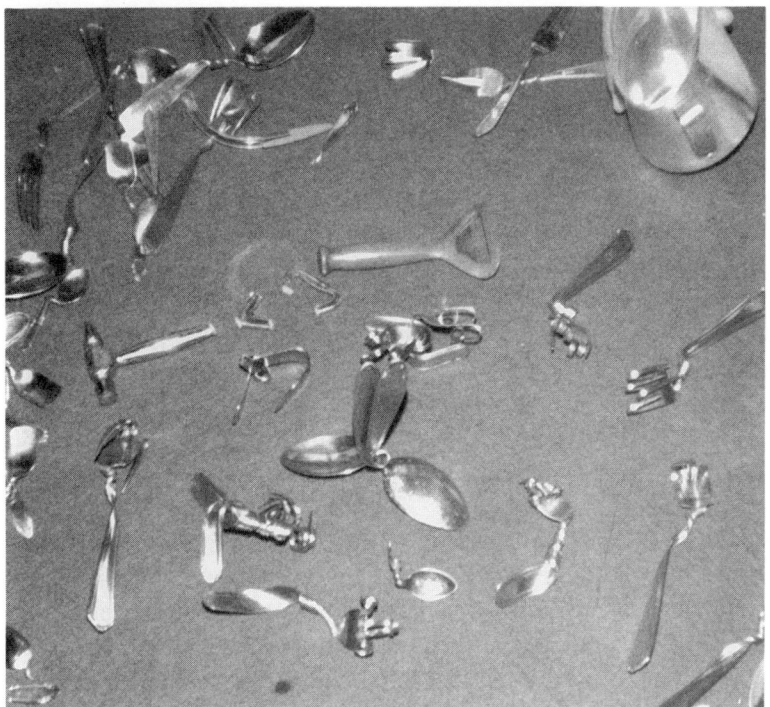

Figure 6–1

taken in a lighthearted manner, for Thomaz realized that he might one day be the target of a witch-hunt or allegations of dishonesty. Even in Brazil, a literal-minded community insists that the only truth lies in the simplistic stimulus-response universe of the behaviorist. Anyone who violates or casts a shadow on behaviorism's strict procedures is perfunctorily accused of fraud. Thomaz insisted on performing all of their experiments stripped to the waist and barefoot.

Over the next two years, Thomaz obliged the Machados and demonstrated a series of astonishing phenomena. Coins, cutlery, and large metal objects and containers were psychically twisted and coiled with ease. Transmutations, note-burning, clairvoyance, and transteleportation of various kinds of objects were also exhibited, always under controlled conditions. There were times when Thomaz could not summon the energy on demand. There were other times when the energy, as if it had a mind of its own, created a totally different phenomena than what had been intended.

As the Machados became absolutely convinced that the man and his powers were genuine, they began to travel to his home in Minas Gerais. They also accompanied Thomaz on many of his cross-country wanderings. As might be expected, the more natural and comfortable settings seemed to provide more powerful and staggering psychic displays. Careful records, photographic documentation, and, wherever possible, super 8 movies all catalogued the extraordinary events. The Machados were very generous in sharing their findings with other investigators. Gary and I were given unlimited access to all their artifacts, chronicles, and photographs.

One lazy Sunday afternoon in July 1979, the Machados were entertaining luncheon guests. Present were Irene Granchi, an English tutor who had a longstanding interest in extraterrestrial phenomena, and Hermano and Bianca Reis from Belo Horizonte. The Reises had allegedly spent two days aboard a flying saucer in 1976, becoming the focus of considerable national interest, particularly when Air Force investigators pronounced their experience "legitimate but unexplainable." The Machados have always been cautious and skeptical about UFO claims, but they, like the Air Force, were convinced that this case had unusual and credible elements meriting exploration.

Thomaz arrived at the Machados' house unexpectedly. In his energetic and engaging fashion, he shifted the focus of conversation from UFOs to metal-bending, the events of the Fasqueira, and to increasing his psychic development. As late afternoon faded into early evening, Thomaz guided the group through the six o'clock "mentalization" and meditation. After an hour or so, he excitedly announced the foreshadowing "click" and rush of energy within him. An assortment of cutlery was placed before him and he was able to snap most of the metal in two.

Metal Transmutations

Thomaz was in fine form that evening. He turned to Bianca Reis and said, "I feel I must do something very special for you." He asked her to remove a cotton rope belt from around her waist and to tie it in as many tight knots as possible. Mrs. Reis did so and cupped the knotted belt in both hands. Thomaz positioned himself six feet in front of her, closed his eyes, stretched out his arms, and began to invoke the energies with what was now becoming his personal psychic litany. He breathed very deeply several times and said, "At this moment, I 'mentalize' with all of the mental, spiritual, and universal forces that your belt will be transmuted into . . . metal! . . . Ra!" Mrs. Reis opened her hands and to everyone's astonishment, the knotted cloth belt was no longer there. In its place was a metal necklace made of tiny, shiny orbs, linked together.

Professor Machado had been quietly filming the sequence. While everyone else was dancing about and celebrating the event, he unobtrusively measured the length of the chain at thirty-five centimeters. Mrs. Reis tried to put the necklace on, but to her disappointment, found it too short. Thomaz instructed her to lay the necklace out on the table and asked everyone to position themselves around it without touching anything. Standing several feet away at the other end of the table, he extended his arms and invoked the mental, spiritual, and universal forces to "make the chain grow in size. Ra!" Over the next five seconds a creative anarchy unshrouded itself and the thin stilts of a clockwork universe began to buckle. Everyone present agreed that they could see the chain growing and silently forming additional metal links. Professor Machado measured the chain again; its length was now fifty-five centimeters long . . . an increase of twenty centimeters in five seconds with seven people observing! Bianca Reis was aglow with excitement as she put the necklace around her neck.

Later that evening, as the Machados were comparing their

notes, they began to speculate about the physics of the events they had witnessed earlier. Was the lengthening of the chain a transmutation of metal? Or could it have been a series of materializations and a quantum restructuring of matter? Are there indeed yet unrecognized whisperings between human thought and the subatomic realm of allegedly inanimate matter? Perhaps, they conjectured, the metal links had been transteleported through what has frequently been referred to as hyperspace. In working with materializing mediums, the Machados have seen a bouquet of flowers, an egg, and various other objects suddenly appear as if out of nowhere. This is certainly a common experience in the hundreds of carefully documented poltergeist cases. (In another experience with Thomaz, Gary and I watched carefully as an American quarter began 'losing' its features. Within seconds, the head of George Washington "melted" away and disappeared. The molecular restructuring resulted in a smooth, round metal wafer.)

Driven by intellectual curiosity and a need to enhance current understanding, the Machados intensified their research and observations of Thomaz. They also consulted with physicists in an attempt to further articulate the materialization-transmutation continuum. Other scientists observed and took part in the experiments. Thomaz would ask someone to hold three or four coins in his tightly clenched fist. Without touch, of course, he focused his energy toward the subject, and when the fist was opened, the coins had become rings. The process was just as easily reversed, and the rings transmuted back into coins—but of another country! The Machados also filmed a subject cutting a piece of a carrot, holding it, and in a few moments opening his hand to find the carrot replaced by a large black olive.

During the early months of their experiments with Thomaz, no one actually "saw" the transmutations because the subjects' fists were always closed. The Machados suggested that Thomaz permit the subjects to keep their hand open during the transmutation. In one test, Thomaz took a paring knife and cut a circular strip of peel from the top of an orange. With cameras rolling and several observers present, he began to bend and compress the peel in between his fingers. After thirty seconds or so everyone present noted a distinct change in the texture of the orange peel. Initially, it appeared to "dry up" and then, very slowly, the surface granulated into a metal-like texture, but still pliable. The "peel" was placed flat on the table. In a few more moments, the circular piece of malleable metal became rigid. Tiny furrows and ridges began to form and a definite design emerged. Approximately one minute passed before Professor Machado picked up the metal object. What had been a piece of orange peel four minutes earlier was now a Kennedy half-dollar.

The Machados continued to be nagged by this curious capacity of Thomaz's psyche. Was it materialization, transmutation, or transteleportation of matter? Or was it a cosmic kaleidoscope being shaken by some totally unsuspected force?

Transmutation of Currency

An even more baffling dimension was to be added in June 1979. A medical school classmate invited Dr. Dessimoni and Thomaz to Paranvai, a growing agricultural town in the Brazilian state of Parana. They were the honored guests at a special luncheon hosted by the mayor, Dr. Jose Vaz de Carvalho, also a physician. Local gossip and the small-town grapevine were responsible for a large turnout of guests, including other politicians, physicians, and representatives from the press. Thomaz was in fine fettle that day. Not only did his psychic "click" announce the onset of his energy almost immediately but it remained present for six consecutive hours.

Dr. Carvalho was openly skeptical about paranormal phenomena. Thomaz began with a series of dazzling metal-bending demonstrations as an introduction to his psychic Pandora's box. Dr. Carvalho's wife was asked to take a one cruzeiro note from her purse, fold it, and clench it in her fist. Dr. Carvalho was seated between his wife and Thomaz. When Thomaz exclaimed his psychically detonating mantra, "Ra!", Mrs. Carvalho opened her hand and unfolded the note. It had been "transformed" into nonexistent currency. In English, "THE JAPANESE GOVERNMENT" was printed across the top while the words "ONE HUNDRED PESOS" were embossed on the bottom. A lithograph of a monument was in the center of the bill—a monument no one has yet been able to identify. In the lower left-hand corner of the note was the mark of a rubber stamp with only the word "COMPILED" discernible. The back of this bizarre hybrid bears bank note markings corresponding to those on the front.

On many occasions, Thomaz has transmuted a piece of napkin into currency or even "increased" the value of a ten cruzeiro bill to one hundred cruzeiros. Changing currency from one country to another is also part of what he refers to as his repertoire of "money transmutations." But where in the world does one find a peso bank note issued by the Japanese government? In some souvenir or magic shop? Perhaps, but not likely.

The absurdity of this symbolic hybrid was strained by an even larger coincidence. Participating in the demonstration that day was a man of Japanese origin and a visitor from Argentina. Thomaz's complex personality is compounded even further by a very strong need to please other persons and to gain their approval. Is it possible that in his unconscious mind, Thomaz created this curious confection, mirroring several of the personalities present in the mayor's home that day? In our experience with Thomaz, we have always felt a strong interaction between our own subconscious and Thomaz's subconscious. Often we have felt exhausted after observing him work, as if he were able to use us as a "battery pack" to sustain the fragile and silent connection between us. In addition, several materializations he produced for us were of personal symbolic significance. Somehow, he seems to create a metaphorical bridge that becomes translated to the language of the subconscious. But the basic issues and questions remain. Is Thomaz able to speak through the voice of nature and literally create matter on subparticle and atomic levels? Or are there energy templates somewhere in hyperspace that he can transform from mental blueprints into an architectural assemblage of molecules? (This theory is covered in depth in Chapter Twelve.)

Several weeks later at his home in Trés Corações, Thomaz was joined by nine friends, all seated around a large wooden table. Thomaz had done several "routine" transmutations of coins into cheap rings. Six of the persons present were complete strangers but nonetheless they began to pester him for a souvenir, just as children will buttonhole a baseball idol for an autograph. Thomaz was very tired but typically wanted to please everyone. He asked each person to take a coin and hold it in a tightly closed fist. Beginning to hyperventilate, Thomaz squinted his eyes and went into a very deep state of concentration. He commanded that all the coins transmute into astrological medallions bearing the respective birth sign of each person present. As he shouted "Ra!", each man opened his hand to find the coin replaced with the medallion Thomaz had requested, each half again as large as the centavo coins. Each bore the correct birth sign of the holders, exactly as Thomaz had commanded.

Great excitement followed, with the men comparing their psychic souvenirs. Someone remarked: "Six of us are complete strangers . . . how could he possibly know our birth signs?" Another said that the phenomenon was "due to an external energy or entity that is helping him." Thomaz, as usual, refrained from explanatory speculations and simply enjoyed the moment and the satisfaction generated among those present.

Psychic Exploits in 1979

As Thomaz's psychic exploits became known, the Machados were convinced of the uniqueness of his gifts. No one else in the world, to their knowledge, possessed such a versatility, range, and intensity of psychic powers. In 1979, Gary, in the capacity of a freelance journalist, was invited to observe Thomaz. Hopefully, his articles would stimulate sufficient interest and attract foreign investigators. Gary became an active participant in the dozens of field observations and data-gathering expeditions.

Several times Thomaz severely tested the Machados' patience, composure, and tolerance. They would agree to meet him in a certain town at a prearranged time. Even though the trip would take many hours or days, they would often be informed that Thomaz had "left just hours before . . . he may be back next week." Once, Thomaz excused himself for a moment in a restaurant and kept a party of twelve of us, including two infants, waiting for six hours before returning. He never offers an explanation and simply assumes that "everything will work out." Some people cannot tolerate what they perceive as his childish, impulsive, and narcissistic behavior. Defenders of Thomaz feel that he is always guided by and listens to his intuition, which he says is the "voice of nature." Rarely does one have neutral feelings about Thomaz.

In spite of all the obstacles, canceled appointments, financial sacrifices, and the punishing strain of long-distance auto travel, the Machados persevered. During their first several visits, they conducted a meticulous search of Thomaz's house, yard, and even his personal effects to rule out possible trickery or illusions. However, the spontaneity of the phenomena, credibility of dozens of witnesses, and Thomaz's typical half-naked dress code led to more practical and periodic "spot checks" of his working environment.

One of the most vexing challenges for the Machados was maintaining the careful balance of objectivity and receptivity at the same time. Thomaz's reaction to scientific scrutiny danced back and forth between cooperative compliance and an irreverent defiance. This was compounded by his need for continual stimulation from his friends and enthusiasts. Most phenomena took place around a large table in his kitchen. In addition to his local drinking companions and his brother-in-law, visiting dignitaries and an increasing number of military observers began to attend the sessions. Thomaz's personality and temperament seemed to derive energy from confusion and disarray. He would also insist that everyone join him in his digressive drinking *"to get loose."* Neither of the Machados drink at all and Gary's limit is one glass of beer. It was a difficult environment in which to maintain a position of detachment and objectivity. Once the dam of Thomaz's consciousness control broke, he would rarely be in the mood to speculate about what he was thinking or feeling during the spontaneous and sometimes capricious production of phenomena. The local townspeople and regular observers were also lacking in interest or curiosity about the sociology of miracles. For most of them, it was perceived as entertainment in the context of a party atmosphere.

March through August 1979 was a period of accelerated psychic growth and creativity for Thomaz. The Machados compared him to a jazz musician who plays the same melody line but always in a slightly different key or with innovative subtleties that weave in and out of the main theme.

Soccer Lottery

Though Thomaz never gambles on the soccer lottery, for some unknown reason he began to favor lottery tickets as a vehicle for his psychic forces. For fifty cents, anyone can purchase a national soccer lottery ticket, which typically lists thirteen matches; by marking an "X" in the box, a bettor can designate a win, loss, or draw. Over sixty million Brazilians participate in the sweepstakes each week. The payoff has ranged as high as one million dollars, and many persons wager on several tickets at once. Thomaz's most common tactic was to have an individual fold a new lottery ticket three times and hold it tightly in one's clenched fist. Thomaz would burn the back of the person's hand with a lit cigarette and shout "Ra!" Upon unfolding the ticket the person would find a mark in one of the boxes, as if a cigarette were held against a paper to create a slight charring.

An astonishing variation developed one day when Thomaz took a ballpoint pen and made thirteen X's on the back of the subject's hand. Thirteen X's were subsequently recorded on the lottery ticket. If Thomaz uses a pen with blue ink, the markings on the ticket will be blue. A pen with black ink will produce black markings. Sometimes Thomaz will place the selected ticket face up on a table and stand back about three feet. While the subject watches the boxes marked with X's, Thomaz commands the markings to "move to a new selection." As quickly as he can say "Ra!", the already fragile psychic boundaries are collapsed once more. The X's shift to totally different boxes, leaving not even a trace in the original location. The "translocation," if that is what it is, happens in a fraction of a second and is not discernible to ordinary examination. One day, Thomaz described an unusually "strong field of energy" and changed the position of the X's five times in succession.

One Sunday afternoon in 1979, Thomaz was introduced to Dr. Enio Lima, a dentist from Rio de Janeiro. Thomaz was in high spirits and felt very positive about a man who was both a professional and interested in paranormal phenomena. Impulsively, Thomaz decided to try something different. Brazilians generally have three or four different identification numbers for taxing, legal, and social security purposes. Dr. Lima had four such numbers, and was asked to purchase a new lottery ticket from a street vendor. On instruction, he folded it three times and held it in his fist. In Portuguese, Thomaz printed the words, "social security," "civilian identification," and "voter registration" and the corresponding numbers on the back of his hand. This time, he did not use a cigarette but simply commanded the event to take place and proclaimed that it would. "Ra!" When Lima unfolded the paper, inside the small boxes were three columns of numbers. Each column corresponded to the words on the back of Dr. Lima's hand—his social security, civilian identification, and voter registration numbers. Once he overcame his "psychological disarray," Dr. Lima went on to document and film dozens of hours of other Thomaz phenomena. These films have been well-received at several parapsychology conferences.

The Machados have always insisted that Thomaz carefully document and authenticate every psychic event whenever possible. Thomaz has been uncharacteristically conscientious about being "scientific." He now assumes the role of a director, particularly if someone is filming the event. The bills used in the experiment are signed and photographed prior to the event. He is fastidious about not touching the note, coin, or whatever object is to be transmuted. For some unexplained reason, Thomaz prefers working with new currency—fresh, crisp bills.

Other Phenomena with Currency

To the best of our knowledge, no one has ever won any money on the sports lottery from Thomaz's paranormal selections. Similarly, rarely has anyone benefited by Thomaz's transmutations of currency from lower to higher denominations. Both authors have held ten-cruizeiro bills and, in a millisecond, each is transmuted into a five hundred or one thousand cruzeiro note. The procedure is always the same: *our* bill, from *our* pockets, and Thomaz never touches the currency. Sometimes during a followup stage, the five hundred note will then enigmatically transmute into a Canadian or American one dollar or five dollar bill.

The geography of Thomaz's imagination is constantly shifting its borders. Another variation is to have someone take a pair of scissors and cut a five hundred cruzeiro note into four even pieces (Figure 6–2). They are placed on top of each other and the person is asked to fold them two or three times. A pause, then the now familiar "Ra!" Upon opening one's fist, the note is fully reconstituted with no evidence of being torn or cut into pieces. With the exception of one staggering, comical absurdity! The four pieces were "psychically glued" together—but in a crazy-quilt fashion (Figure 6–3). Two of the back pieces of the bill became the front and were in the wrong arrangement with respect to left and right. The Machados have a large collection of various currencies that were torn in two and psychically reconstituted with the two halves facing "backwards" like bookends.

Unfortunately, no one has yet approached the Brazilian Treasury Department for permission to certify the serial numbers of the bills that have been pushed back and forth across different psychic boundaries. To do that, formal petition to the govern-

94   Miracles and Other Realities

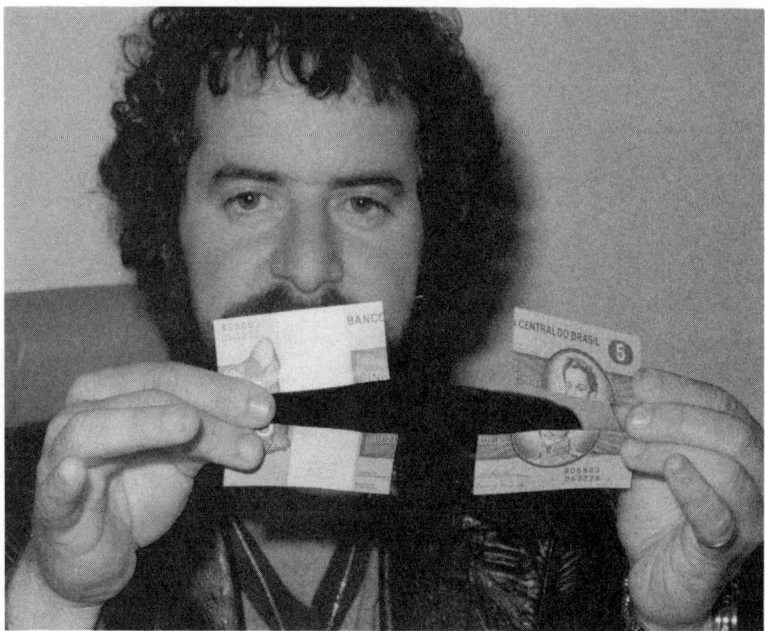

Figure 6–2

ment would be necessary to obtain a record of the currency. Then, the currency record would have to be cleared through the Brazilian SNI or Secret Service along with justification for the request.

In 1980, Thomaz developed another important relationship with Elson Montagno, a young Brazilian physician. During their first meeting Thomaz asked for Dr. Montagno's steel Cross pencil from his breast pocket. Montagno extended the pencil; Thomaz took the top lightly between his thumb and index finger, and the steel pencil suddenly bent into a forty-five-degree arc. Dr. Montagno was then instructed to take a currency note from his pocket, record the serial number, and sign the bill. As usual, Thomaz stood well back from Dr. Montagno and did not touch the bill. He was then asked to fold his note three times and hold it tightly in his closed hand. Dr. Montagno was then invited to imagine a sample of his own blood materializing within the en-

Figure 6-3

closed note. Thomaz closed his eyes, appeared to be straining, then reached out and touched the back of Dr. Montagno's hand with his finger, shouting "Ra!" Dr. Montagno unfolded the bill and discovered a large spot of fresh blood in the center.

Note-Burning

Needless to say, that was not his only meeting with Thomaz, but the first of a series of emancipating experiences for Dr. Montagno and some of his colleagues. During a subsequent session in September 1980, Dr. Montagno went through much the same procedure with another cruzeiro note. This time, Thomaz declared that "something important" would appear on the bill. He then took a cigarette and burned the back of Montagno's closed fist as if to mark the bill through his hand. When the cruzeiro note was unfolded, a series of burn markings spelled out "October 14" on the edge of the bill. Neither Thomaz nor Dr. Montagno could attach any significance to the date. Several weeks later on October 14, Dr. Montagno received a letter from Dr. Nashold of Duke University formally accepting him into the neurosurgery residency program of Duke Medical School. A discomforting coincidence? Or another reflection of our unclaimed heritage to a flowing connectedness that is not held in a tight mechanistic grasp?

The Machados were continually being challenged by the recurring question: Does Thomaz utilize telepathy, clairvoyance, or "X-ray vision"? Or perhaps some other chunk of irrationality still undiscovered in the diversity of psychic process? For example, when American businessman Jim Jensen was asked to hold a folded dollar bill, Thomaz announced that his driver's license number would be burned on the note. The charred numbers that appeared were not Jim's driver's license number from Oregon, but his Social Security number. Coincidentally, Jim has an Idaho driver's license that also records the Social Security number above the operator's number. The numbers were not organized into the typical xxx-xx-xxxx order that appears on a Social Security card. The burned numbers on the bill, however, were grouped this way.

On rare occasions, Thomaz will entreat a divine source for guidance. One evening in July 1979, Lada, Gary, and several observers spent almost five hours recording and documenting various phenomena. Lada was particularly frightened by the thought of never regaining her sight. She began to sob and Thomaz in a very moving and loving way, took his cousin in his arms and held her tightly. Both wept as Lada tried to explain how difficult it was for her to participate in his marvels without being able to see them. Thomaz asked her to take a cruzeiro note, fold it, and hold it in her fist. He went into an almost trancelike state and petitioned for an answer directly from the Almighty. If it were God's will that Lada would see again there would be a message of some kind burned on the bill. He placed a lighted cigarette against the back of her hand and she unfolded the bill.

"DEUS" ("GOD" in Portuguese) was boldly charred across the length of the currency. The circuslike atmosphere was suddenly transformed into a gathering of emotional, profoundly affected, and connected human beings.

Many of the steps of the "note-burning" phenomena are loosely anchored to logic. For example, in order to obtain a charring on the notes, Thomaz literally burns the back of the subject's hand. In materializing fresh blood inside a folded bill, Thomaz simulates cutting by running a dull butter knife against the back of the subject's closed fist. Sometimes he "cuts" a cross or crude geometrical design on the hand, and that design will "bleed through" onto the folded bank note. In several experiments, the blood samples taken from the bills matched the blood types of the persons being symbolically "cut."

Thomaz's explanation for these phenomena is somewhat literal and mechanistic. He believes that the heat of the burning cigarette "somehow passes through the hand onto the paper." This undistinguished explanation was challenged one day by Gary and an army friend of Thomaz's, Sergeant Palomino. They convinced him to try an experiment. The police officer went through the usual ritual, folding the bill from his wallet and holding it tightly. Thomaz was asked to visualize the outcome *without using a cigarette*. He agreed but still clung to one comforting habit from his old process. He "commanded" that a lucky date and number appear on the bill, and asked those present to visualize or pretend that he was burning Palomino's hand. "Ra!" As the officer opened his hand and unfolded the banknote, he discovered that the word "branco" (white) and the date "1–1–1999" was charred onto the bill.

Thomaz was shocked by that unexpected outcome. He genuinely believed in a simple cause-and-effect relationship between heat and the psychokinetic transfer of energy through the hand onto the currency. This marked the beginning of Thomaz accepting the possibility of, in his words, "pure mind power." He added that perhaps it was necessary to have certain rituals that would make the experience more acceptable to those who did not understand the "power of the unconscious wish-making." In other words, what was beginning to stir in Thomaz's consciousness was that a literal perception of reality reveals limited answers. A more emancipated vision of his awesome phenomena would suggest an underlying connection and resonance among all matter and persons.

Reconstituting Notes

This important shift in his thinking was accompanied by even more provocative "experiments." The Machados and Gary were present when Thomaz, in a somewhat reflective yet whimsical mood, asked one of them to take a new bill from his billfold. Gary removed a ten cruzeiro note, carefully recorded the serial number, and signed his name on the bottom of the bill. Thomaz took the note in his hand, struck a match, and to everyone's astonishment set the note on fire. He allowed it to burn until it was almost three-quarters destroyed. Blowing out the flame, Thomaz managed to salvage about twenty percent of the original bill. The remnants were crumpled, along with whatever ashes he could scrape together, into a little stack in the center of the kitchen table. Standing back with arms outstretched and palms facing toward the burnt residue, Thomaz "commanded" the bill to "reconstitute from all its parts." He began to breathe deeply, his face turned crimson, and his eyes remained fixed in a trancelike gaze. In a few moments, the ashes moved slightly and the fragment of the note began to enlarge. Fortunately, Professor Machado filmed the whole process with a motor-driven 35mm camera. The sequences of destruction and reconstitution are clearly documented. The ten cruzeiro note regained its original size in about thirty seconds. The serial number matched the original note, which was slightly charred in places as if it had been held close to a flame.

Following the raw excitement and rejoicing over this success, Thomaz tried to explain what had happened. He believed that he had caused the note to *"reorganize itself from all its parts."*

However, there were still ashes on Thomaz's hands and fragments of the burned paper on the floor. He had been unable to retrieve all of the ashes and not all of the parts were available to form the whole.

Thomaz still seemed to be confined by the mechanistic clutch of the conventional universe. As he began practicing his new psychic accomplishment for other observers, however, his interpretation of the phenomenon changed—as if he had somehow gained access to a more profound decoding computer or information source. During the course of several conversations I had with Thomaz in December 1982, he talked about "energy blueprints," which are the basis of the form of all matter. He feels there are different "templates" for all the billions of separate objects in the world. By "tuning in" to a specific ten-cruzeiro note, for example, he could "multiply" or reconstitute any number of identical bills.

I was excited by his explanation. It was very similar to a captivating new hypothesis introduced by a respected British scientist, Rupert Sheldrake. Sheldrake (1981) proposes that all matter is governed by both known energy forces and by invisible organizing fields—fields determined by laws outside of space and time and therefore devoid of energy. Nevertheless, they are causative and serve as blueprints for both form and behavior. Thomaz had never heard of Sheldrake or his hypothesis of morphogenic, "form-causing" fields (M-Fields). A tantalizing speculation is that Thomaz, with his highly amplified paranormal abilities, unconsciously tuned into the "M-Field" hypothesis. (Sheldrake's ideas are discussed in detail in Chapter Twelve.)

The range of phenomena that are catalyzed by Thomaz fluctuate to varying degrees. Psychic tasks depend both on the demands and difficulty of the situation. For example, the charring of dates, messages, or "lucky numbers" onto currency and lottery tickets has been repeated hundreds of times. Once Thomaz has mastered an "experiment," he finds little challenge in duplicating the achievement. However, he has performed the reconstitution of a burnt bank note only a dozen times. Because of insufficient practice, he has failed several times, and friends have been left with fragments of burnt notes as souvenirs.

Energy Catalysts and Energy Drains

Other important and often overlooked dimensions in the success or failure of psychic displays are the conscious attitudes and unconscious biases of the observers. We have mentioned how we came to the realization that Thomaz was using us as an unconscious source of energy. Seventy percent of over two hundred observers who had also participated in Thomaz phenomena acknowledged that they also felt "exerted" or "drained" after watching Thomaz perform. One judge stated that he felt like he had done "several windsprints" at the end of a two-hour observation period with Thomaz.

I have worked with many healers all over the world and have experienced a similar "energy drain" effect at the end of their sessions. One healer, sensing my exhaustion, openly acknowledged that he uses observers or helpers as "batteries" for additional energy.

Thomaz goes one step further. Skeptical or unconsciously negative observers "drain off" the available energy and can adversely affect the outcome. He attempts to maximize success by having all observers hold onto a metal object. If a phenomenon is taking place outdoors, he insists that everyone remove their shoes and stockings so as to "connect with the magnetic or electrical energy of the earth." It is indeed a strange sight being among a dozen barefoot persons all waving bent cutlery. Sometimes, this seemingly absurd ritual will be punctuated by a loud crack or snap in the air. This will be immediately followed by at least two or three persons experiencing a light electrical tinge or "run" of electricity through their entire bodies.

While Thomaz seems to go through cycles of developmental spurts and psychic plateaus, he finds it important to have present prominent civic officials and professionals who are unconditionally supportive of his unusual powers. One such person, who was to be a major influence in the direction of Thomaz's psychic development, entered Thomaz's life in 1979. Flavio Zanata is a successful businessman and the owner of the largest macrobiotic manufacturing plant in Brazil. He spent several years in Japan studying oriental medicine, herbal practices, acupuncture, and what is referred to as "alimentation." During their first meeting, Zanata mentioned to Thomaz that he was reading an inspiring essay entitled "*The Limits of Man.*" Thomaz asked him to take three coins out of his pocket and hold them tightly. After the customary "Ra!", the three 1970s coins had been transmuted into three 1920s coins out of circulation for years, a routine demonstration for Thomaz, but Zanata promptly tore up the essay and scattered the pieces of paper in the air.

The friendship and special bonding between the two men was immediate. Zanata was invited to Thomaz's thirty-second birthday party three weeks later. The birthday was an important and memorable event in several ways. Zanata witnessed an incident that marked a new ordering of experience stemming from Thomaz's powers. As a consequence of the unusual occurrences that day, Thomaz reinterpreted the explanation and significance of being struck by lightning on his twelfth birthday. The new theory also provides further insight into the mystifying properties of Thomaz's psyche.

CHAPTER SEVEN

First Contact

A new world is only a new mind.
    William Carlos Williams

M arch 16, 1979, was Thomaz's thirty-second birthday. Though birthdays are very special events in Brazil, it is the responsibility of the "birthday boy" to organize all the festivities. During the week before the party, Thomaz was uncharacteristically quiet and pensive. More than once he remarked that he had been receiving strong intuitive impressions that his birthday would signal a very important and memorable event.

He also felt a "strong urge and pull" to celebrate his special day with Vera and Noe. And so, on Thursday, March 15, Thomaz, his wife Lygia, his cousin Lada, and Flavio Zanata drove the two hour trip from Trés Corações to Divisa Nova. Noe had inherited his father's farm and abandoned his own pharmaceutical practice for a more rural and relaxed life-style. In addition to ten acres of land, the property includes a small lake and a large, rustic house. Sonia teaches school in the district's only elementary school. Besides Thomaz and his friends, Noe, Sonia, their thirteen-year-old son, Rogerio, and Maria Salles, a maid, were all staying at the house.

The group spent Thursday evening and all day Friday swimming, walking, drinking beer, and generally enjoying the fresh air and countryside. On Friday, dinner was served at 5:30 P.M., followed by a huge birthday cake. Thomaz was reserved and detached throughout the dinner. Noe went to bed early; Thomaz half-heartedly entertained the rest of the group by bending some cutlery and psychically burning "messages" onto two banknotes. His behavior became increasingly more distant and aloof, until finally at 11:00 P.M., he suddenly announced that he needed to go off and be by himself. He added in a rather peculiar manner that if he didn't return, no one should worry because he would be "protected."

UFO or Hallucination?

Thomaz walked away from the house, then suddenly veered in the direction of the lake. As the group curiously watched his departure, they were bewildered by Thomaz's gait. His body rhythm first slowed down and then became jerky and mechanical. In Zanata's words, "he began to walk like a robot." A moment later, a small, silver, ball-shaped object "materialized out of nowhere." It hovered just a few centimeters above Thomaz's head and remained there.

Alarmed, Zanata and Thomaz's nephew Rogerio followed Thomaz. They saw him stop at the edge of the lake. Still moving like an automaton, Thomaz "examined, one by one, several fishing poles he had left planted in the soil that afternoon." He then paced agitatedly along the bank. Suddenly, though he was wearing a leather jacket and boots, he walked into the water. Zanata could see him floating on his back with arms outstretched. The moon was full that night, and in its light both men could see that Thomaz's head was mostly under water, except for his nose. Without warning, a thin, silvery bolt of light appeared and silently radiated from Thomaz's forehead. Zanata thought for a moment that he was hallucinating or losing his senses. Rogerio quickly affirmed that both of them were seeing something totally absurd—but very real. Zanata even pinched himself to make certain he wasn't the victim of a contagious hallucination of some kind.

After about thirty seconds, Thomaz stood up completely covered with mud. He seemed dazed. He gasped for air and had difficulty in keeping his balance. Zanata, distressed about his friend's condition, approached and asked if he could help. Thomaz held up his hand, signaling for silence. Then he turned and, "stumbling and staggering," found his way back to the farmhouse. Without stopping to talk to anyone, he went directly to the bathroom. Still wearing his clothes, he stepped into the shower, where he remained for more than a half-hour. Dripping wet, he staggered out and mumbled that he had experienced a "contact," without explaining what he meant by the word, and disjointedly added that three words remained firmly imprinted in his memory from the lake episode: "metal, fire, and heat." The only other information he volunteered was that the "contact" had been terminated because Zanata and Rogerio had followed him to the lake, contrary to his instructions.

At this point, Lygia excitedly pointed to a mark on Thomaz's forehead: It looked like a second-degree burn the size of a silver dollar and was positioned between and just above his eyebrows. Thomaz appeared dumbfounded when he looked at himself in the mirror. He touched the area with his finger cautiously. Then, without comment, he turned and went directly to bed.

The next morning, everyone awakened early—except for Thomaz who remained in a deep sleep until noon. While he slept, there was some confusion as Zanata had lost the stem of his prized pipe during the previous night's strange adventure. Everyone joined in the search of both house and grounds without success. To compound matters, Zanata also had an unbearable toothache. Finally, he took Noe's advice and went to see the local dentist, who examined him and said there was nothing he could do.

Just as Zanata returned to the farm, Thomaz awakened and was brought up to date on the morning's activities and the missing pipe stem. While Zanata was describing his pipe, Thomaz felt an "electrical tingle" in his body and Zanata heard a "clicking" sound on top of the television set in the living room. There, on the top of the set, was his missing pipe stem, though the room had been thoroughly inspected that morning. Thomaz, uncharacteristically, was not particularly surprised or excited. He sensed that "something would happen" when he felt the "electrical signal" in his body.

Later that afternoon, everyone sat on the veranda bursting with curiosity. They hoped Thomaz would explain or interpret the inconceivable occurrences of the night before. Thomaz did, in fact, make several abortive efforts, but he seemed perplexed and frustrated. After he admitted that he could not "find the words to explain," Zanata, sensing his friend's uneasiness, changed the subject. He began talking about "money transmutations" and an American dollar bill that had been transmuted from a ten cruzeiro note. Jokingly, he teased Thomaz that he would never allow him to see the American currency again as his glance "might change it back to Brazilian money." Thomaz replied that it did not matter, he could find the note without anyone's assistance. Lying back in the hammock, he focused his concentration. After a few moments, he said he was "looking through the walls" into Zanata's room—but that the dollar bill was not in that area. Turning his head slightly, he "looked through" another section of the house and located a man's black handpurse, a fashion common among Brazilian men. He "saw" the note inside the purse, along with a pipe and an unopened pouch of pipe tobacco. The purse, he said, was under a metal can on a kitchen shelf. Despite everything Zanata had experienced with Thomaz, he was stunned. Not only was Thomaz's clairvoyancy, "X-ray vision," or remote-viewing accurate, but Zanata had completely forgotten about the tobacco he had purchased before leaving Rio de Janeiro.

This event seemed to rekindle Thomaz's enthusiasm. He declared that he was experiencing an "exceptional surge of energy—more than usual." Zanata was asked to find a lime and place it on a small table. He was instructed to take a coin out of his pocket and put it next to the lime. Thomaz, with his eyes closed and arms outstretched, began to vibrate like a tuning fork. Slowly, as though uncertain of itself, the ten centavo coin began to levitate. It rose several centimeters above the tabletop, and then abruptly imploded into the lime. Poof! It vanished that quickly.

The astonishment and perplexity of the four observers were predictable. Finding no marks of any kind on the surface of the lime, Zanata sliced the fruit in half. Embedded in the center was the ten centavo piece, as if an invisible sword of consciousness had silently sectioned away another cherished version of reality.

Fueled by his success, Thomaz asked Lada to hold a match in her hand. He attempted to ignite it mentally but failed. Instead, the wooden match "drooped over" from whatever energy influences were intruding into its structure. Thomaz followed this by burning a bank note and reconstituting it from its ashes. Zanata, in exasperation, blurted out: "For Christ's sake, you are collapsing scientific laws one by one, yet here I am suffering from a simple toothache. Please do something about it!" Thomaz seemed very unwilling to attempt anything, claiming he wouldn't know where to begin. But when Zanata insisted, Thomaz reluctantly asked for some cotton. There was none in the house, so he accepted a Kleenex instead. Placing the tissue over the inflamed area in Zanata's mouth, he asked for a razor blade. With some understandable misgivings, Zanata reminded Thomaz that "an inflammation is the presence of a foreign substance." Ignoring him, Thomaz lightly scraped the surface of the Kleenex with the razor blade. Shifting deeper into an absorbed state, he quietly remarked that it was becoming difficult to contain the energy building up inside him. "Ra!" Zanata staggered slightly and then took the Kleenex from his mouth. It was dripping with pus. Everyone, including Thomaz, was startled. Zanata experienced almost immediate relief, and both the infection and its symptoms disappeared by the end of the day.

On the basis of this experience, Zanata began encouraging Thomaz to focus his energies in a more constructive and socially relevant manner. As always, Thomaz listened carefully and agreed. Just then, as though placed there to test Thomaz, a farmhand who had been making a delivery to Noe and witnessed the "psychic healing" spoke up. He scoffed, belittling the episode as "hypnosis," and insisted that everyone was being deceived. Thomaz asked the man to take a bank note, fold it, and hold it tightly in his hand. Without even so much as his customary "Ra!" the man's hand began oozing a small rivulet of blood. Unfolding the bill, he found the inside of the note smudged with blood. Uncharacteristically, Thomaz teased the man to taste the blood and confirm that he was "hypnotized and hallucinating."

The perplexing events of that weekend established a precedent for similar incidents in the future. The "birthday contact" proved to be only the first in a series of inexplicable reconsiderations of reality. It was followed by other "contacts" on holidays, special occasions, and anniversaries. Over time, the pattern changed and the "contacts" increasingly became a regular aspect of Thomaz's repertoire.

Following a "contact," a circular, reddish "burn" appears on his forehead. Thomaz is totally exhausted and confused. Eventually, he enters a peacefully euphoric state. He is "unable to find words" to express the experience and his efforts to explain are usually baffling and confusing to observers. For one or two days following these episodes, Thomaz feels "very electrified." His psychic faculties are amplified; many of his innovative talents develop at this time and there is a burst in the number of psychic effects.

That memorable birthday served as yet another milestone in Thomaz's development. It reinforced a special bonding between Thomaz and Zanata. While the Machados provided Thomaz with a sense of worthiness and scientific validity, Zanata steered him into uncharted areas, particularly healing. As a successful businessman, Zanata convinced his young protégé to use his powers as a source of income. Thomaz spent the next several months traveling extensively with Zanata. He began to charge a fee for psychic services and for observing his "psychic experiments." It was an exciting interval for everyone. Thomaz's powers were getting stronger and more diversified. His alleged "contacts" also provided the intriguing prospect of possible parallel universes.

Second Contact

The second "contact" occurred in late July 1979, which also marked the beginning of Gary's research on Thomaz. He was invited to live with Thomaz in his home on Trés Corações for eight days. The Machados arrived a few days later and Thomaz was quite flattered over the undivided attention of a noted journalist and two scientists. On the last day of Gary's visit, July 29, Thomaz offered to take his guests on a tour of the nearby towns and countryside. In what has now become a hallmark of his traveling style, Thomaz invited other friends and a caravan of three cars was formed.

The last stop of the tour was Pouso Alegre, where Thomaz introduced everyone to his uncle, a retired physician. The uncle also joined the entourage, which by now had grown to fifteen persons. Thomaz felt strongly that they should make an excursion to the Fasqueira. The group arrived at the site of Dr. Morais' old farmhouse at 4:30 P.M. Thomaz animatedly began to re-create all the sequences of the "lightning episode" of his twelfth birthday.

At precisely 6:00 P.M., Thomaz ushered the group to the nearby grotto that housed the statue of Nossa Senhora de Lourdes. He guided them through the evening meditation; everyone felt quite moved and buoyed by the experience.

It was the middle of winter in Brazil, chilly and very cloudy. Someone suggested that Thomaz "energize the sky"—break up the threatening storm clouds. It was an incongruous sight. Wearing cowboy boots and leather jacket, Thomaz stretched out both arms and began inhaling and exhaling very rapidly. He then held his breath for about ninety seconds. Exhaling slowly, he commanded the skies to clear. Awestruck, the group watched the clouds part. Within ten minutes the sky was perfectly clear. Thomaz simply remarked that "with harmony," anything was possible.

That idea has been a recurring echo in many civilizations. Psychologists Krippner and Villoldo (1976) describe how Rolling Thunder, a Shoshone medicine man, also seemed to "harmonize" natural laws. In 1974, Villoldo was present during the dry season in Nevada. Rolling Thunder stated that a brief shower would settle the dust for the evening's dance ceremonies. It was a cloudless sky, when suddenly puffs of cloud appeared and a shower drenched the dancing ground before them. The clouds then disappeared.

I was with Villoldo when he taught members of a seminar on shamanism how to create openings in the clouds by participating with the energy flows of nature. Toward the end of the week, we would arbitrarily point to different parts of the overcast sky. Three of the more talented members of the group were able to "poke holes" in the clouds at will. As physicist Bohm (1983) has noted, the potentially transformative power of human consciousness lies in our rediscovering the unity and connectedness with the universe. It is therefore not surprising that the disciplines of physics and parapsychology often join forces. Certain theoreticians in both disciplines suggest that there are no "things," but only interconnections between things (LeShan, 1978; Walker, 1975).

As dusk turned into evening, everyone in the group felt a sense of calm and serenity, partly in response to Thomaz's diminished intensity. For him Fasqueira is a sacred place, the fountain of energy that mysteriously flows through his veins. Most of those present joined him in going barefoot. He kept prompting everyone to "soak up the energy from minerals in the ground—it will change your metabolism." The calm mood was a welcome contrast to the turbulent and sometimes chaotic evenings spent around Thomaz's kitchen table.

With the clear sky and romantic setting, the group—more as poets than as researchers or journalists—began to look at the stars. Then Gary noticed that one of the stars was moving in a most uncharacteristic pattern; it was rocking back and forth. Someone else gasped—another star in another quadrant of the sky was also winging back and forth in a narrow arc. The prevailing feeling was akin to walking through a wax museum and seeing two of the figures begin to breathe and move. As they began to scrutinize the heavens more closely, other stars, ten in total, were identified as behaving strangely. Some would swing back and forth, others moved in diagonal lines and two were seen to make "sharp right angle" motions. Subdued at first, Thomaz became quickly aroused. He stretched out his arms and began chanting "Ra! Ra! Ra!" Everyone present joined him. Becoming more and more carried away with excitement, Thomaz declared that the "suspicious stars" were "ships" and that one of them was going to land.

Though everyone present had experienced a number of "impossibilities" with Thomaz's unique and diverse manipulations of matter, this phenomenon was promising to be the most provocative anarchy of all. The "stars" or "ships" continued with their stellar entertainment. Criss-crossing back and forth in diagonal lines, the "lights" appeared as a deliberate defiance against the stable background of the southern constellations.

Thomaz continued his deep heavy breathing. He said he was receiving some kind of communication. One of the "ships" would be landing soon and everyone would have the opportunity to see it. With a mixture of apprehension and elation, the group continued chanting and shouting. In a few moments, two blinking red lights appeared at ground level to the right of the gathering. Everyone was overwhelmed with anxiety and fear, shivering with bliss and scientific curiosity.

The flickering red lights continued to move even closer, accompanied by a strange humming noise that grew increasingly loud. Suddenly the lights stopped moving. Two dark silhouettes emerged from them and began approaching the group. Everyone was struggling with the apprehension of an interplanetary encounter when the mood was shattered by an authoritarian voice, "What the hell are you doing here?"

Two policemen had responded to a neighbor's complaint about "a group of drug-crazed hippies" screaming out by the lake. Professor Machado stepped forward to deal with the situation. Identifying himself, he explained that he and his colleagues were "conducting research in mind sciences." His explanation did not have the intended effect on the two rural "hillbilly" police officers. They started to round up the group for arrest, convinced that everyone was intoxicated or on drugs. Fortunately, Thomaz's uncle, the retired physician, recognized one of the officers and managed to defuse the situation. Issuing the usual warnings, the two policemen departed. As the group watched the "extraterrestrial craft" with its flickering red light move away, they broke the tension by joking and laughing at themselves. It had been so easy to be mesmerized by their fascination with the "lights in the sky."

But the evening was not over. Thomaz had remained silent throughout this interruption—he was cataleptic, still captivated by the events in the heavens. He appeared to be in trance. A hush came over the group as one by one they confirmed that the "stars" were still performing their celestial acrobatics. Suddenly, Thomaz ran off murmuring, "Don't follow me." He ran up a small hill and Gary's friend Martha saw a small ball of light just beyond Thomaz. It had a reddish-yellow hue. A few moments later, Thomaz screamed and this was followed by the sound of his body falling to the ground and rolling back down the hill. Several of the group ran as fast as they could and found him unconscious in the grass.

Just five minutes had passed since the police officers departed but it seemed like an eternity. There was disagreement on what to do. Dr. Dessimoni expressed concern and wanted to examine

Thomaz. The Machados felt that the best thing to do under the circumstances was wait. Seito, Thomaz's mechanic friend, could not resist going to aid his unconscious friend, who might be seriously injured. He touched Thomaz on the shoulder and called him by name. At that instant, Seito's arm catapulted in the air and Seito cried out that he received a strong electrical jolt. This was immediately followed by Thomaz's body entering into epilepticlike spasms. Then, absolute stillness.

Thomaz began to utter soft sounds. They grew louder and seemed to be a strange and unidentifiable language—a language with a distinct rhythm, subtle intonations, and pauses, as if formulating a declaration or message. Then, Thomaz got up slowly, his face frozen and his eyes focused in a fixed gaze. He walked toward the lake, entered the water to just above his knees, and remained there for several minutes, seemingly oblivious to his surroundings. There was absolute quiet as Thomaz walked out of the water, got into his automobile, and drove off.

The group dispersed quietly. Gary, Martha, and the Machados went directly to Thomaz's house in Trés Corações. No one was home but they decided to wait. Two hours later, people straggled in, including Thomaz. He was in good humor but had the conspicuous "monogram" on his forehead. It was circular and it appeared as if his skin were inflamed. Etched in the center of the redness or irritation was an "m" on its side.

Thomaz was reticent about the incident at the lake. He said that a "ship would have landed" had it not been for the untimely arrival of the police. He also mentioned that he received a "communication" but was unable to share it at this time. He referred to the entire adventure as a "contact."

The following day, Gary was scheduled to return to Rio with the Machados. They stopped at Thomaz's house on their way out. Thomaz had just awakened. He seemed refreshed despite the exhausting experiences of the preceding night. The red circle and imprinted Σ were still on his forehead. The next day, Gary called Thomaz's house from Rio, concerned whether Thomaz had experienced any physical repercussions from the extraordinary experiences at the Fasqueira. Lada, Thomaz's cousin, answered, saying that Thomaz had been "totally electric" all day, performing all sorts of phenomena and creating new marvels. His friend, police officer Palomino, had stopped by and Thomaz asked him to bring a fresh raw egg from the refrigerator. Thomaz held it in his hand for ten seconds and then asked his friend to break it open. It was hard-boiled. Palomino ate the egg, quipping that he should have held it for only five seconds since he prefers soft-boiled eggs.

This had been Gary's first exposure to Thomaz. In eight days he witnessed a total of seventy-three psychic phenomena. During this period he filled four notebooks with observations and compiled nine hours of tape-recorded interviews with credible witnesses. He probably had enough material to occupy several parapsychologists for years in analyzing and collecting the data. The assault on his sensibilities, culminating with the intensity of the final evening at Fasqueira, left Gary in a state of discomforting numbness. How could he possibly report such an account? At best, it would sound like a myth or fairy tale; at worst, like the plot of a B movie. What would the narrative do to his credibility as a journalist? Fortunately, there were fourteen other witnesses, including a parapsychologist, engineer, and three physicians. Everyone was in agreement about the process, details, and sequences of events.

UFO Theories

Most bothersome was how to reconcile the concept of "harmony" and "flowing connectedness" with "dancing stars" and UFOs. Brazil is a large country but certain "hotbed regions" have reported a significant number of UFO sightings. The Brazilian Air Force has published data that UFOs are not stars, aircraft, satellites, meteorological phenomena, ball lightning, swamp gas, or insect swarms. Then what are they? Does anyone know?

In a recent symposium on theories and speculations on the origins of UFOs (Bearden, 1980), a number of prominent astronomers, astrophysicists, and space scientists advanced several explanations ranging from objects entering and leaving underwater civilizations to the actual extraterrestrial spacecraft.

More recently, several authorities have proposed the "ultraterrestrial theory": interdimensional beings living in parallel universes. The newest proposal is the "psychic projection theory": UFOs are merely "planetary poltergeists" generated by the psychic energy of the earth's collective unconscious or by one individual's unconscious. Roberts' (1981) imaginative conjecture is that there are several states of origin. The most provocative is that they come backwards in time from the future. The atoms that structurally compose the UFOs are guided by different laws of nature than from other universes. As they magnetically realign the molecular symmetries, the craft is caught in a "dilemma of form." This partial transformation could account for the conflicting reports of shape and size or the ephemeral nature of the "sightings."

Not one scientist, however, has satisfactorily explained the much more common paranormal phenomena, such as telepathy, precognition, or psychokinesis. Perhaps we have not yet learned how to interpret the many psychic sources of information even though the information probably makes sense on an unconscious level. As the "message" filters its way to conscious awareness, it somehow becomes lost or misinterpreted in the translation. Perhaps the meaning of the phenomena is intended in a metaphorical manner. Somehow, we keep insisting on wrenching the information into a literal, mechanistic physical interpretation.

Possibly the most agonizing question for me was whether to include Thomaz's "contacts" in this book. Gary had considerable experience with the Brazilian Air Force on sightings. His reporting assignments also led to interviewing parapsychologists and UFO theorists. He was definitely much more comfortable with this aspect of the Thomaz enigma. Despite my extensive experience with paranormal healing phenomena, the idea of UFOs seemed total anathema to me. To arouse the reader's imagination by speculating is one thing; to write and risk ridicule from scientific colleagues is something quite different. After several months, I concluded that I would be intellectually dishonest if I did not include these incidents. In other words, was I reacting emotionally as if the limiting beliefs of science and psychology were true? Roberts (1981) helped crystallize my thinking. What we are writing about are indeed psychological facts. Until science includes the full spectrum of psychological events into the physical-scientific paradigm, we are only dealing with a very narrow and diluted version of "official reality." Paranormal events are too common to be explained away on the basis of fraud, neurotic needs, or subconscious distortions. The "contact" phenomenon was here to stay with Thomaz. There would be enough data to satisfy both the scientifically curious and the scientific "witch-hunters."

More Contacts

Toward the end of 1979 Thomaz frequently remarked that he was in communication with "extraterrestrials" or "energy beings." He would point to the clouds and say that they were "really ships." On January 5, 1980, Thomaz was at his home in Trés Corações. Lygia, now his wife after an emotional roller-coaster courtship, was six months pregnant. Living with them were Lada, her mother Danusa and brother, Tacinho, a victim of Down's Syndrome. Thomaz's friend, Paulo Costa, manager of the Tourist Bureau, had dropped by for a visit. At about 2:00 P.M., Paulo excitedly pointed to five silvery objects in the sky. Thomaz merely shrugged, "It's them," he said.

After the regular six o'clock meditation, several members of the group had lingered to chat and gossip. Suddenly, without warning, Thomaz seemed to be "seized and pulled" by invisible forces. Because he was shirtless, his family could observe bruises and scratches appearing on his arms. According to Lygia, it was "as if he were struggling with an invisible man." Even though he resisted, he was actually pulled through a door and outside into the backyard. Then, as suddenly as the incident began, it was over. Visibly shaken, Thomaz said that the "contact" was terminated and that "they" had "gone away." He then became more agitated and insisted that Lygia call his friend, military commander Antonio das Gracas Santos, and ask him to come over immediately.

Later that night, the commander, his wife Marlene, Paulo Costa, Lygia, and Thomaz tried to make sense of what had happened. Thomaz explained that the "intruders" were from "Aphron-V," an alleged "parallel universe," and that they wanted him to accompany them. They told him he might have to be gone for an indefinite period of time—Lygia might have to take over the management of the pharmacy.

The group was discussing various alternative plans and contingencies when the lights went out without warning. Commander Gracas checked the fuse box but found everything in order. Glancing outside, he saw that the entire neighborhood was without electricity. Then, just as one of the group was lighting a candle, the back door was flung open and a strong gust of wind blasted into the house. Thomaz instructed everyone to raise their arms, palms forward, a gesture he said that would signify peace with no intention of aggression. Rising, Thomaz attempted to close the kitchen door, but couldn't. He paced the floor uneasily for a few minutes and then asked Lygia to bring him his Polaroid camera. Commander Gracas was invited to accompany him out to the yard, where both men saw a small ball of dazzling light hovering at eye level several yards away. It began to move and landed on the welcome mat at the bottom of the stairs leading to the kitchen. The mat caught fire at first and then extinguished itself. Examining the mat the commander could find no evidence of fire or charring. Five minutes later, the lights in the house flickered back on. Incredibly, everything in the house—plates, glasses, table lamps, paintings, clothing, and books—was on the floor in total chaos. Just as incredibly, nothing was broken.

While the group was cleaning up, the lights went out again. Both the commander and Thomaz went outside through the kitchen door in time to see the mat catch fire once more and again snuff itself out. Immediately afterward another fire burst into flame next to one of the large trees in the yard. Gracas then saw yet another spontaneous fire flare up under the picnic table. Flames licked through the wooden planks, but no trace of singeing or searing was found when the table was examined later.

Thomaz became very agitated and ran to his meditation room in the basement of the house, locking the door behind him. For several minutes the sound of a scuffle could be heard. When the door flew open, Thomaz was on the floor, calling for Lada. She went to him, knelt, and cradled his head in her lap. He murmured that he needed metal; someone handed her some bent silverware always available in Thomaz's house. He held a fork in his hands as Lada pressed a spoon against his forehead. After fifteen minutes or so, his energy seemed restored.

He returned to the kitchen, found his Polaroid camera, and again invited Commander Gracas to join him in the yard. The others were cautioned to remain in the living room. Before Thomaz and Gracas went outside, Thomaz mentioned to his friend that "one of them had materialized in the form of a doll," but that the materialization process had been incomplete. Precisely at that moment, a strange form appeared. It stood just outside the kitchen door, behind a screen door that was propped open. Although the lights had come back on, it was difficult to distinguish the features of what Gracas referred to as "the creature." Thomaz managed to take a photograph, causing the creature to produce a low-pitched, "whiny-shrieky" sound, and suddenly vanish. The two men rushed to the door and saw it again at the bottom of the back stairs. Thomaz took a second photograph. This time, there was a "whimpering." As Thomaz and the commander descended the stairs, the creature disappeared.

Proceeding to the yard, they saw the creature again, about fifteen yards away. Gracas described it as "about five feet four inches in height, with one arm or 'limb' slightly extended . . . Both limbs could move, but the right limb seemed more immobilized. . . ." With no hesitation Thomaz approached the creature, his right arm extended in greeting. The moment his hand touched the creature's limb, Thomaz fell to the ground but was not injured. The strange visitor made a piercing, shrieking sound which Gracas described as "that of an animal being attacked."

As if it were playing a cosmic game of hide-and-seek, the creature vanished again, reappearing in another part of the yard. Gracas helped his friend to his feet, offering to protect Thomaz with his revolver. Thomaz told Gracas that the creature meant no harm and that he would not allow the use of the pistol in any case. As they were returning to the house, flashes of light punctuated the darkness. Some flashes were just above ground level; others exploded over the treetops. They were scattered over a wide radius, in no apparent pattern, similar to the bright popping of camera flash bulbs. The colors varied, but were predominantly silvery-blue, reddish-yellow, and orange. As many as ten or twelve lights sometimes flashed on and off simultaneously, looking like a deceptively innocent psychedelic light show.

The two Polaroid photographs revealed the creature to be greenish-brown, very short, and with poorly defined body configurations. Its head appeared to be about seven inches in diameter, with two dark circles where the eyes would be in a human face. The limbs were barely discernible. Its appearance was similar to descriptions of other alleged "sightings" in diverse parts of the world.

The house looked as though it had been ransacked by burglars and everyone pitched in to put things in order. During the cleanup process, Thomaz announced that he had received an important message—"special instructions" to install a yellow light on his roof and to build an "energy captor" in his backyard. The "energy captor" was nothing more than a metal pole imbedded in a circular block of cement. He was also advised to paint his meditation room black to enhance the visibility of "light beings" as they materialized. Finally, he was instructed to build a wooden pyramid in his den: The diagonal of the base should measure five feet and it would "facilitate re-energization" for anyone meditating within its enclosure.

The rest of that month was hectic. Paulo Costa painted the

meditation room black. In accordance with another of Thomaz's detailed instructions, he also sketched a "ship" on one of the walls. Dion, a friend of Thomaz, constructed the pyramid, and several other friends assisted Thomaz with the yellow light and "energy captor." It seems that people were to hold on to the pole during electrical storms in order to "build up energy."

Thomaz's behavior during this time was erratic. He drove around town in his jeep, stopping suddenly, pointing his camera at the sky, and then driving off wildly to another vantage point to take more photographs. Occasionally, he was accompanied by his brother-in-law, police chief Loyola. Though Loyola could not see anything in the sky, when the photographs were developed most of them contained clusters of disc-shaped objects. Thomaz identified these objects as "craft" and could not understand why no one else could see them. Other friends accompanied him and were allowed to take the photographs, using Thomaz's Polaroid camera. Thomaz simply pointed when he could "see" the "craft." His friends rarely saw anything but dutifully snapped the shutter. Without fail the "flying discs" appeared in the color prints.

On February 2, 1980, the Machados arrived; they had decided to assess personally all the data that they had been hearing about back in their laboratory in Rio. Professor Machado spent the first evening carefully examining one hundred seventy photographs. All had been taken by Thomaz or in his presence. Just after midnight, in the midst of their examination, a flash of light exploded through the kitchen window. After this, Thomaz became very withdrawn, seeming to be meditating or concentrating. Quietly he announced that he felt the presence of "intense energy fields" both inside and outside the house. Dr. Gloria Machado announced that there were now "several light explosions" taking place in the backyard.

After a few moments, Thomaz snapped out of his absorbed state and ordered everyone to take off shoes and stockings. As the group ran out into the grass, the yard became an electric circus. Each "light" had a flash duration of one to three seconds. The light appeared to have a nucleus that would dissipate after each strong burst. Several times Thomaz attempted to advance further into the yard. He could go just so far and then no further; it was as if he had run into an invisible shield or barrier. The lights were at distances varying from two feet to forty feet above ground. There were also flashes in between some of the branches, silhouetting the trees in an eerie diorama.

Several members of the group went to the small platform on the roof where the flashing yellow light was housed—the area was now designated by Thomaz as a "UFO PORT." Because it was a damp chilly night, they decided after a few minutes to go back inside the house. Thomaz accepted Professor Machado's suggestion that the yellow light be turned off. Just as he flicked the switch, all the lights in the house went out, making the exploding, dancing lights in the backyard much more visible and incandescent. Huddled in the den, the group had an excellent view of the spectacle in the yard. Suddenly, there were two flashes of a bright light behind them—the "energies" had moved into the house. Thomaz became crazed with excitement, screaming "Ra! Ra! Ra!" over and over. The others joined him and the room crackled with enthusiasm and tension.

After several minutes, Mario Machado asked for quiet. He wondered if the "lights" possessed some form of intelligence. On previous occasions, the lights had responded in a rudimentary fashion—one flash for "Yes," none for "No"; with some correlation between the questions and answers. Hoping for more sophisticated communication, he asked the lights for a signal corresponding to the letter "A." Almost immediately, the group heard a brief, high-pitched sound, rather like someone saying "e-e-e-k." Machado then said, "B," and the same sound was emitted twice. For "C," there were brief squeals. One member of the group, a local attorney named Donalson Xavier de Carvalho, interrupted the process, suggesting, "Now the letter 'D,' but with a long, low sound." The "source" responded, producing a low-frequency blare lasting twenty seconds. Someone likened it to the whistle of a docking boat. The group was elated, convinced that they were participating in an historic encounter with life from another reality. Unfortunately, the combination of euphoria and electric joy interfered with Machado's strategy for establishing a code; the whole situation became unmanageable, and by 2:30 A.M. the phenomena stopped altogether. There was no more light or sound.

The next afternoon, the group reassembled at Thomaz's home. Present were the Machados, Donalson de Carvalho, and Josefino de Carvalho, president of the local bar association, Lygia, Lada, and two other attorney friends. Thomaz had driven off to tend to business at the pharmacy. Professor Machado, in his typically meticulous fashion, was reviewing and summarizing from his notes the implausible events of the preceding night. His remarks were interrupted by the sound of a car horn. Thomaz was back and wanted everyone to follow him immediately—"the sky is full of flying objects," he said. Following him in two cars, they went to the top of Cortia Hill, the highest landmark in the area. Excited, Thomaz pointed to the sky, but the others could see nothing but blue sky and puffs of clouds.

Thomaz kept taking photographs. Twenty minutes later, however, both the Machados began seeing forms in the sky. They no longer needed Thomaz to show them where to point their cameras. For two hours, they took photographs. Of the fifteen people present during this experience, only Thomaz and the Machados saw "objects" in the sky. When the film was developed, Mario and Gloria found they had a series of sixteen photographs of what appeared to be "discs in formation" in various positions. The authors have examined both the negatives and the prints of the Machados' "ships." They are indeed disc-shaped and look very much like classical photographs and drawings of alleged UFOs. Thomaz's Polaroid images were identical to those of the 35mm prints obtained by the Machados.

After dinner that evening, the entourage went to Thomaz's home. At approximately 11:00 P.M., the backyard was again filled with a retinal spectacle of lights. Everyone went outside to observe. Then, hearing strange noises coming from the house, Dr. Machado went inside to investigate. A chair was flying through the air, even though no one was in the room. She called her husband and shortly everyone joined her in the kitchen. Soon thereafter, "poltergeist-type energy" was noted: glasses flew off the shelves, chairs rose and crashed against the wall, and other objects began "moving through space." No one was struck or injured, but some of the glass objects broke. Standing by the back door, Dr. Machado saw the welcome mat at the bottom of the stairs catch fire, burn for thirty seconds, and go out. Again, there was no evidence of scorching. As she returned to the kitchen, a box of matches began winging through the air. In mid-flight, the box opened and matches went flying in all directions.

Things seemed to calm down around 11:00 A.M. But just as the group began to organize their thoughts about the flamboyant events they had witnessed, they were confronted with defiance of common sense. What appeared to be a rock catapulted through a corridor window, breaking the glass. The rock literally flew down the hall, crashing with great force against the door of the meditation room. The door was forced open by the impact and the rock fell to the floor just inside the room. It proved to be granite and, according to the Machados, looked like a "jagged parallelogram, eight inches by ten inches." The top plane was covered by small hieroglyphic inscriptions. The Machados began taking photographs while Thomaz declared that "they" had sent him a message and that he would find a way to translate the cryptogram.

As the reader would guess, being with Thomaz is a disquieting experience. Every day we spent with him seemed full of intrusive anomalies and indecent rearrangements of our tidy world views. But the introduction of the "contact" phenomena was truly irreverent and bizarre. It was no place for cerebral chauvinism. Though it would be cowardly to ignore these phenomena, how does one integrate such "absurdities"? Until 1980, I had carefully given wide berth to anyone interested in UFOs. Now I had to rethink my position. Are they really UFOs? Could most of it be poltergeist activity influenced unconsciously (or consciously) by Thomaz? Were the objects photographed by the Machados real craft occupying space in the sky or were they psychokinetic transmissions of thought forms onto the film? There is certainly evidence of "thoughtography" in the literature. Eisenbud (1968) and Fukurai (1931) have worked with gifted subjects who can paranormally project images onto unexposed film in tightly sealed cameras. However, their psychic photographs do not have the clarity, contrast, and consistency of the Thomaz material. Contagious hysteria was also a hypothesis that we considered but we discarded that in the face of subsequent data.

Two weeks after these turbulent experiences, several persons who had UFO experiences during the same period were interviewed as part of our research; none had been in Thomaz's vicinity at any time, and one eyewitness had never even heard of Thomaz.

João Jose do Nascimento owns a bicycle shop in Trés Corações. On January 29, 1980, he was in his shop with a friend. It was late at night, taxis were not easily available, and João offered to drive his friend to the bus station. On the way home he saw a "firelike" object following him. At first he thought it was an "unusually large star" and that its apparent motion was caused by the moving car. To make certain, he drove behind a hill and stopped. The "object" followed him, hovering in the sky. He hid behind an apartment building and scrutinized the object closely. It "was like a star . . . huge, round form . . . had a big headlight . . . the light transformed into a flash and formed a pattern like a Spanish fan. . . ." João decided to drive on home, but for no apparent reason his car stalled. Finally, it started, and the "object" continued to follow him. He rushed into the house to find that his son, Vincente, had been drawn to the window by the "strange light." Vincente described it as "a fire in the sky . . . turning around . . . there were small lights on it changing colors from orange to green to blue . . . it was onion-shaped."

During that same twenty-four-hour-period, Edson Dias da Silva, a truck driver for a land development project, arrived at the site. It was 5:00 A.M. and he had walked to work. He saw a strange light in the sky that "descended suddenly." It was reddish-yellow, with a number of multicolored lights encircling its perimeter. He rushed into the office to call the police. Suddenly, another similar object appeared and shot upwards with such velocity that it disappeared within seconds.

The "flying objects" created such a shock for real estate broker Roberto Francisco Sentana that he rear-ended an automobile stopped in front of him. It was during the day and several people on the street were "looking at something in the sky." He looked up and could see the "shadow of a saucer." The driver of the automobile he struck had also stopped to examine the "object." Suddenly, two more objects appeared, both with distinct disc-shaped forms. They "hovered for a moment and then flew off at great speed."

When Thomaz was informed about the independent sightings, he repeated what he had been saying all along. "They" were from a parallel universe called "Aphron-V." The "visitors" have a particular interest in him, he says. They are attempting to "create circumstances" so he can accompany them to their reality.

During these episodes, Thomaz began to withdraw for longer periods of time, questioning the purpose and meaning of his earlier experiences. Most noteworthy was the emergence of simple, utterly frail human qualities in Thomaz. His new experience attracted new friends with certain doctrinaire biases. Thomaz responded to some of their persuasive suggestions. Perhaps the sky bolt that struck him at age twelve was not lightning. In his own mind he had revised his own history. Now the lightning had become a "special ray fired from a spacecraft."

CHAPTER EIGHT

The General and the Psychic

Man is made by his belief . . . as he believes, so he is.
Bhagavad Gita

It was only a question of time before Thomaz would be introduced to Brigadier General Alfredo Moacyr Uchoa, retired from a distinguished military career spanning many pursuits. An engineer, Uchoa had been assigned as a young officer to several posts with the engineering corps. Following a period of administrative duties, he became part of a confidential project of the Brazilian Air Force to gather and collate data on the increasing number of UFO sightings. That project was to be only the beginning of his intense interest in UFOs.

Following his discharge from the military, General Uchoa established a university in Brasília, attracting scientists interested in anomalous phenomena as they relate to social issues. Out of this effort came a special team organized by Uchoa to probe the "extra or intraterrestrial objects or sightings." The author of five books and a number of scientific papers, he is a soft-spoken man who discusses issues in a careful, considered manner. An impish sense of humor punctuates the seriousness of deliberations about "phenomena." Intellectually, he oscillates comfortably between theories of hyperspace and Walker's quantum tunneling wave-packet collapse proposal. However, UFO "contacts" most stimulate his scientific curiosity; he sometimes refers to them as a "siren song leading me into the boldest enigma of all."

The general owns a farm just within the town of Alexania, in the state of Goias, approximately one hundred miles from Brasília. A two-hundred-mile arc north and east of Brasília is the focus of a disproportionately large number of sightings. In 1969, Uchoa and his research team observed several appearances of a "silvery-blue sphere" over Alexania. In every sighting, the "sphere" maneuvered, turned sharply, and disappeared in trajectories that ordinary aircraft were incapable of. Most of the sightings were confirmed independently by townspeople who had no knowledge of the general's research interests.

Contact with Extraterrestrials

Uchoa wondered if it would be possible to connect psychically with these extraterrestrial visitors. He approached Wilson Gusmao, an excellent deep-trance medium. After several unsuccessful attempts, Gusmao made contact, and began talking in a "broken, mechanical, computer-speech fashion." During contact, his body movements became stilted and robotlike.

From 1969 to 1973, the group established communication with their visitor who identified himself as Aramak. (The complete chronicle of their interchanges has been documented by Uchoa in a diary format). The most stunning aspect of the communication was the materialization and appearance of Aramak during several sessions. All members of the research team agreed on Aramak's physical description: "A humanoid appearance . . . between five feet two inches and five feet four inches in height . . . his lips were very fine or thin, centered low on his head, giving the impression that he had no teeth . . . His trunk was slim, but his throat, head, and shoulders were quite large . . . He wore a skin-tight uniform and a wide belt punctuated by three distinct buttons." Aramak always greeted the group with his right arm bent upwards, palm facing forward. While his description sounds like a character from science fiction, the group's illusion of earth chauvinism disappeared forever.

In mid 1973, General Uchoa's thirty-year-old adopted daughter, Bernadette, contracted the dread Chagas disease, which is transmitted by the bite of a small tropical beetle. The symptoms are fever, myxedema, or hypothyroidism, and enlargement of the glands, spleen, and liver. There is no known effective treatment; it is almost always a fatal disease. Bernadette had been hospitalized for five months at the modern Armed Forces hospital in Brasília. On July 14, 1973, a medical grand rounds was convened and the summary entered in her medical chart read "critical . . . medication for comfort . . . no further treatment indicated."

In desperation, General Uchoa summoned his team for a crisis session with their contact. Aramak instructed the group to meet at noon on July 17, 1973, at "kilometer 19" on the road south of Brasília. They were to bring Bernadette with them. Just as they were approaching their rendezvous point, a "bright blue light" appeared above the horizon and settled on the road almost one hundred seventy-five yards away. Aramak appeared and the medium Gusmao relayed instructions to Bernadette while the research group observed. Weakly, she approached Aramak. He appeared to give her two injections, though he held nothing in his hands. His "invisible syringe" caused two "biting pains"—one in her left arm and the other on the side of her neck. A golden light illuminated the whole area as both Aramak and the bluish ball disappeared back over the skyline.

After that pivotal encounter, Bernadette began to recover almost immediately and she has since resumed a normal life. Her physician at that time was Dr. Bonfim Albrahao Tobias, a heart specialist. He is currently medical director of Brasília's Santa Lucia Hospital. In a recent interview with Gary, he acknowledged that all the professional personnel associated with the case considered it an "extraordinary, miraculous cure."

Jahn (1982), in a provocative perspective on psychic phenomena, has likened the world of the paranormal to a vast, fog-shrouded swamp. Within it resides a bewildering array of creatures, alien to our normal manner of cataloguing experience. Some of the scientific explorers who have ventured into this misty domain have returned, claiming that all such life is illusory. Only the gullible would see things that are not really there. But there is no question that at times something surfaces from the depths to "flash momentarily in the light of human experience." Then, the "activity" or phenomenon disappears before it can be photographed or calibrated. The reports of the psychic naturalists are usually treated with disdain or even worse, believed to be fraudulently obtained.

Each new age seeks a broader context so that the fullest magnitude of human beingness can be expressed. General Uchoa has taken a courageous public stance on these matters. He would like to see a loosening and a new understanding of anomalous phenomena from the tyranny of scientific restraint and rigidity. Fortunately, Brazil is a country where personal and subjective experiences are "facts." So-called paranormal events are commonplace and are described every day by conspicuously normal persons.

Thomaz met Uchoa following his first series of "contact phenomena" late in 1979. They established an immediate rapport and Uchoa began to travel with Thomaz whenever possible.

In the ensuing months, Thomaz became obsessed with "sighting and contact" episodes. Fortunately, Uchoa was available to provide a stabilizing influence for his young friend and at the same time provide validation for Thomaz's experiences from the Air Force dossier of photographs.

Extraterrestrials and Hieroglyphics

Because of Uchoa's stature in Brazil, Thomaz made great efforts to win his new friend's respect. He began to modify the meaning of his twelfth birthday; within a relatively short time, the lightning at Fasqueira had become reinterpreted as a "ray from an extraterrestrial craft." Everyone who knows Thomaz wonders

The General and the Psychic

about the source of his powers but he too is searching for answers. After meeting Uchoa and recognizing his prestige and his philosophy, Thomaz was very comfortable with a spacecraft interpretation.

While it is relatively easy to speculate over social influences upon Thomaz's world views, other features of this hypothesis pose very annoying challenges. Thomaz had translated the hieroglyphics on the rock that had crashed into his home the night of the "poltergeist activity." According to Thomaz, the message said that he was now being visited by "energy beings" who would continue to make themselves visible in the form of light-flashes. He was provided with the names of the four different colored lights. A second rock appeared later—just as mysteriously as the first. It contained additional information that the "electrical experience" on his twelfth birthday had not been caused by lightning: He had been struck by a "special ray of light from an interplanetary spaceship."

Another event that occurred about this same time appears to substantiate Thomaz's translation of the inscribed rocks. As mentioned in Chapter Six, Mrs. Bianca Reis, a housewife from Belo Horizonte, was allegedly abducted and spent two days aboard a spacecraft. The only memento she was permitted to keep of her experience was a small sheet of papyrus with strange glyphs inscribed on it. The material was translated for her psychically by a well-known psychic, and its content compelled her to locate Thomaz. They compared the inscriptions on the papyrus with the hieroglyphics on the rock, discovering the two sets to be identical—the translation received by Mrs. Reis corresponds almost word for word with Thomaz's version.

It would be simple to increase the stockpile of paradoxes on this issue. For example, Beloff (1983) has proposed a "super-ESP" hypothesis to account for so-called mediumistic channeling of spirit messages that he attributes (rather than the deceased person) as the source of the message. Similarly, one could postulate a "super-psychokinesis" and "super-ESP" premise for the inscribed rock and papyrus. Thomaz has repeatedly demonstrated his capacity for triggering and detonating a number of realities, such as transteleportation, telepathy, and psychokinesis. A person with a distinctive affinity could certainly select the facts that happen to fit their theory. I tend to agree with Beloff who suggests that "normal" explanations are sometimes far more implausible than a frank acceptance of psychic realities.

General Uchoa also speculated actively about these "zone of mystery" experiences. He felt that the "energy" or "light forms" connected with Thomaz were advanced beings from another universe. His writings also emphasized that it was unwise to accept the light explosions literally. It is much too easy to accept the appearance of Thomaz's "space friends" as necessarily physical reality. As Watson (1979) has pointed out, there is a strong psychic component in UFO phenomena and enthusiasts will go to extraordinary lengths to justify a physical explanation. The same caution should be observed with Thomaz who has repeatedly demonstrated that "mind" can manifest in many forms, possibly even creating physical reality. At times, I am convinced of the physical existence of Thomaz's intra/extraterrestrial contacts; on other occasions, I feel that the phenomena can be accommodated by an explanation of psychokinetic materialization of personal and collective unconscious thought forms. Either way, one can still feel justified based on the "evidence."

Thomaz's Growing Popularity

The challenge of researching and documenting Thomaz's phenomena was becoming more and more like running a gauntlet, especially in late 1979 and 1980. His reputation had begun to spread and people from all over Brazil flocked to his home. On some weekends, as many as a hundred people might mill about his house and property. The heightened psychological atmosphere created a pervading anxious expectancy—waiting for something "psychic" to happen.

Compounding the "edge" in the air were the differing motivations and expectations of the visitors. Some were professional and amateur researchers who had come to objectively and "officially" validate, or negate, Thomaz. Some had come with a sense of privilege and awe at being witness to new magnitudes of reality. Others were stimulated by religious or mystical incentives—anyone who could perform miracles of such consequence must be a true avatar, or son of God. They expected to be anointed with a special misting of cosmic bliss. Many of the visitors came for the sheer entertainment value. They were open to all types of magic and would subscribe promiscuously to anything out of the ordinary. Of course, there was the whole spectrum of Ufologists, who were anxiously awaiting a special sign to sanctify their pet theories. What was missing was a social scientist to consider the sociology of miracles. Here was a new order of experiences unfolding and everyone was reacting in a traditional and predictable fashion. Are intellectual and emotional straightjackets that comforting?

Light Energies

General Uchoa's experiences with Thomaz's "light energies" began literally with a baptism of fire. Thomaz, in his usual impulsive fashion, had interrupted a late evening social gathering and asked the general to "drive him around town." Then he decided they should make the two-hour drive to Uchoa's farm at Alexania. With them were the general's daughter and granddaughter in the back seat, and, following, two carloads of Uchoa's friends and colleagues who had decided to join in. About one third of a mile out of town, "four explosions of light" suddenly burst inside the general's sedan. Thomaz reacted as if this were his first psychic experience, screaming with delight at each "light." His enthusiasm soon spread to everyone in the car. For the duration of the trip, a full two hours, there were dozens of light explosions in light blue, dark blue, light red, dark red, orange, green, and yellow.

Mauricio Panisset, a physics teacher for a federal education agency, was driving the car behind Uchoa. He noted that some "light forms" jelled or "took form" more slowly than others. All the passengers in his car observed "distinct, cloudlike light forms" around Uchoa's sedan, appearing both outside and inside the vehicle. Extinguishing his headlights, Panisset could also see "colored streamers of light" inside and around the car in front of him. The streamers were less luminous than the other light forms and were not accompanied by explosions.

An exhilarated group arrived at Uchoa's farm. Despite the late hour, they stayed up comparing their observations and found them generally in accord. They agreed on the colors, intensity, and position of the curious and aberrant eruptions of light. After a few moments, Thomaz walked away from the group and disappeared into a nearby cluster of trees. Soon he began to shout for the general to join him. Before Uchoa could get out of his chair, a series of multicolored lights flashed within a thirty-yard radius. When Uchoa and Panisset went out they were unable to find Thomaz. Calling Thomaz's name, Uchoa was instantaneously illuminated by and totally immersed in a silvery-blue light form for a mind-boggling five minutes. While Uchoa began to humorously refer to this experience as his "instant illumination," at the time he was quite fearful. Panisset, who witnessed the episode, accompanied the general back to his house, where they found Thomaz on the porch chatting excitedly with the others. They had all seen the light form create the envelope of light around Uchoa. Thomaz referred to the silver-blue energy as "Kryptus." Kryptus, he said, liked the general; bathing him in light was a demonstration of affection.

The energy light forms have been witnessed by hundreds of observers. They have appeared inside and outside buildings, above tree level, and simultaneously in different physical locations. Their capricious and protean dance has even been captured on videotape. On rare occasions, the bedazzling flashes will manifest when Thomaz is not even in the same room or building.

New Psychic Realms

Two weeks later, General Uchoa invited ten of his associates to Trés Corações to join forces with the Machados and Gary. They were intrigued with the luminous pulsations of the lights, but equally important was the fact that Thomaz was going through another evolutionary leap in his mastery of physical time/space. Shortly after their arrival, one of Uchoa's guests became distraught; she had left her documents in Brasília. Her concern was understandable—in Brazil, people must have their identity cards with them at all times or risk being detained by authorities. Everyone joined in the search and the car in which she had been riding was examined thoroughly. She remembered leaving her document pouch on the hallway table in her apartment. Thomaz spoke to her briefly; suddenly, the hair on his arms became "electrified." He announced that he would bring the documents from Brasília. His eyes closed and he began deep breathing. Two minutes later, he started to speak in a peculiar stutter. "They were coming . . . they are going to fall on the table . . . they have arrived . . . no . . . they are inside your car . . . not in the glove compartment . . . somewhere in the back seat. . . ." General Uchoa, accompanied by his brother, a psychiatrist, rushed to the car. Lying on the back seat were her documents.

Transmutations of Organic Matter

Later that evening, Thomaz performed a demonstration he had never done before: He psychically transmuted and revitalized dead organic matter into a living organism. After dinner, Thomaz asked the general's brother to take a piece of grilled beef from his plate, hold it in his hand, and close his fist tight around it. Sitting across the table from Dr. Uchoa, Thomaz closed his eyes, held his arms up, palms out, and prepared to be radiating energy. "Ra!" When the psychiatrist opened his hand, everyone present was at first stunned, then inflamed with excitement. The piece of beef had been replaced with a live cricket. When the emotional impact of this incredible event had been absorbed, someone noticed that one of the cricket's legs was injured. Concerned about the creature's suffering, Thomaz began to probe the leg gently with his pocket knife, attempting to restore or effect a cure. It was midnight and the restaurant was closing. The group talked Thomaz into reluctantly "dislingando" (disengaging) from the cricket's injury.

The general placed the injured cricket in a napkin and the group moved on to Thomaz's house. Moments after their arrival, Thomaz asked the general to replace the paper napkin with a cruzeiro note. Uchoa folded it gently around the cricket and held it in his right hand. Thomaz appeared to be mobilizing energy, radiating it into the banknote. He held this position for some time, explaining that he was "mentalizing" healing energy for the insect's leg. When the bill was spread open, everyone was shocked. The cruzeiro banknote was charred and the insect inside was dead. Thomaz apologized, explaining that he had "exaggerated the energy." Despite the scorching effect, Uchoa had not felt any heat in his hand.

Thomaz was perplexed and dissatisfied with the damaging effects of his "healing energy." Once more, he instructed Uchoa to close his fist around the banknote and the lifeless cricket. This time, with a steady chant, he implored "the powers of the universe to put things back in order again." When the general opened his hand, everyone was dumbfounded. The cruzeiro note had been restored to its original state and the cricket was miraculously revived. The only blotch on this inexplicable marvel was that the cricket's injured leg was no longer attached to its body. It was somehow psychically amputated and was lying next to the cricket inside the general's palm.

A sense of numbness and reverence swept over the group. Even Thomaz gasped and seemed stunned. This did not last long, however. He became uneasy and announced that the "electricity is everywhere in my body." His behavior seemed a combination of childlike puckishness and a determined sense of control and focused will. Once more he asked the general to make a fist around the cricket and its dismembered leg. Thomaz invoked "transmuting energy from the universe" to change the cricket into "something else—something whole—Ra!" Uchoa felt no movement. However, when he opened his hand a large shiny cockroach had replaced the cricket.

One of the women gasped and shrieked. She was phobic and terrified of cockroaches. Thomaz tried to make light of the situation, joking that the creature would "fly off to find a mate."

Nothing happened. Then Thomaz became very somber and said he would try to do something to resolve the situation. For the last time, the general was asked to close his fist around the captive cockroach. Shutting his eyes, Thomaz petitioned the "universal energy . . . to return all matter to its original states . . . but with a 'sign' interpreting what had happened." Cautiously, Uchoa opened his hand. In the center of his palm was a morsel of cooked beef, flanked on either side by a cricket leg and a single leg of a cockroach.

Is our reality that fragile? Can consciousness be used like a weaving loom shuttle to treat life in such a fickle fashion? Is the mind of man the microcosmic counterpart of the universal mind? This would suggest that the only limits to human capacities are self-imposed.

The General's Dinner

The following day, still more of the general's friends arrived in Trés Corações for a special dinner in honor of Uchoa. The general is well-known and respected throughout Brazil for his writings. In addition to the military contingent, many of the town's distinguished citizens were also invited—forty guests in all. The usual after-dinner speeches praised the distinguished honoree. Then Uchoa spoke for a half-hour on psychic and UFO research. He candidly admitted that the Air Force has a large collection of photographs, film, and classified data on alleged sightings of spacecraft. In the midst of his prepared talk, he turned and pointed to Thomaz, who was seated in the back of the room and unusually quiet. Directing his remarks to Thomaz, the general said that investigating the paranormal would do more to provide insights into the persistent mysteries of life than "ten thousand brain studies." Parapsychology, he said, could ultimately unfold the evolutionary process and bring about the inevitable liberation of consciousness. "Thomaz represents the razor's edge and living vision of the future mind," Uchoa pronounced.

Thomaz was overwhelmed at being celebrated by such an eminent person. In a few moments, however, his quiet humility gave way to a sparkling, impish animation. He announced that he wanted to produce a "psychic souvenir" for everyone present. Uncertain at first of what he would do, he was suddenly inspired. He would demonstrate one of his more common phenomena, but in a manner never before attempted.

Eighteen of the general's closest comrades were asked to take banknotes out of their pockets and mark them in some way. This was done, and the notes were gathered and handed to Uchoa. He was instructed to divide the currency arbitrarily and present nine bills each to the two men sitting on either side of him. They, in turn, were to fold the cruzeiros and hold them tightly in their right hands. Thomaz walked around the table to where they were sitting and announced that he would "psychically singe" a lucky color and significant date onto each of the bills through the men's hands. Lighting a cigarette, he burned the back of each fist. Colonel Kamer, Commander of the Brazilian Army Sergeant's School, screamed out in pain. The banknotes were then taken by the general and returned to the persons who loaned them. Each bill had a color and date charred on its face. The placement of this extraordinary psychic imprint varied on all eighteen banknotes. The room was galvanized with excitement. Thomaz never looked more pleased with himself. Uchoa attempted to make a brief speech about "superminds" but was overcome with emotion. Instead, he concluded his address in a tearful embrace with his young friend.

The manifestations of that day added to Thomaz's growing reputation. More of the general's military friends became interested in his miraculous displays. Surprisingly, they never mentioned military or political application of his powers; they seemed to have a genuine interest in unclogging old visions and sparking a wider perception of reality.

Transteleportation

During the summer of 1982, a group of Uchoa's friends were invited to the farm to spend more time with Thomaz. A caravan was organized and several cars departed from Brasília at 2:30 P.M. on a Friday afternoon. The general had other engagements and would join his friends later that evening. At approximately 3:00 P.M. the caravan pulled into a truck stop where Thomaz entered a small luncheonette to buy cigarettes. He never came out. Two of the group went inside to look for him, but the employees denied seeing anyone of his description. It was a small area and anyone coming through the door could be seen easily. Baffled, they called Uchoa in Brasília, who advised them to go on to Alexania and to call him again from the farm.

The caravan arrived at the house a few minutes after 6:00 P.M. To their astonishment, Thomaz was sitting in the patio area nonchalantly chatting with Uchoa's caretaker. They asked how long he had been there and the caretaker's wife answered, "Since a few minutes after three." Impossible! That was the precise moment he had entered the luncheonette. She was adamant about the time; she remembered well, she said, because she had been urging her husband to tend to certain errands in town in preparation for the guests. Also, a bank deposit had to be made before the 4:00 P.M. closing time. She recalled distinctly "pushing my husband out of the house at 2:55." A few minutes later, she said, a total stranger had walked up and asked if this was General Uchoa's home. It was Thomaz! She had invited him in and made him a fresh cup of coffee. He seemed confused, and to use her expression, "not with it." Just as he started to sip from the cup, there were several explosions of bluish-white light. Questioned by the group, Thomaz proved to be totally unaware of what had taken place. He remembered entering the luncheonette and recalled "suddenly being outside a strange house I had never visited before."

Transteleportation was a totally new and unexpected phenomenon for Thomaz. He was to have several similar experiences in the future. However, at no time was he able to exercise any conscious control over the heretical violation of this basic law of nature. Rogo (1982), in a comprehensive review of miracles, described several instances in which religious and mystical notables have publicly demonstrated levitation and translocation. Dr. Joseph Lapponi (1974), medical officer to Popes Leo XVII and Pius X, documented four mysterious transportations of the Pansini brothers, aged ten and eight years, respectively. In the most incredible experience, they were in Ruvo, Italy. A few moments later, they were on a boat at sea almost sixty miles away heading towards Trinitapoli. Shortly afterwards, they "vanished in an instant" before the presence of Bishop Berardi as they were recounting their experience to their mother. More recently, Geller (1975) was allegedly transteleported while window shopping in Manhattan to Dr. Puharich's home thirty miles away. He experienced a feeling of "running backwards a couple of steps . . . then being sucked upward." A few seconds later, in Ossining, New York, he crashed through a screen eight feet above the ground, injuring his shoulder as he landed. Puharich was assured of the credibility of the experience after validating the reports of observers in Manhattan.

Change in Thomaz

With the transteleportation incident at Alexania, Uchoa became even more convinced that extraterrestrial energies—perhaps friendly and unfriendly—were influencing Thomaz.

After his first experience of transteleportation, Thomaz suddenly exhibited uncharacteristic flashes of insensitivity. For example, an engineer from Rio, who viewed Thomaz as a messiah, lost his job and adopted the role of disciple, following his "psychic brother" all over Brazil. He also declared that he too possessed paranormal powers, although none were evident. While not directly responsible for this man's behavior, Thomaz did nothing to discourage it.

The general began to express some concern about the changes in his friend's life-style. He used the expression "negative forces" when discussing Thomaz's increasing merchandising of himself. Thomaz's fees for "psychic consultations" have far surpassed the excessive spiral of Brazilian inflation. His current price for a conference and demonstration ranges from two thousand to five thousand dollars depending on how much time he spends with the client. Though Uchoa did not dispute his right to charge for a "psychic show of miracles," he feels it unethical to profit from the treatment of human disease and misery. Brazil's finest healers and psychic surgeons, he might have argued, never ask for money and always refuse any donations. While this attitude reflects in part the general's spiritista orientation, the fact that Thomaz charges money for healing automatically brands him a fraud in some Brazilian circles.

Even more discreditable, Uchoa felt, were Thomaz's sprees of drunkenness, womanizing, and self-indulgent unreliability. Uchoa believes very strongly that anyone gifted with such supernatural powers should set a "Christian-like example" for others. However, just as his psychic energies often burst forth unexpectedly, so does his control over impulses. He immerses himself totally in eating, drinking, and sex. Lygia, his wife, has been a pillar of patience in tolerating her husband's gusto for life and unrestrained self-gratification.

Uchoa finds such crude behavior frustrating and incomprehensible. On the other hand, a fair portrayal of Thomaz must include the fact that he has been the source of spiritual inspiration for many of his friends. One of the most touching experiences for the general took place during a transmutation. Thomaz had Uchoa roll a small ball of paper and hold it between his thumb and index finger. As Thomaz radiated energy, the general could see a "golden halo of light around his head and shooting out from his fingers." He felt a sharp pain in the finger that held the paper wad and saw that the paper had been transformed into a miniature bust of Christ. Exquisitely fine detail depicted the wounds and bleeding around the head of the crucified Jesus. The bust was truly a work of art and Uchoa was deeply moved.

Space Ray Theory of Fasqueira

During most of 1980, Thomaz continued to refine and defend his new "theory" about being struck by a ray of light from a spaceship, a theory that made him feel more comfortable in his attempts to understand and explain his astonishing powers. Somehow, it was also a very plausible explanation to many of his advocates, who could not negate the visual proof of more than one hundred photographs of what appeared to be spacecraft as well as several hundred sightings by reliable witnesses. Yet with time, Thomaz's protean mind would come to favor other theories. New friends and new influences were entering his life: The "space ray" explanation would eventually yield to yet another startling interpretation in Thomaz's continuing metamorphosis.

Despite Thomaz's changing views of himself, the extraterrestrial theory began to develop unsolicited support. During the summer of 1980, a nineteen-year-old paraplegic from São Luis, Brazil, Antonio Alves Ferreira, was acclaimed for his extraordinary powers. He was accompanied to Rio de Janeiro and São Paulo by a state district attorney. He was taken to two university research units for investigation and also spent nearly a week in Professor Machado's laboratory. Under various controls, he repeatedly demonstrated metal-bending abilities. Simply by looking at or thinking about various metal objects, he caused them to bend, twist, or collapse. He was never permitted to touch the articles and frequently was in a room separate from the metal. Spontaneous poltergeist phenomena would also manifest during his concentration periods: Objects catapulted across the room and furniture suddenly displaced itself.

Ferreira insisted that he acquired his powers three years earlier when he was abducted by extraterrestrials. During his examination, he was given a "potion" to accelerate his latent psychic powers. Throughout all testing procedures, the youngster impressed everyone as sincere and ingenuously honest. Scientists Hynek and Vallee (1975), respected authorities on UFO phenomena, feel that extraterrestrial sightings and the "awakening of man's psychic abilities" are intimately related. They provocatively suggest that civilizations of a superior intelligence are perhaps another dimension of ourselves—a part of our own consciousness yet outside our time and space boundaries. The "sightings" would serve to stimulate our imaginations. Gifted persons like Thomaz, Geller, and even Ferreira could be physical representations or intimations of an even greater mental and spiritual heritage.

Hero Worship

Although one would have to labor to perceive Thomaz as a symbol for spiritual growth, perhaps there is a lesson in his behavior that is not immediately apparent. If he didn't drink and womanize and was more considerate about social obligations, people might deify him much more readily. In some of his more pensive moments, Thomaz has acknowledged that psychic powers do not necessarily constitute wisdom. They are simply signposts to what should be a path of inner searching and development. Knowing that many people tend to worship gurus and psychics, Thomaz, by his scandalous behavior, might be suggesting (perhaps unconsciously) that those who treat him as a divine being can lose their sense of individual identity. There is evidence that several persons stopped their weekly religious pilgrimages to Trés Corações and began to put Thomaz and psychic phenomena in a more realistic perspective.

In my own experiences with Thomaz, I have oscillated from hero worship to disgust. Some of my greatest frustrations occurred while waiting for psychic phenomena to happen. There would either be an explosion of marvels or long periods of waiting impatiently. On the other hand, Thomaz has done more to help me redefine my world view than all my previous experience with psychics. One of my most valuable learnings was that psychic phenomena cannot be "arranged" to meet pressing time schedules. Since the energy seems to transcend our time and space boundaries, we must look for different laws of causality. Perhaps that is why there is such despair in many parapsychology laboratories today. We have no conceptual categories for anomalous phenomena. If they don't fit into a neat mechanistic-Newtonian scheme of the world, they are fraudulent or don't exist. Somewhere, there is a middle ground between the analytic endeavors of reason and the ephemeral shadows of paranormal experiences.

CHAPTER NINE

Divine Inspiration

There are two ways to be fooled. One is to believe what isn't so. The other is to refuse to believe what is so.
Søren Kierkegaard

At 11:00 P.M. on December 7, 1980, at the Veranda Restaurant in Pouso Alegre, Thomaz performed his typical transmutations. Luis Macedo removed the gold foil from a cigarette package and placed it on the table. Another witness, Edson Provesan, folded the foil several times and clutched it in his closed fist. Thomaz wanted to "create a present" for Macedo's wife, Nazare.

He tightened all the muscles in his body, held his breath until he turned crimson, and cried, "Hra!" Provesan felt nothing in his clenched fist. He opened his hand and what had been a piece of foil "was now a solid, circular golden medallion, seven centimeters in circumference and one-third of a centimeter thick. It had a gold color, texture, and weight. On one side, five radiating rays of light and on the other, all the symbols of the astrological zodiac . . ."

Witness to Dematerialization

At 1:30 A.M. an affidavit, initiated and prepared by Judge Almir Paulo Lima, a lawyer and former police chief who retired after seventeen years on the magistrate's bench, was circulated among those present. Among the witnesses were several professional persons, two politicians, and Dr. Elson Montagno, a Brazilian neurosurgeon who recently completed postgraduate studies in Berlin. (Dr. Montagno's work with Thomaz is discussed in Chapter Six.) The affidavit began:

> We who sign this affidavit saw what is described . . . what for others may be totally impossible and absurd . . . what we witnessed is an expression of Truth . . . and nothing which will be related took place under hypnosis or any other type of altered awareness . . .

We possess several similar affidavits and in interviewing the witnesses, we were consistently impressed by their sincerity and innocent boldness. By openly acknowledging their experience of "impossible realities," they risked rejection and ridicule by friends, and especially scientists.

This document, however, concluded with a hair-raising absurdity that could easily be thought of as an insulting hallucination. Just after midnight—"Thomaz and all the witnesses went to a locale known as the Fasqueira . . . and there, we observed Thomaz dematerialize in front of our eyes four times . . . In his place appeared a large number of lights . . . bluish white, red, green, yellow . . . with Thomaz reappearing in his place . . . before dematerializing again. . . ." Materializing? Dematerializing? Seeing a person transform into light energies? Heretical at best and more like the stuff of a poor science fiction writer at worst.

Nevertheless, in August 1982, Dr. Montagno (1982) presented his observations of several Thomaz phenomena, including the materialization and light occurrences he witnessed that night at the Fasqueira. The occasion was the Centenary Conference of The Society of Psychical Research and the Parapsychology Association, held at Cambridge University in England. Many of the world's leading parapsychologists and physicists were at the conference. Dr. Montagno's observations were of an area at Fasqueira that was fairly visible because of adjacent street lights. He went on to say, "Then followed a sequence of events which I now find difficult to present because they are so incredible. These included apparent distortions of Thomaz's body; at one stage he seemed to shrink to a very small size, another time his body seemed to expand. He also appeared to levitate and to disappear suddenly and also gradually. . . ."

Dr. Montagno considered the possibility of being in the presence of a skilled magician but, "there were no stage props and no assistants." The hypnosis hypothesis was difficult to sustain as there were no suggestions nor an element of expectation. During the review that evening and next morning the events and memories of the observers were in complete accord. While Dr. Montagno's paper probably divided the house of faith and reason more than ever, there were also encouraging stirrings in the audience.

Some of the more thoughtful scientists approached Montagno after the presentation and speculated about "fragile psychic boundaries . . . and . . . psychological stepping stones to other realities."

Communicating Paranormal Experiences

It seems that our current concepts of ourselves may be so limiting that often we confine our experience to fit our reality. Not Judge Lima. During a visit with him at his home in Lavras he stated, "Thomaz turned into lights; it was no optical illusion or collective hallucination." He also reminded us of the validity and objectivity of psychological experiences, which represent truths that cannot necessarily be categorized, neatly labeled, or broken down into true/false, clear-cut contrasts to be assimilated by the everyday mind. So far we have found it easier to cramp our ex-

Divine Inspiration

istence and homogenize our consciousness—anything but challenge our perception of what is real and possible.

But what about Thomaz, who "turned into lights—just three meters in front of twelve witnesses?" Thomaz somewhat prosaically stated that he had not planned to dematerialize that night. He added that the process was subjectively similar to his transteleportation to General Uchoa's farm in Alexania—"I only knew it was happening when it happened." All efforts to elicit further recall from Thomaz about his dematerialization experience led to one verbal quandary after another. He acknowledged that he suddenly appears in Aphron-V, an apparent parallel universe in another dimension: "It is the most beautiful place I have ever seen . . . such vivid brilliant colors. . . ." Then, he usually adds that it is "inexpressible . . . beyond words," stopping in mid-sentence with a somewhat perplexed yet enraptured expression. Sometimes, he breaks down into tears, unable to continue.

Apparently Thomaz's conscious framework is too limited to interpret the multidimensional nature of this deeper, more complex consciousness. Masters and Houston (1966) have described how drugs or life-threatening illness can often serve to scatter our usual focus of consciousness. When this cultural trance is broken, we move into other ways of perceiving and organizing data. Only then can we capture glimpses of alternate realities.

A second problem in communicating "paranormal" experiences is a linguistic one. In a thoughtful interview, physicist David Bohm (1983) suggests that mystical experiences are too difficult to communicate because our language is inadequate for the task. These limitations force us to compress perceptions into linear expressions, into a mechanistic interpretation, thereby diminishing the perception. Our language is geared to a lower level of experience. According to Bohm, poetry comes closest to describing the unexplored territory of higher human consciousness. I might add that metaphors, allegories, and parables also offer possible bridges to the open skies of consciousness.

The physicist Fritjof Capra (1975) expressed a similar concern. The world, he postulated, is in the midst of a "giant paradigm shift." We are experiencing a massive transformation of values, perceptions, and consciousness. Again, we "do not possess the vocabulary or terminology" to distinguish the subtle gradations at the extremes of external events and internal experience. But is imprisonment by language a new condition? Capra discussed the dilemma of scientists at the turn of the century, who were faced with a similar situation when they were first exposed to the subatomic and quantum worlds. "In their struggle to grasp this new reality, scientists became painfully aware that their basic concepts, their language, and their whole way of thinking were inadequate to describe atomic phenomena."

It is no wonder that Thomaz cannot find words to express himself when he somehow "bleeds through" into other pulses of consciousness. His vocabulary is sprinkled with psychological terms related to "energies" or "realities," but probably no more so than the average layperson. His attempts to clarify phenomena are usually rooted in nature or natural philosophy. Thomaz declares that he somehow harnesses "the cosmic energies" that are omnipresent in nature. He is especially attracted to water and its "energy." Similarly, whenever possible, he also enjoys walking barefoot on the rolling grassy hills of Minas Gerais. When one walks barefoot, he says, one's body attracts the energy from the minerals of that very rich soil.

Thomaz's Energy Force

According to Thomaz, the natural forces of energy have a much more profound meaning for him than they do for most people. He feels his body opening up like the aperture of a camera lens. He can accommodate either strong electrical fields or draw in the more subtle energies from rain, immersing himself in a lake, or walking on mineralized earth. Several persons living in proximity to microwave towers have reported experiencing an increase in their telepathic abilities (Becker, 1982), which suggests that the presence of smaller and faster frequencies allows a wider spectrum of information to "come through." Perhaps the lightning that struck Thomaz at age twelve biased or polarized the biomagnetic fields of his body so that he can now interpret more information. Sound engineers can increase the clarity or reduce distracting background noise on a magnetic tape simply by introducing an electrical current into the plastic (Lichota, 1985). This causes particles to align, with less randomness in the molecules on the tape, and results in less distracting "noise" or bias. Therefore, a broader spectrum of signals, or clearer information, can be lifted from the more organized field. There may be some universality to the laws of electricity that could apply to a macroelectrical phenomenon such as lightning and its possible "liberating" effect on energies.

Energy is such a vital and recurring theme in working with Thomaz that we must approach it from many different angles. In Chapter One I described how we actually "saw" energy during a reconstitution-mending session. As Jim Jensen held together two jagged pieces of a broken chicken bone, Thomaz squinted his eyes and "lost" himself in focused concentration. Within ten seconds, a blue, hazy mist enveloped the junction of the broken bone like a delicate cloud. It was clearly visible for a moment until the familiar "Ra!" and was followed by the healing of the bone. Interestingly, metaphysical literature almost always refers to the "vibrations of blue light" (Lapponi, 1974) as the color associated with healing.

Energy in such a visual context has rarely been reported, but many people have recounted feeling or sensing energy fluctuations. Both of the authors have experienced sensations of lightheadedness, fatigue, and occasional hyper-alertness while observing phenomena. Thomaz openly acknowledges that he taps into the "body resources of observers" to facilitate these events. He will sometimes rearrange the seating positions of persons in the room so that he can draw more readily from "compatible energies."

Different flows of energy are often related to the state and flow of consciousness of those present. Thomaz constantly refines his ability to distinguish between different gradations of energy, such as the difference between metal-bending and note-burning forces. However, he is also aware that the consciousness of those in the room can create invisible intersections and detours that can partially determine what will occur. More and more he recognizes an interaction effect between himself and those in his psychic environment. More and more, those who have spent considerable time with Thomaz are learning to identify, and allow themselves to resonate with, the luxurious activity of his energies.

This interaction effect poses some interesting questions. How would the "energies" be affected in the presence of skeptical observers, those who have difficulty trusting subjective experience? How does allegiance to official scientific beliefs interact with subjective realities? Do beliefs, subjective or objective, form their own level of consciousness? Does one's psychological experience change if it is filtered and modulated through scientific measuring devices? These questions and concerns have been raised repeatedly by parapsychologists in a number of scientific journals (Batcheldor, 1982; Beloff, 1983; Jahn, 1982).

Dr. Roll's Research

During August 1981, William G. Roll went to Brazil to investigate Thomaz and to measure and quantify his energy in specific ways. Dr. Montagno had convinced Dr. Roll that Thomaz was indeed a "paranormal in a class by himself" and worthy of thorough examination and research.

Dr. Roll's credentials and background as a parapsychologist are outstanding. He has authored several books and dozens of scientific papers and is currently Professor of Psychology and Psychical Research at West Georgia College, Carrollton, Georgia. I met Dr. Roll during the Cambridge Conference where he, Dr. Montagno, and I shared a symposium on the Thomaz phenomena. He is an honest, careful, and conscientious researcher

Divine Inspiration

who has devoted most of his life to assessing a wide range of anomalous occurrences.

The "Thomaz project" was approached as a combined field investigation and laboratory study. Dr. Roll brought with him twelve miscellaneous metal items sealed in plastic containers. His instruments included thermometers, a compass and leaded shield, a special apparatus measuring psychokinetic activity, and a light-sensitive color video camera and recorder.

Suspicion of Fraud

Unfortunately, Roll's two-week visit still echoes with controversy, hurt feelings, and misunderstandings. Dr. Roll had agreed to "pay" Thomaz for his full-time participation during the project, specifically a Panasonic PK–801 video camera and JVC video recorder as a "fee for service." However, at the end of the two-week project, Roll accused Thomaz of fraud and of simulating some of the results. As a consequence, he was not given the video unit. What really happened during the investigations? Was Thomaz indeed guilty of fraud and trickery? If so, why would he resort to such activity since he has demonstrated a dazzling display of psychic powers time and time again?

Dr. Roll reported several instances of metal-bending that were apparently real and impressive. He also acknowledged that he could find "no normal explanation" to account for the materialization of "burn marks" on a soccer-pool betting form that was folded and clenched in his fist. Thomaz later "straightened or restored two bent keys" by stroking them lightly between his hands. Dr. Roll then witnessed a series of "light flashes" that appeared to be of paranormal origin. The flashes occurred in and above moving automobiles "between Mrs. Hooks' hands" (she had joined the investigation from her home in Texas; the research was made possible by a grant from Mr. and Mrs. Hooks), and in other places, including a restaurant. Another time, Dr. Roll produced a compass surrounded by a protective shield of lead. Despite the shield, Thomaz was able psychically to rotate and spin the compass needle with ease. Monsignor Arlindo was present during this experiment and reported that Dr. Roll kept repeating to himself, "That's impossible, that's impossible."

Nevertheless, Dr. Roll also cited several incidents he feels were fraudulent. One evening, Thomaz was able to influence the lights in his house and in the neighborhood lamppost, making them go off and on at will. According to General Uchoa, Dr. Montagno went to the utilities control center in Pouso Alegre the next day and discovered that a relative of Thomaz's was employed there as a technician. This raised the possibility in Roll's mind that a clandestine collaboration had created the effect and that the phenomena might have been fraudulently produced. However, Air Force Captain Claudio Capparelli was also present on the night of the alleged phenomena and during the next day. He reported (and we subsequently verified his report) that no relative of Thomaz's had ever worked at the utility company. Technicians at the utility company also acknowledged that the area of the city in which Thomaz resides was "without electricity—unknown causes" that night. I am convinced a misunderstanding or breakdown in translation accounts for Dr. Roll's information. Yet, the allegation still stands.

In a paper delivered at the Cambridge Conference (Roll, 1982), Roll mentioned several episodes of metal-bending that he felt were suspicious and fraudulent. In one instance, Thomaz held up a bent knife for his dinner companions to see. However, Mrs. Hooks, who was sitting next to Thomaz, saw him remove the knife from the table and then heard what she described as a "cracking sound" under his seat and assumed the knife was bent with physical force. In another display during a videotaping session, Thomaz drew attention to a bent fork he was holding. The start button on the camera had inadvertently been pressed and the full event was recorded. Upon replay, Thomaz was shown taking one of the forks from the table, placing it beneath the surface of the table where he made some movements with his upper arms, and then producing a bent fork. The movements were in-

Divine Inspiration

deed suspicious; both Drs. Montagno and Roll feel that this was blatant deception.

During dinner one evening, Dr. Roll was sitting across from Thomaz and observed him "quietly take a saltshaker off the table." Thomaz replaced the saltshaker and emptied the contents onto a plate. He appeared to be attempting to transmute the grains of salt into something else. He then invited several persons to taste and smell the substance, now found to be camphor. Dr. Roll stated that it was "reasonable to assume" that an exchange of saltshakers had occurred below the surface of the table. Perhaps. In December 1982, I sat next to Thomaz in a restaurant under similar circumstances. Thomaz pointed to a saltshaker and announced the presence of "transmutational energy." I picked up the saltshaker, tasted the contents (salt), and screwed the cap back on. We were videotaping the entire dinner because of the spontaneous occurrences that take place under such circumstances. I held the saltshaker up so the camera would capture the whole sequence. One minute later I unscrewed the top; the entire contents was camphor. Thomaz had not touched the salt container.

Later that week, Drs. Montagno and Roll were with Thomaz during a UFO sighting. Thomaz borrowed Dr. Roll's Polaroid and took several photographs. Oblong shapes described as conventional images of UFOs appeared on the film. Upon returning to the United States, however, the two researchers duplicated the UFO pictures by "aiming the camera at some trees and holding a sheet of transparent plastic with oblong shapes painted on it in front of the lens. The Polaroid print showed blurred UFOs between blurred tree tops, as in Thomaz's photographs.

Again, the possibility was raised that Thomaz's pictures might have been produced in the same manner. Perhaps. But there was no reference to the dozens of witnesses who have taken photographs of alleged UFOs with their own cameras corresponding to the images on Thomaz's Polaroid.

Both of the authors feel that Thomaz may have resorted to trickery on occasion. The most suspicious instance occurred on the last night of our visit with him in November 1981. It had been a long day; Thomaz had been drinking excessively and he was very tired. Yet at three o'clock in the morning, he wanted to do one more favor for Jim Jensen and his daughter, Julie. While they were lying face down during an acupuncture treatment, they both heard sounds suggesting Thomaz was ruffling through their hand luggage and papers. Neither Jim nor Julie looked to see what was happening, but they both reported it was "highly suspicious." A short time later, Jim was counting his money and discovered that what had been twenty $100 notes had "increased" to twenty-two. However, two $100 bills were missing from Jim's wallet. Under the circumstances, trickery is certainly a major consideration. It is also possible that Thomaz psychically transteleported the money from Jim's billfold to Thomaz's hands as he was counting. That is a routine feat in his psychic repertoire. Though there was no "smoking gun" in this instance, the implications suggest some measure of fraud, or at least, intent. Thomaz was confronted about this incident but denied the allegations.

Investigating the degree and frequency of possible fraud with Thomaz, the authors interviewed several persons who acknowledge that "on occasion" they suspected Thomaz would resort to trickery or "substitution." Even General Uchoa, who has witnessed and documented almost every conceivable Thomaz phenomena, felt that "perhaps one in two hundred cases, he will do something 'promiscuous' when the energy is not flowing."

Fraudulent activity among psychic subjects has been reported by several researchers (Rao, 1973; Rhine, 1974). There is even suggested evidence of a well-known stage magician and professional skeptic creating a fraudulent situation in an effort to disprove real psychic experiences (Panati, 1976). *Psi* phenomena contradict and seriously challenge already established scientific laws based on sound research. Under the circumstances, it is understandable how scientists who have built their careers on conventional views of the physical world suddenly lose their objectivity and allow emotions to influence their perceptions. But that is not the issue here.

If a psychic has proven abilities, why cheat? Having demonstrated so many convincing and genuine psychic phenomena, why would Thomaz risk being branded a fraud over a half-dozen crude attempts at deception?

Perhaps one of the most important factors in psychic activity is spontaneity. Physicist Hasted (1981) discusses how systematic and controlled laboratory studies lower the success rate of telepathy. It is difficult to be spontaneous under laboratory conditions. Many of us who have worked with Thomaz have attempted, unwillingly, to squeeze him into the confines of our tight time schedules. It has been frustrating for Thomaz. Because of his extreme desire to please everyone, he will try at times to accommodate our expectations of his performance. If the energy is not available, he may be tempted to gain acceptance by meeting our needs with deception.

Unfortunately, Dr. Roll visited Thomaz while he was still mourning the death of his best friend and brother-in-law, police chief Ovidio Loyola. Thomaz was depressed but felt obliged to meet with Drs. Roll and Montagno and their party. He canceled all appointments for two weeks and pledged himself to work with the Roll group exclusively. Despite the inner turmoil and grief, he attempted to conform to the demands and experimental tasks designed for him. The question must be entertained about Thomaz's effectiveness under the circumstances. Do emotional warps interfere with the activation of psychic powers? Can one illuminate certain portions of the psyche while laboring under a conscious cloud of depression? Where are the laws we can turn to that govern such mental processes?

Fraud and Other Psychics

My first experience with fraudulence in the psychic world occurred in 1974 in the Philippines. I had been standing next to one of the better-known and more reputable healers for over two hours on a Saturday morning. This was a man who was investigated and filmed by a group of scientists and his healing abilities were declared to be real (Meek, 1977). Yet that morning, I observed him demonstrating extremely crude, inept, almost adolescentlike attempts at deception. He saw over one hundred patients and not once did he produce a real materialization or "psychic opening." Most of his materializations of tissue were clumsily manifested from under a towel and detection was simple.

Despite his scandalous behavior, I returned to observe him the next morning. Once more, I stood next to him and had full access to everything within a four-foot radius. For the following two hours, he was a "spiritual superman." He was definitely in a deeper trance, and his psychic diagnoses, materializations of tissue, and psychic surgery all reflected another seemingly absurd but dramatic reality. At one point, he invited me to put my hand inside one of the several barehanded openings he created. The patient was a rather thin man and my hand went "in" up to the second knuckle of my finger. My fingers were covered with blood as I removed them from the "opening," which quickly sealed over as he removed his hands. How could he be imprisoned by a highly formalized reality one day, and then, within twenty-four hours, slip away to the outskirts of consciousness? It outraged my intellect at the time, and to this day I still don't have any answers.

I wondered if healers might have an exaggerated cosmic metabolism without their awareness. On another occasion, I observed a lesser-known healer palming an object of some sort while preparing to make a psychic opening. Something went wrong and an "opening" appeared spontaneously at the site where he was preparing to make a psychic opening. He appeared shocked. Whatever was in his hand was thrown into a container under the table, and he then proceeded to remove tissue that was being materialized psychically.

The issue of simulation among psychics has been discussed by several researchers (Krippner, 1976; Meek, 1977). One intriguing speculation is that simulating a psychic feat activates, or is conducive to, the real effect. In other words, pretending something is occurring intensifies and, on occasion, creates the possibility of the pretended phenomenon becoming a reality.

Pretending to the point of not distinguishing fantasy from reality is common among children from most cultures. Psychologist Barber (1982) has written a thoughtful article on the role of fantasy and imagery in hypnosis and parapsychological phenomena. On the basis of his investigations of fantasy-prone individuals whose imagination and imagery is "often as real as life," he suggests that an imagined event, if intensified, can crystallize into reality. Anthropologist Alexandra David-Neel (1931) described her own experiments in Tibet where a powerful concentration of thought created a "tulpa," or materialized thought form, that took on a life of its own.

Simulation and fakery among psychics is indeed a Gordian knot. On one hand, there is the very real motivation to deceive and cheat. On the other, there is the use of make-believe to stimulate the richer and more open levels of the unconscious. Because of both the intensity and childlike quality of Thomaz's imagination and imagery, simulation can serve the function of detonating phenomena. Compounding the effects of his own unconscious dramatizations are the outside influences and interpretation of his powers by friends and well-wishers.

"Bleeding Christ" Miracles

Shortly after Dr. Roll's visit, Thomaz (in one of his several relocations), moved to Lavras, a town near Trés Corações, where he spent four months helping Dr. Dessimoni establish a small clinic. Thomaz's role was to provide "energization sessions" for the patients. He also inspired some of the more chronic cases with demonstrations of the force of mind over matter. During this period Thomaz became uncharacteristically quiet about his extraterrestrial friends, his "lights," and their influence on his powers.

Dr. Dessimoni had noted a subtle change in his friend several months earlier. He had accompanied Thomaz during one of their several visits to São Paulo, where Thomaz purchased homeopathic remedies, visited friends, and attended to clients. During this visit, Thomaz watched Pope John Paul II on television address a large public gathering. He was rather quiet and dreamy while listening to the Pope's message. Suddenly, he bolted upright and announced that a strange wave of energy was coming over him. He seemed quietly excited, yet perplexed. It wasn't an energy that he was familiar with. He ruled out the now familiar pulsations of metal-bending, transmutational, note-burning, and healing energies. He closed his eyes and concentrated for an unusually long time. Then, he opened his eyes and in a very bewildered manner blurted out "the word 'blood' is echoing in my ears . . . I am overwhelmed by the word 'blood'."

Dr. Dessimoni knew that these "energy rushes" were signals that something of note was about to happen. While Thomaz kept repeating the word "blood," his friends rummaged through the house to see if they could locate anything unusual. Dessimoni walked by a portrait of Christ in the living room. He stopped and was astonished to see what looked like fresh blood flowing from the crown of thorns around Christ's head. Taking a bit of the substance on his finger, he tasted it and declared that it was indeed blood. Everyone gathered around the portrait and for the next thirty minutes watched in wonder as the blood oozed slowly from Christ's head. Several of the group joined hands and said the Lord's Prayer. One person took out a Bible and read certain verses. With the Pope's voice in the background speaking of peace and brotherly love, everyone present rejoiced in the intensity and touching inspiration of the moment.

The "bleeding Christ" manifestations have happened to Thomaz more than fifty times since that day in São Paulo. It is one of the paranormal events that Thomaz never consciously intended or attempted to precipitate; it is entirely spontaneous and the only predictive sign is the flooding of Thomaz's consciousness with the repeated word "blood." Monsignor Arlindo Mombach, Captain Claudio Capparelli, and Professor Machado have been present and witnessed the "bleeding" several times. Because of the circumstances, and because they actually saw the blood materializing from a portrait or through glass, they are convinced that the phenomenon is real. Professor Machado had one sample of blood examined at a medical laboratory. It was established as "human type A," which is not Thomaz's blood type.

Bleeding or weeping portraits and statues seem to be one of the most common types of events classed as "miracles." Rogo (1982), in a comprehensive and critical investigation of remarkable phenomena, states that it is most common in traditionally Catholic countries and "that a book could be written about this miracle alone." In one of the more typical examples cited, a lawyer living in Maropati, Italy, awoke one morning in 1971 to discover that a Madonna, hung over his bed, was dripping blood from under the glass of the painting. The liquid was seeping from the Madonna's eyes, heart, hands, and feet. The bloodlike substance also spread out and formed crosses on the wall, "as if a magnet were drawing the blood in four directions at once." At first, blood flowed from the painting daily and then it slackened off to brief trickles. Needless to say, scientific and church authorities were called in and validated the "miracle." The blood was examined and established as human.

Rogo also reported that in 1975, a twenty-eight-inch-tall statue of Christ in the home of a Philadelphia housewife suddenly began to "bleed." It was just after Easter and she was kneeling and praying before it. She then gave the statue to her priest, who testified to the authenticity of the miracle. When placed out of reach on a shelf ten feet above the altar, it continued to bleed for up to four hours at a time. In another instance, in the small town of Porto das Caixas, Brazil, a three-hundred-year-old wooden statue of Christ began to bleed during the mass. It bled for thirty-three minutes on the first occasion in 1968 and has dripped blood intermittently from the crucifixion wounds to this day. Three million persons have since visited the small church and observed the materialization of blood.

Dr. Louis Souza Aguiar, an eminent Brazilian physician, was

appointed to head a medical commission formed to investigate the hundreds of purported "miracle cures" which took place in the church. The commission's report, described by Rogo (1982), declared that twelve cases could be identified as "miracle healings"—"with no rational explanation." However, Denis Eischer, a reporter for Rio's largest newspaper, *O DIA*, has a regular column in which she describes cases of "spontaneous cures" and "special blessings" that have touched the lives of hundreds of persons at Porto das Caixas.

Most authenticated instances of bleeding portraits, miracle healings, and associated paranormal phenomena have involved persons with a strong sense of faith in a divine realm. This is particularly true of mystics, shamans, saints, psychic surgeons, and faith healers. Not only do these persons demonstrate a special sensitivity to spiritual dimensions, they alter their consciousness in order to participate in these different realities. Prayer and devotion are the most common consciousness-focusing activities in Catholic countries, although meditation and fasting are also utilized to open up into the richer and more dramatic levels of the unconscious or supraconscious.

Seeking Spiritual Answers

But what about Thomaz? Why did miracles usually associated with piety suddenly begin erupting at this point in his life? Were these intense symbolic encounters a reflection of a more personal animated dream? Or were they dramatic exteriorizations of the ego dilemmas he was experiencing? The reasons may never be known, but Thomaz was beginning to want more out of his life without knowing where to turn. His recent experiences with researchers had left him hurt and disappointed. He was tired of wandering from town to town and changing residences every few months. While earning larger amounts of money from his psychic demonstrations, he still yearned to be a healer and to be accepted as such by his friends. Consciously, and perhaps at deeper levels, he was searching for another identity, something

Divine Inspiration

other than that of an accomplice to, or instrument for, extraterrestrial forces. On the one hand, he was grateful for the stamp of credibility he had received from General Uchoa and his colleagues. On the other, he was beginning to chafe under the constant presence of the curious and the sensation seekers who saw Thomaz merely as a projection of their own metaphysics.

It was probably no coincidence then that during that period of concern and introspection about purpose in his life, Thomaz turned to and developed his friendship with Monsignor Mombach. During this period of heightened spiritual concern, there was a proliferation of "Christian miracles"—bleeding Christs, materialization of religious medallions, and transmutations of tinfoil into small icons of saints. The more time Thomaz spent with his well-meaning new "scientific" friends, the more he began to consider other internal spiritual dramas as explanations for his powers. He began to speculate that he might be a divine messenger from God, specially chosen to receive the benediction of His gifts. After all, weren't "weeping Madonnas" and "bleeding Christs" always associated with the divine providence of miracles? His new followers added fuel to the emerging one-man Brazilian passion play. They recalled, for example, the time when Thomaz had walked into a hospital room and a mistakenly diagnosed "deceased" man came to life. They searched for other links between the miraculous acts of Christ and Thomaz's staggering array of psychic talents. After all, Thomaz could transmute nonorganic substance into organic matter—isn't that what avatars are worshipped for? Perhaps the lightning bolt that struck Thomaz at Fasqueira was really a "Divine Light," a luminescent baptism. And so on.

Though these interpretations may insult many intellects, earthly devotees and God-makers have always clogged their vision by trying to infuse new life into old dogmas. As Roberts (1981) points out, we haven't learned to distinguish between psychic morality dramas and psychic facts that can be interpreted literally. These kinds of unconscious distortions will continue until we realize that our inner life is just as varied, multidimensional, and rich as our external world. The intellectual and superstitious debris around the paranormal serve as mental dams and even sterner definitions of "who we are."

Once again, Thomaz found himself in a quandary. In his innocent search for meaning he had allowed himself to be imprisoned, at times, by the varying needs and dogmas of his groupies and devotees. Sometimes he succumbed to their idolization and worship, but most of the time Thomaz vacillated between basking in the glow of his admirers to repudiating their unwarranted beliefs. But what was real? With his new interest in the spiritual life of the Church, Thomaz abandoned the theory that his powers came from extra or intraterrestrial visitors and began to see the Fasqueira event as a baptism by the cosmic light of Christ. Was there yet another interpretation that would lead him to turn one more mental corner?

CHAPTER TEN

Transmutations and Transformations

The trouble with the future is that it usually arrives before we are ready for it.
>   *Arthur H. Glasgow*

With Thomaz's increased popularity and spreading international reputation, more and more individuals are imposing their perceptions and values on what he is and what he should be as a psychic. For some, he is an avatar, his powers deriving from a divine source. These devotees ignore his outrageous behavior and impute his drunken mumblings with significance and meaning. Others, primarily upper-middle-class professionals who are well-grounded in such spiritual philosophies as Rosicrucianism, Theosophy, Buddhism, and Brazilian Spiritism, acknowledge Thomaz's powers but treat him with cynicism and dissaffection because of his "distorted spirit." For them, Thomaz is mocking the spiritual needs of the people by charging for his services. A smaller group, associating Thomaz with UFOs, sees him as a modern Prometheus bringing to earth the light energies of extraterrestrials. They are convinced that Thomaz is "plugged into a different circuitry" heralding a new technology of the mind.

The largest group of followers includes many actors, musicians, writers, and students. For them, Thomaz fulfills the public appetite for mystery and enchantment. They see him as an artist and performer endowed with a very special, magical charisma. While he is perceived as a hero from a mystical world, they do not impose a tyranny of excellence on him. His powers are generally ascribed to his ability to harness universal forces and blend them in harmony with unknown laws of nature. As one forty-year-old musician said, "Thomaz is the Michael Jackson or Mick Jagger of his field. He is tops. But we cannot expect any more of him than we expect of ourselves." A writer from Rio de Janeiro stated, "To know Thomaz is to break out of our dull, limited perspective of the world. Then, to realize that all knowledge, wisdom, and limitless creative potential lies entirely within ourselves. Thomaz can open your mind, your soul, but he is not like a nanny who must walk with you every step of the way."

More and more of his friends and followers are accepting Thomaz's preposterous antics, bad manners, and scandalous behavior along with the "illuminations of the spirit," they experienced. After all, how can we condemn a man who "dehypnotizes" us from the trance of our limited concepts?

In interviews with hundreds of persons who witnessed or participated in Thomaz's demonstrations, the one phenomenon mentioned most often as having the greatest impact on the observer is transmutation. As one Brazilian lawyer declared, "once you have seen Thomaz transmute matter, change one basic element into another, the magic of alchemy brings about an alchemy of the soul."

Alchemy Throughout History

Christ's Biblical feats and public demonstrations of transmutation have been discussed and commented on by scores of religious authors (Carrington, 1935); however, it was the medieval concept of alchemy that charted new terrains of consciousness. The alchemist, through charms, spells, and elemental chemicals, sought the transmutation of lead and other base metals into gold. The techniques were based on ancient mysteries and magical practices. According to Berman (1984), gold was indeed produced in one experiment conducted in 1666. It was witnessed by Helvetius, physician to the Prince of Orange, and was verified by a number of witnesses, including the philosopher Benedict de Spinoza, who was also involved in the case.

Alchemy, however, was much more than a search for gold. One of the central notions was that all matter possessed rudimentary forms of consciousness. Berman described a number of techniques practiced by alchemists that were aimed at bridging the division between the conscious and unconscious parts of the mind. These included meditation, fasting, yogic "prana breathing," the chanting of mantras, and visualization. Corresponding to these mental exercises were physical operations consisting of dissolution, distillation, and purification of minerals using various chemical compounds. The alchemist would then attempt to meld a rich interplay of various altered psychic states with the physical techniques to create the transmutation of matter. Thus, the alchemist did not try to grapple with matter, he tried to blend with it.

Jung (1973) discussed alchemy at length as a sacrament ritualizing a deeper aspect of our being. He viewed the essence of the alchemist's art as a metaphor for the psychic process of personal transformation and self-realization. Thus, the crux of alchemy was the discovery of one's own true nature. Everyone is potentially divine ("pure gold") but must go through a series of cleansings and psychic transmutations along the path of spiritual evolution. Alchemy represented an attempt to deepen our understanding of nature's secrets. To achieve that goal, the practitioner had to probe the primal depths of the unconscious and chart the imagery, symbolism, and dreams that speak from the deeper side of our nature.

One of the last important practitioners of alchemy was Sir

Isaac Newton. Unfortunately, his records and diaries describing his mystical pursuits remain relatively obscure. Ironically, his public experiments contributed both to the discrediting of alchemical notions and the beginnings of the scientific revolution. The idea that all of nature is mental and interactive gave way to a model of the mind that was mechanical and isolated from its surroundings.

Thus, magic, myth, and alchemy served an almost desperate need for helping one maintain a sense of spiritual identity. Perhaps for the alchemist, as for us today, it was comforting to think that our presence permeates the world and that all forms of creation are interconnected at some fundamental level. Science, with its linear and "rational" logos, alienates us from nature and makes rigid distinctions among "things" and people. Perhaps we must broaden our sensibilities and discover a way of reenchanting ourselves with our psychic roots and with each other.

Where does one begin to achieve this reconnection? Perhaps by leaving our minds open to all possibilities, by not forcing closure, and by not creating sharp polarities in our thinking. In the alchemical and magic traditions, this state of openness permitted polarities and differences to resonate with each other.

In an open system, the two polarities of mind and matter might be brought into a more resonant, interrelated, and ultimate "ecstatic merger." Somehow, I suspect that is what Thomaz, the medieval alchemists, and other psychics mean when they say "in harmony with nature."

Thomaz's Transmutations

Thomaz has never read any of the mystical treatises, nor does he even know they exist. Yet, in his own way, he reenacts in rural Brazil these Old World rituals and experiments, lore and discipline of the medieval alchemists. His first transmutations were spontaneous; they happened when, as a teenager, he attempted to imitate the feats of a Chinese circus-tent magician. Marbles were transformed into candy for his playmates. Then, slowly, he acquired the "psychic skill" that enabled him to change paper napkins into various denominations of currency. Since 1979, Thomaz has been consciously experimenting and tinkering with his powers, like a skilled craftsman. He will work with a piece of aluminum foil taken from a cigarette package and transmute it into an attractive, exquisitely detailed medallion. Many who have observed this process describe it as "an almost mystical experience."

Researchers have speculated that some of Thomaz's transmutations are apports rather than the metamorphosis of matter. "Apports" are objects that materialize suddenly out of thin air and they are common features of spiritualist seances and poltergeist activity. Thomaz claims to be able to distinguish between apport and transmutation energies and on occasion will identify the difference for observers. For example, the sudden appearance of a lost billfold he ascribes to apport activity.

Beginning in 1980 Thomaz no longer required that objects be held in the participant's closed fist and allowed his transmutations to be observed out in the open. On one occasion, we saw him cut a piece of tinfoil into the shape of a rather crude triangle. He poked at it with a toothpick and then became glassy-eyed, appearing to fall into a deep, internally absorbed trance. He began a deep, rhythmic breathing, the palms of his hands radiating energy into the metallic foil. Fifteen minutes later, the fragile union of time, causality, and matter began to dissolve before our eyes. The tinfoil "straightened" into a triangle and slowly hardened into a piece of hard silverlike metal. What was now a pyramid-shaped medallion was etched with the appropriate markings of the pyramid on the back of an American one dollar bill. We could actually see the engravings furrowing and forming in slow motion. Our parochial boundaries of mind seemed too small for what we had observed. This ritual has now been witnessed and photographed hundreds of times.

Since then, Thomaz's inventory of objects has grown. His transmutations now include astrological medallions, animals, charms, religious medallions (usually of Catholic saints), and an unusual number of phoenix birds with outstretched wings. He has also transformed an orange peel into a Kennedy dollar, grains of rice into colored rocks, a wedge of cheese into a bronze replica of the Great Pyramid, and, of course, a piece of raw meat into a live cricket.

Thomaz's transformations can rebelliously assert their own peculiarities and logic. If Thomaz forgets to "seal" the newly organized matter by proclaiming "*definitivo*," the object may revert to its original form. For example, on Gary's night table stood a bronze pyramid Thomaz had transmuted from a triangular-shaped piece of cheese the week before. One morning, Gary woke to find the pyramid gone; sitting in its place was a wedge of smelly cheese. Similarly, Thomaz created a beautiful bronze medallion for me but forgot to "seal" it. Several days later, it too renounced its new form and returned to being a prosaic piece of tinfoil. Now, when Thomaz works in his home or in restaurants, someone usually reminds him to pronounce "*definitivo*." This eliminates the concern that a precious souvenir will display an outlandish fickleness and abandon its new owner.

Transmutation experiences with Thomaz have an unusually electrifying effect on those present. The process seems to activate a substratum of the unconscious in which certain echoing memories are stored. Perhaps Thomaz is reinstating our sense of wonder, reminding us of something we already know but have forgotten. Additionally, observers often experience a bond to each other. Sometimes they weep quietly and frequently express the feeling that "God (or nature) is alive in everything."

Transmutation is a recurring theme in most of Thomaz's conversations and especially in his six o'clock group "mentalization" sessions. He invites everyone present to "transmute war into peace, hate into love, diseased organs into healthy ones, cancerous cells into healthy tissue, and fear or negative thoughts into compassion." With great feeling, he guides the group through each organ in the body, asking them to assist in transforming the world's illnesses to a healthy state. The meditation concludes with guided imagery of the clouds, sunrise, flowers, birds in flight, and an invitation "to be one with nature, so you can be one with God."

Psychic Healing

Despite what appears to be his magical control of physical matter, Thomaz considers himself to be an "alchemist of the soul," a healer. He earns his living in this way and is paid outrageous sums of money for healing. His "clients" come from all over Brazil and from other countries in South America. Most of them have serious chronic illnesses that have not responded to conventional medicine.

Though Thomaz may be the world's most powerful phenomena-producing psychic, his healing efforts have been at best equivocal. Some of his clients have responded very favorably; others gain only temporary relief before the illness recurs. However, his "failures" add a much more human dimension to his capacities and pose interesting questions about his energies. Does his invisible "power plant" pulse only certain bands of energy? Are there special qualities a healer must have that have not yet surfaced in Thomaz? Just as he has developed certain psychic skills, might he also eventually create subjective psychic openings that will tap into healing realities?

It is indeed ironic that Thomaz is not a superb healer. Raised in a medical environment, he learned to infuse various remedies with energy to increase their potency. Throughout his pharmacy days, he gained a wide knowledge of homeopathy, herbs, and many natural elixirs. At one time, he considered medical school but was unable to meet the academic requirements.

Psychic Surgery

In 1979 Thomaz's powers developed yet another tributary—psychic surgery. Late one evening in July of that year Thomaz was beginning to tire of performing psychically for his friends. The several people present included two physicians and Amanias, a thirty-six-year-old journalist who had worked as an agricultural supervisor and inadvertently inhaled pesticides for over seven years. His skin had turned yellowish and according to him, "my blood is poisoned. I am anemic." Suddenly, Thomaz turned to Amanias and said, "your time has come." Thomaz's expression changed; he appeared to go into a deep trance and began to speak Portuguese with a European accent. Everyone moved into the living room where a makeshift "operating table" was prepared.

The two physicians agreed to assist. Thomaz asked for cotton, salt, and four pairs of scissors. The salt was sprinkled liberally onto the cotton that was placed on Amanias' abdomen. The scissors were positioned around the cotton like the four points of a compass. Within moments, the flesh "parted and opened," and everyone agreed they could see inside the body. Thomaz took one of the scissors and began to probe inside the opening. Over the next twenty minutes, he removed four dense blood clots, each slightly larger than marbles. The clots had a horrible stench and several persons complained. Thomaz "ordered" the odor to disappear and to be replaced with a pleasant fragrance. The clots very quickly took on the odor of a French perfume. The opening appeared to close by itself and Thomaz's facial expression and accent returned to normal. He seemed very perplexed and kept asking, "What happened?" as he had no recollection of what had transpired.

Thomaz had never entered an "unconscious trance" before and several persons present thought he might have incorporated a spirit entity. Amanias felt very weak after his "paranormal surgery." Two days later he regained his strength and lost all his previous symptoms. Two weeks later, however, Amanias' skin turned yellow again and the old symptoms returned. Thomaz stated later that Amanias did not achieve a permanent cure because he would not follow the diet instructions that were prescribed.

Several other "surgeries" were performed in a similar manner. In his typically innovative style, Thomaz dispensed with the cot-

Transmutations and Transformations

ton, salt, and scissors. Instead, he would pass a razor blade lightly over the afflicted region. This motion would usually result in a superficial cut but no bleeding. The patient's body seemed to open and Thomaz would probe inside the body with his fingers and remove tissue.

Once, Thomaz "operated" on Dr. Gloria Machado, who had complained of severe stomach distress and a recurring sharp pain in her abdomen. Thomaz removed six bladder stones, authenticated later by the hospital laboratory. Dr. Machado's abdominal pains disappeared the day after the operation and she later remarked, "It was truly a miracle."

A short time later, Thomaz refined his technique once more. Dispensing with the razor blade, he began to "open" the patient's body by kneading the skin with his bare hands—a procedure almost identical to the one used by the Philippine healers. Even with this refinement, lasting cures were elusive. The patient would experience a general improvement for several weeks but the symptoms would gradually return.

All of Thomaz's "surgeries," with or without instruments, were performed with no anesthetic, antiseptics, or antibiotics. There was no evidence of hypnotic induction, and the patients rarely experienced any discomfort.

The most dramatic and sensational "surgery" took place during the fall of 1980. What distinguishes this psychic operation from all the others was that Thomaz was over one mile away when the "surgery" occurred. Neurosurgeon Montagno accompanied Thomaz to a hospital to see a patient who had asked for psychic healing by Thomaz. The patient was suffering from an inflammatory condition in the right side of her abdomen. Thomaz was left alone with the patient but nothing transpired. Within a half-hour, he and Dr. Montagno decided to go on to a restaurant for dinner.

At the restaurant, Thomaz was upset that he was not able to perform "surgery" at the hospital. Then, Dr. Montagno made a strange request: "Why don't you try and do the surgery from the restaurant?" Thomaz looked puzzled but acknowledged that he was still emotionally linked to the patient. He began to gaze at his right hand with a "blank preoccupied stare." Thomaz became uncomfortable at this point with "images of gall bladder and blood spreading over the table," but snapped out of his dazed condition and finished dinner.

Later in the evening (still at the dinner table), according to Montagno, "Thomaz suddenly cried out, 'Oh! The gall bladder!'" He opened his right hand, showing "a round object, which could have been a human gall bladder or large clot of blood." There was also blood on the table. Thomaz then closed his hand again and implored that the gall bladder be "returned to the patient" and that she be cured. Dr. Montagno reported that when Thomaz opened his hand again, "we saw a brown stone of about one half cubic-inch, dark blood, and pus." The air was pervaded with the odor of infection. Dr. Montagno later had the stone analyzed at his hospital's laboratory and it was identified as a human gall bladder stone.

Remarkably, the next morning, the patient was symptom-free and had risen from her bed and walked around the room unassisted. When asked if she had any unusual experiences the night before, she replied that around midnight she had the "impression of being transported to some other place."

The implications of the event were mind-boggling, and Dr. Montagno felt strongly enough about the experience with Thomaz to present his findings at a scientific meeting at Cambridge University (1982).

With Thomaz, each new dazzling psychic display sparks an infinite number of questions. For instance, since he is a frustrated physician, does his psychic antenna tune into the spaceless realms of consciousness for ways to affirm his personal needs? Unconsciously, Thomaz has apparently tuned in to an energy blueprint or information field that gives him techniques for psychic surgery. He has successfully imitated the visual effects of both the Philippine and Brazilian psychic surgeons. But why hasn't Thomaz been more consistently successful in his healings? Is his unpredictable and somewhat egocentric personality simply incompatible with a "healing consciousness"?

New Treatment Method

Thomaz no longer performs psychic surgery, adopting instead a different treatment approach that is perhaps better suited to his nature. He requires that first-time patients begin with a several-day orientation. The orientation program includes attending the six o'clock "mentalizations," following Thomaz and his entourage to various restaurants, and listening to the complete account of how Thomaz was struck by lightning and acquired his powers. This is followed by a psychic diagnosis. If the problem is primarily physical, Dr. Dessimoni conducts a medical examination. Then, according to Thomaz, "before the real treatment begins, I must turn his head around," through demonstrations of bending metal, materializing medallions, imprinting symbolic messages on currency with blood, and so on.

Once the patient's faith in Thomaz's powers is established, he is escorted into a basement room in the clinic, referred to as the "energy chamber." There, Thomaz "injects energy" into his patient, performs chiropractic manipulations, administers acupressure and, sometimes, deep muscle massage. Almost always, his treatments are accompanied by the explosive flashing of his "energy friends," Kryptos and company. His patients generally leave the treatment refreshed, relaxed, and satisfied. But are they healed?

Thomaz's greatest successes have been with skin problems, asthma, various allergies, bronchitis, and nervous disorders, all conditions with a strong psychological component. Could it be that having "one's head turned around" creates a placebo effect, mobilizing the patient's belief and expectancy that he will get well? Cousins (1977), summarizing a number of placebo studies, stated that the positive healing response of placebos ranged from thirty-five percent to seventy-eight percent. Placebos, of course, suggest the significant interaction between mind and body. Is Thomaz simply a placebo therapist who knows how to take advantage of this powerful interaction? Does it really matter *how* the patient gets well? Ultimately, all healing is self-healing. The challenge is to find the best means of stimulating one's subconscious and the healing forces of the mind-body. This can be done with a witch doctor's rattle and incantations, the dramatic materializations of psychic surgery, by wearing a white coat and carrying a stethoscope, or stopping the intellect cold by transmuting a coin into a medallion. It all depends on the patient, the illness, and the healer.

One dramatic disorder, multiple personality, illustrates how powerfully mind can affect physical functioning (Abrams, 1983). In personality A, a person may suffer from severe allergies but lose that allergy in personality B. In other cases, personality A may need strong prescription lenses, but personality B has perfect 20/20 vision. Is this a more subtle flow of transmutational energy? What does it take to mobilize such powerful and sudden "healings"?

Thomaz does have healing abilities and many persons have paid him large sums of money and feel it was well worth the experience. Some who were not cured said they would have gladly paid even more because what they saw changed their lives. One such person, Senator Teotonio Villela, was one of Brazil's most popular politicians. An outspoken critic of the country's military regime, he was an avid crusader for democracy and free elections. Senator Villela was unsuccessfully treated for cancer by conventional medicine and went to see Thomaz for "energization treatments." He received sufficient strength from the sessions to prolong his life; he campaigned actively and relatively pain-free until the day of his death. His son, a physician, felt that Thomaz's treatments were both positive and beneficial. How would one classify the senator's case? Was it a success or failure?

Accelerating Biological Processes

Experiences such as this make it difficult to evaluate Thomaz's abilities as a healer. Sometimes his treatments are no better than what one would expect with a placebo. Other times he mystifies everyone by successfully traveling through unfamiliar terrains of healing. Paradoxically, although his healing outcomes are unpredictable, he has consistently demonstrated the ability to accelerate basic biological processes. For example, he has frequently stimulated a tightly closed rosebud to open into full bloom within one minute. He has also caused bean sprouts to grow so fast their maturing can be seen with the naked eye. In another instance, corn kernels several days old were briefly "energized," placed in a closed refrigerator, and three days later sprouted into cornstalks.

The most provocative and far-reaching of all his "biological experiments" defied the basic laws of life itself. On four occasions, Thomaz has taken fresh, unfertilized eggs and "hatched" them into live chicks. The first incident occurred in 1982 in the company of several friends and observers. He experienced a rush of energy, but this time identified it as "totally different from anything before." Responding to an "inner voice," he requested that fifteen eggs be purchased at the local market and placed on the table before him. Thomaz slipped into a very deep trance with eyes open but unfocused. Very slowly, he picked up each egg one at a time, stared at it for thirty seconds, and then rested the egg against the middle of his forehead. He performed this curious ritual with each egg. His eyes remained fixed and staring throughout. He then cracked the eggs one by one and broke their contents into a large flat bowl (Figures 10-1 and 10-2).

Thomaz then began hyperventilating. His chest was puffed and his face taut and crimson. He stretched both arms out, palms down over the eggs, and began pulsing and vibrating energy into the bowl. The observers, which included a physician, a psychiatrist, and a local district judge, watched very closely. Slowly, the yolks began to change their texture, solidifying and becoming darker. Different densities began forming and within five minutes, the fetal forms of baby chicks could be identified (Figures 10-3 and 10-4). As one observer stated, "It was like watching the high-speed sequence photographs of developing embryos that used to appear in *Life* magazine."

Thomaz sustained the throbbing energy, spurred on by the gasps of those present. The embryonic forms continued acceler-

Figure 10-1

Transmutations and Transformations

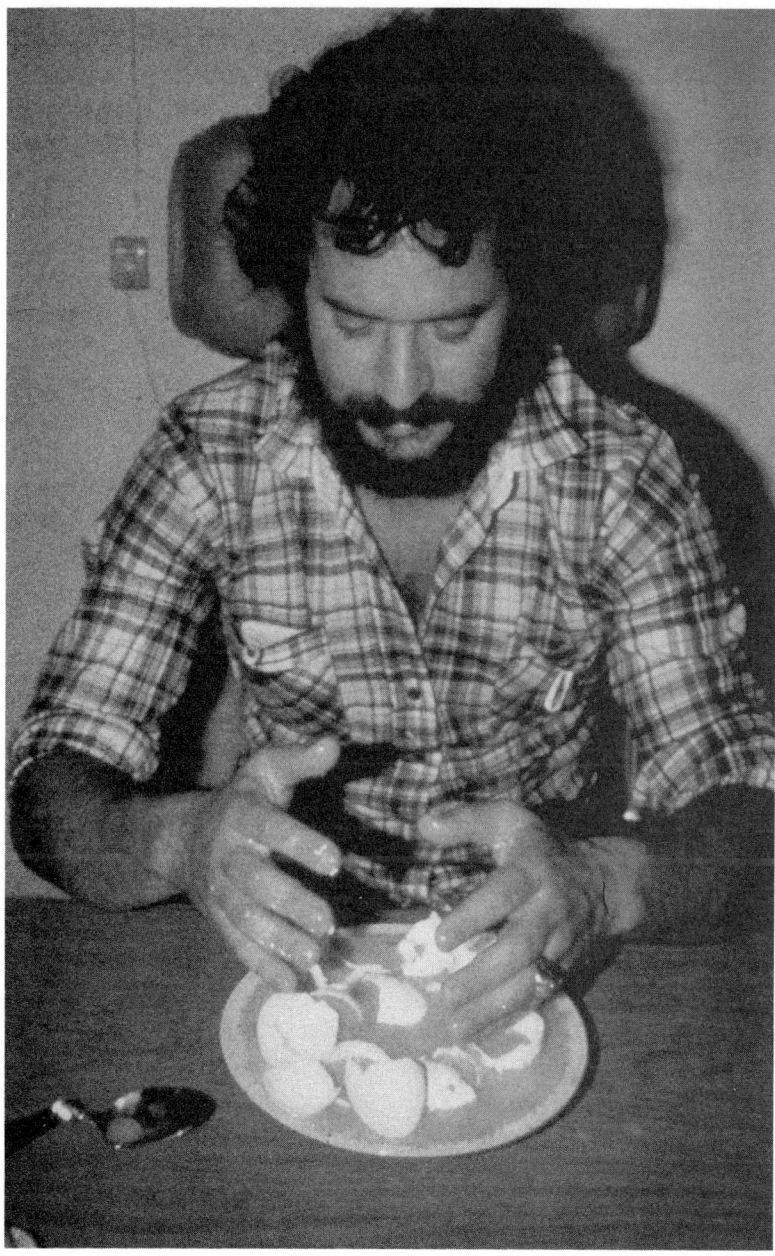

Figure 10-2

Figure 10-3

Transmutations and Transformations

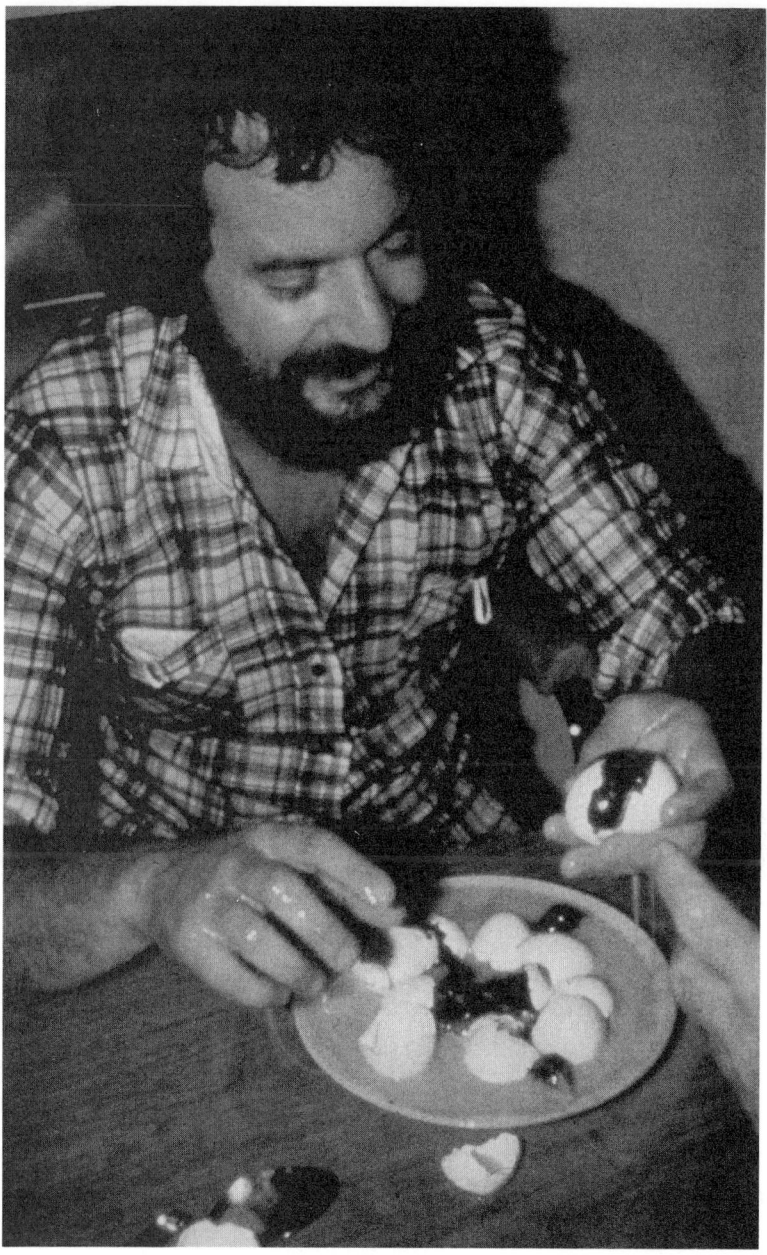

Figure 10-4

Figure 10-5

Transmutations and Transformations

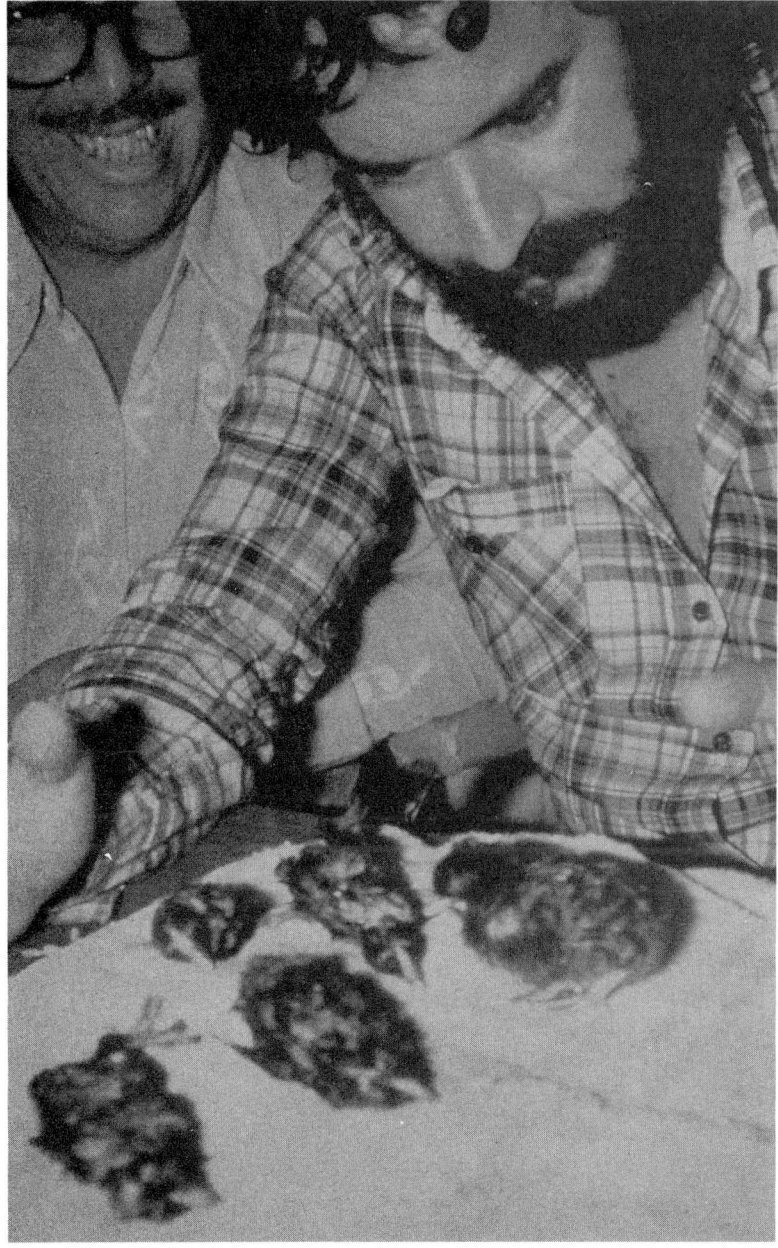

Figure 10-6

Figure 10-7

ating and changing as if connected to a cosmic metabolism. Over the next two minutes, the internal organs of the embryos could be seen through thin membranes. After nine minutes, the first sounds of life were heard—the "cheep-cheeping" of little chicks. From the fifteen eggs, nine baby chicks were hatched (Figures 10-5, 10-6, and 10-7).

One of life's deepest mysteries unfolded there, just like that, in all its simple nakedness. Pandemonium broke loose. People wept and embraced each other; some knelt in prayer. The physician present, Manolo de Menezes, said, "I cried. All of us did. I live with life and death. Just to see life becoming before your eyes is a deep religious experience. Yes, I cried and cried. People can say whatever they want about Thomaz. He may be the most irresponsible person in the world. But anyone who can animate the spark of light into unfertilized eggs has a very special relationship with the Divine. It was simply a miracle."

Five of the nine chicks died within three days. In the next three demonstrations of the same "miracle," only half of the chicks survived. When last seen, the rest were thriving and pecking their way around the backyard. Two were served for dinner.

While one can rejoice in the reverence and magnificence of the occasion, there are no categories to contain the invisible environments of Thomaz's mind and energies. Gary and the other observers present that evening acknowledge that they will never be quite the same again. Gone forever is the simple innocence of knowing what is "real and possible." Instead, as Gary stated during one of our introspective sessions about Thomaz, "There are simply too many things that are real—but not within our officially recognized order of reality."

Having visited other realities such as Aphron-V, Thomaz is not limited by "the impossible." Having seen the other potentials of his parallel universe, his conscious mind has been released from the bondage of "the impossible." How does one even begin to make sense when you have experienced a significant derangement of your sensibilities?

With Thomaz, it is tempting to write about every phenomenon that we have observed or have evidence in fact. We have sufficient documentation, interviews, and photographs to fill a six-hundred-page book. All the miracles and marvels, however, would become stupefying after awhile. After all, how many "oohs-ahhs" can one endure? But we would like to share one last experience. It reflects not only the new dramatizations of Thomaz's psyche but also captures some of the glory and possible terror of his psychic atmosphere.

Visit from Kryptos

During the latter part of our visit in 1981, we accompanied Thomaz to Fasqueira, where he wanted to meditate and "recharge" himself. Included in our party were Gary, Jim Jensen, his daughter Julie, my brother Andy, psychologist Eloise Garmon, Thomaz's cousin Lada, his wife Lygia, and three other friends. Immediately upon our arrival, Thomaz said he had to go off alone. He asked us not to follow as he slipped through a barbed wire fence and headed for a wooded area. Ignoring his instructions, we did follow him but stayed twenty to thirty yards behind.

Suddenly, and for the next half-hour, the area was flooded with explosions of light—Thomaz's now familiar "energy friends." We drifted back to our cars for a better view. The range of flashing eruptions spanned a radius of three hundred yards and some were above the nearby trees.

Thomaz came back and joined us where we were assembled. He walked slowly and seemed quite dazed. A large, circular angry-looking burn had appeared on his forehead. He asked us to remain calm as we were soon going to witness an extraordinary event. Walking with a peculiar gait, as if he were a somnambulist, he entered his automobile and drove away. Rapid bursts of light and energy followed his car, exploding both inside and outside the disappearing vehicle.

In a few minutes, we saw his automobile returning down the same road. This time energy flashes revealed two silhouettes in the front seat. The car parked fifteen yards away from where we were congregated and Thomaz got out of the passenger seat. He had not been driving. But who was? In a robotlike gait, Thomaz approached us and announced, "Kryptos has taken on a humanoid form. You can see him, but you must not touch him or you will receive a strong shock. Go to the car one at a time and you can look at Kryptos."

Our hearts were pounding with fear and excitement. One at a time we approached the driver's side of the car. Standing two to three feet from the car, we looked inside and then slowly backed away. After all of us had shared this most extraordinary encounter, Thomaz got back into the passenger side. A strange noise emanated from under the hood, not the usual coughing growl of a starter. With Thomaz lurched over on his arm against the window, the car let out a low-pitched whining sound and slowly moved away. Bursts of light followed, illuminating both the interior and exterior of the car. Thomaz was still slumped against the window on the passenger side.

To affirm our sanity and assure ourselves that our minds weren't outraged by hallucinations, we went back to the clinic to record our experiences on tape. We had no biological guarantees that we weren't hallucinating, but we had to placate the questioning chatter of our logic-driven "left brains."

There was general agreement that the "thing" (Kryptos) was humanoid but not human. It appeared as if it might be slightly lower on our evolutionary ladder. Its skin was muddish-dark, the shoulders were broad, and its head was almost touching the roof of the car. We had been able to distinguish shoulders, neck, chest, and rather primitive facial features. It acknowledged our approach by raising one of its arms as if saluting. The eyes were dark but at times took on a subtle green glow. The creature's trunk moved slightly as if it might be breathing.

We found, not unpredictably, some discrepancies in our perceptions. One person thought the "thing" had hair. Another could not perceive any facial features. Three of our party did not see or sense the green glow from the eyes. However, we all agreed it was "very ugly—but very real."

While we were waiting for Thomaz to return, we considered several possible explanations. We even wondered if Thomaz had fraudulently produced a lifelike dummy. But Gary and I had arrived at the Fasqueira in Thomaz's car. We had observed nothing unusual in the front or back seats. When the automobile "drove off" and returned, we could visually track his lights and the car had not stopped. How could he have driven the automobile, slumped over as he was in the passenger seat? (All Brazilian automobiles are four or five-speed stick-shifts on the floor.)

A second possibility was that he had mentally materialized a "tulpa" or thought-form, which can be very real and human in appearance. (This practice, developed in Tibet, is described in much greater detail in Chapter Eleven.) Finally, perhaps it was a phenomenon that simply could not be explained in our limited categories of experience. Psychological facts in one psychological system may seem quite senseless in another.

We spent two hours waiting for Thomaz to return and hoping he would provide some kind of explanation. Just as we decided to go home at 2:30 in the morning, we spotted Thomaz's white Ford coming down the dirt and gravel road leading to his house. Something was not quite right. Usually, Thomaz catapults the short distance in fourth gear at sixty miles an hour. Now, the car was approaching very slowly, almost hesitantly. As the car got close enough to be illuminated by the overhead streetlamps, we could see that there was no one in the driver's seat. Thomaz was slumped over on the passenger side.

The car went past us twenty-five yards, pulled into a neighbor's driveway, turned around, and pulled up in front of Thomaz's house. I ran up to the passenger door and opened it. Thomaz staggered out, very groggy. I noticed that the keys were in the "off" position and the hood of the car was cool to the touch. No engine heat! Thomaz was stumbling, as if intoxicated, but there was no odor of liquor on his breath.

He behaved as if bewildered or in a trance. We all joined hands and sat in silence for more than a half-hour. Somehow, questions did not seem appropriate under the circumstances. The "burn" on his forehead was more crimson and swollen than ever. Finally, glassy-eyed and gasping, Thomaz acknowledged our presence with a nod. He broke the silence and began to speak slowly and haltingly. "I was with Kryptos . . . we went to Aphron-V . . . life there is so beautiful . . . everyone is at peace . . . the colors . . . the colors are magnificent . . . I want to tell you what it is like . . . but there just aren't any words . . . there is no way to explain."

We went home and went to bed. Before returning to Rio de Janeiro the next day, we stopped to say goodbye to Thomaz. He was still groggy and uneasy. He had not returned to his usual high-spirited, joking, outgoing self. As we embraced, he said several times, "There is no way to explain . . . every time I go there it becomes more difficult to return . . . they want me there . . . but I haven't finished my mission here yet . . . I know you want answers . . . but they are all inside you . . . I hope you will understand. . . ."

On the drive back to Rio, we wondered if we should even share the experience with anyone, certain that arrogant amateurs and professional skeptics would respond with fanatical hostility. The six hour drive through rolling green hills, the scents of smoke houses and eucalyptus provided us with the opportunity to relax and unwind. Eventually, our conversation drifted into the everyday reality of soccer, racquetball, French cuisine, computers, and the stock market.

Effect on Thomaz's Character

We know the profound effect Thomaz has had on our psyches. But, we wonder, how does he cope with being so different? How does he function in day-to-day activities? How does he relax? What does he think about life, the state of the world, science, religion, or love? Does he have the usual problems balancing his checkbook, keeping to a budget, getting along with his wife, or being a good father? Does he feel blessed or hexed because of the unexpected and uncalled-for "divine surprises" of his powers?

There is no question that the spontaneous and erratic outbursts of his energies pose problems for Thomaz in his day-to-day living, but he has no alternative but to take them in stride. For example, quite often his keys, which he usually keeps in his trouser pocket, simply vanish. Once his keys disappeared and despite Gary's assistance they could not be found. Thomaz borrowed a friend's automobile and accompanied by Gary went to a nearby town where he bought medicinal leaves. They stopped for lunch at a roadside diner. As the waiter was pouring coffee out of a metal coffee pot, the "lost" keys slid out of the pot and plopped into the cup, almost breaking it.

Sometimes, bank tellers and waiters who know Thomaz are reluctant to accept his currency. Is it real or a paper napkin that will transmute back to its original state after Thomaz leaves?

No matter where he is staying, Thomaz rarely wakes up before noon. He may choose to spend the afternoon hours boating on his lake or cruising around town. Or he may experience a sudden flash or inspiration and decide to travel to another city in a moment's notice. He avoids anything that has structure or routine. If he decides to change his residence, which is often, he may close a deal on a new house within hours. If he wishes to refurnish his home, he will drive a truck to the store and load it with new furniture. If he decides to eat dinner at a restaurant one hundred fifty miles away, everyone must accompany him. Thomaz usually gets his own way.

On the other hand, there are sharp polarities and disparate sides to his makeup. He can be charming, gentle, caring, and sincere, and he often displays a totally captivating childlike sense of awe. However, he can also be extremely egocentric, rude, profane, obnoxious, and totally insensitive to anyone's needs but his own. Recently, his egocentricity has added a new dimension; he will spend hours looking at videotapes of himself. Frequently, he insists that visitors and friends join him, even though they may have seen the tape four or five times.

Is Thomaz an interesting conversationalist? Only if you are interested in hearing about the lightning episode and all of his stories about the phenomena he has produced over the years. They are the same stories, sometimes repeated unmercifully. If someone eases the conversation into politics, sports, or economics, Thomaz quietly withdraws and puffs slowly on his pipe. He feigns interest but is really waiting for another opportunity to take over center stage.

Most of his friends and acquaintances consider Thomaz a good and loyal friend. However, most of the persons who know Thomaz are with him because of his psychic abilities. The true test of friendship would emerge if he were to suddenly lose his powers.

More and more, Thomaz plays the role of a superstar. He loves to be flattered, adored, and showered with compliments. He has also grown accustomed to having gifts thrust upon him by admirers and devotees. He reciprocates all of this attention by joking with his followers, throwing parties, and telling even more dramatic stories about himself. He is a superb host and entertainer. He loves to be photographed and interviewed. However, if you spend a lot of time with Thomaz, occasionally a fissure will appear in his outward mask or camouflage. A trickle of real feeling will come through, like a tear slowly welling up in a child's eye.

Once, just before Christmas, we caught Thomaz in one of his rare, reflective moods. Tears were streaming down his face. He looked at us and smiled weakly. He tried to speak but there was a knot in his throat. He reached out toward us and we went over and embraced each other. Overcome with emotion, he said, "It's so hard, so hard to try and be everything for everybody. You guys just don't have any idea. I try, I really try so hard, but there are so many expectations around me. There are times I just have to be by myself, but that's hard, too, because you forget how to be yourself."

This moving confession suggests that the "psychic superstar" is not the real Thomaz. If indeed he disappears into a void and reappears in another dimension, it would be easy to understand how being a "normal guy" just wouldn't fit into that context. It also explains why Thomaz goes off on his own every so often to fish or walk through the forest, where there are no expectations to be superhuman and no need to perform. These are probably the only times in his life he can afford the rare indulgence of being normal.

Recently, Thomaz has slowed down his frantic lifestyle and devotes more time to his family and small farm on the outskirts of Pouso Alegre. There are still streaks and eruptions of the unpredictable psychic "wild man." However, if someone approaches him as an avatar responsible for the fate of the world, as happens, Thomaz is just as likely to shrug and walk away. This new simplicity may be just another temporary facet of the Thomaz kaleidoscope. Or it may be a reflection of a moderate and more mature Thomaz who is beginning to connect with the human side of his nature.

CHAPTER ELEVEN

Perspectives

> Thinking within a fixed circle of ideas tends to restrict the questions to a limited field. And, if one's questions stay in that limited field, so also do the answers.
>
> *David Bohm*

Historical Understanding of Thomaz's Abilities

As we reflect on our experiences with Thomaz, there still remain many unsettling thoughts and questions in our minds. Is Thomaz some kind of hyperspace anomaly who has ruptured through the technological skin of our species? Could he be a forerunner of the modern-day shaman bringing with him a new mythology of time, causality, and matter? Are his powers real or is he a master magician and illusionist? Was he born without the tight genetic filters that usually censor the barriers between the ego and the unconscious? Or does he represent a glimpse of the future—casting its shadow back over time? How does Thomaz fit into the history of miracles or the shamanic models of inner realms? What about the "uncommon sense" claims of thousands of psychics and contemporary psychic researchers in laboratories throughout the world? Is he really extraordinary or are there historical and modern-day precedents for his supernatural amazements?

Psychic researcher George Meek (1977) annotated one hundred twelve miracles cited in both the New and the Old Testaments of the Bible. These range from miracle healings of the blind and lame to the materialization of matter, apports from space, levitation, and a variety of spirit communications. Father Thurston, a Jesuit scholar and priest, co-edited four lengthy volumes devoted to the lives of 2,532 saints. Parapsychologist White (1982) carefully analyzed his reports and established that varying degrees of psychic abilities were reported for twenty-nine percent of the saints. These feats varied, but included clairvoyance, healing, production of apports, and bilocation. A typical example is that of Blessed Angelo of Acri, who died in 1739. He was seen simultaneously tending a flock of sheep and conducting Mass at different churches.

Rogo, in his intensive study of miracles (1982), cites levitation as the most commonly eye-witnessed marvel among saints. More than two hundred separate cases have been documented. The most authenticated evidence corroborated the levitation of St. Teresa of Avila (1515–1582) and of St. Joseph of Cupertino (1603–1663). St. Joseph's levitations usually occurred in full light, outdoors, and were seen by hundreds of witnesses. St. Teresa's levitations were so disquieting to her that she frequently prayed they would not happen. However, at least twice she levitated before a group of nuns who tried to surround her so that others would not notice this unseemly behavior. More recently, reports of levitation in good light with reliable witnesses were reported in the lives of St. Gemma Galgani and Padre Pio, who died in 1913 and 1968, respectively. According to Rogo, there were two well-documented accounts of Padre Rio's "sudden invisibility" in front of dozens of witnesses.

One of the most frequently cited psychics of the nineteenth century was Daniel Douglass Home. A group of scientists and responsible investigators were present during a demonstration in London on December 13, 1868, when Home levitated, floated out a second-story window, and then returned (Hasted, 1981).

Anthropologists have been reporting on shamanism and associated magical abilities in different cultures for more than one hundred fifty years. Their observations have included such feats as "fire-walking" and fire-immunity (Dougherty, 1982) and weather control (Barker, 1978). Bogoras (1904) observed a Chuckchee shaman make a psychic incision on a teenage boy, put his hand inside the boy's body, remove tissue, and close the opening without a scar. Anthropologist Halifax (1979) watched a shaman materialize foreign objects "through" a patient's skin. This was accomplished by making passes above the person's body to "draw" out the substance.

Tulpas and Other Apparitions

While many trained witnesses and scientists have observed psychokinesis, precognition, telepathy, and healing during shamanic seances (Harner, 1980), one of the most startling displays of materialization was reported by Alexandra David-Neel (1931). An anthropologist, she spent fourteen years in Tibet apprenticing and studying various mystical practices at the turn of the century. Through daily periods of focused concentration and sustained visualization, she created a *tulpa*, or materialized thought-form. Initially the "tulpa" was ghostlike and wispy. Slowly it took on the shape of a "monk, short and fat, of an innocent and jolly type." After several months of prolonged concentration and appropriate rituals, the monk "grew gradually fixed and lifelike." David-Neel's *tulpa* accompanied her on journeys and began assuming more and more independent and lifelike behavior. He was able to "walk and stop," and was mistaken for a real llama by a herdsman. However, over time her thought-form took on other human qualities and became very troublesome or "malevolent." David-Neel then spent several months of "hard struggle" to dematerialize and disperse her mental creation.

Materializations? Thought-forms that become lifelike? It is times like this when faith, logic, and evidence nudge and collide with each other discomfortingly. Yet materialization is a recurring theme of "residue of the unexplained" with Thomaz. Instances of the imaginary becoming real have also been described in the psychological literature. Dr. Morton Schatzman (1980), an American psychiatrist, wrote a book about a woman named Ruth who, through an intense effort of will, could "see" apparitions. Though it might be logically satisfying to assume the woman was psychotic, she was not. In an ingenious experiment, Schatzman established that if one of Ruth's thought-forms stepped between her and a source of flashing light, her evoked response, measured by an electroencephalograph, was completely inhibited. This suggested that her mental apparition functioned like a physical object. Similar to David-Neel's *tulpa*, Ruth's apparitions took on a life of their own. They appeared indistinguishable from living persons.

Harvard psychologist George Estabrooks (1957) experimented with sustained suggestion and concentration through self-hypnosis. He reported creating a bear which was so substantial and vital that he sometimes mistook it for a real one. At times, it took on a personality of its own and would jump out at him unexpectedly from behind closed doors.

How can organized particle fields appear suddenly from the seeming nothingness of space? And then, how can the interaction of mind and matter result in just the opposite—the sudden disappearance of elementary particles into . . . where? Physicist Bohm (1983) has postulated a fundamental energy matrix below the universe of known particles and objects. Do the psychics themselves have a conscious awareness of this magical topography of a new mythology of matter? I doubt it.

Mexican Curandera

Psychologists Krippner and Villoldo (1976) described a series of fascinating experiences with Doña Rosita, a Mexican "curandera" or healer. Her metaphor for healing was a freshly laid raw egg provided by the patient. Prior to healing, the eggs were secretly scratched or marked so they could be easily identified by the researchers. Rosita would stand in front of the "patient" and make passes with the egg over the entire body, praying aloud. The procedure lasted for several minutes. Rosita then broke the egg into a glass of cold water. If the person was healthy, a normal yolk would plop into the water. At other times, Krippner and Villoldo observed freshly laid eggs yielding twiglike objects, a "black lumpy substance" that had the texture of ashes or burned wood, and "portions of plant—buds, seeds, and a flower." Rosita diagnosed from these symbolic transmutations of matter and was generally accurate about the nature of the illness troubling her patients.

I visited Doña Rosita three times, twice for personal healing and once to film her healing sessions. Following the surgical removal of a cartilage in my knee, I experienced continued and troubling discomfort and could not play any sports without a heavy knee brace. I supplied my own egg, which was coded and marked in two places. Following a "cleansing," Rosita broke the eggshell and what appeared to be a normal yolk dropped into the water. She said, "Mira, mira" ("look") and pointed to a dark brown spot in the yolk floating inside the glass. Neither my companion nor myself took our eyes off it and we watched as the spot slowly grew larger. Simultaneously, the yellow yolk seemed to vibrate and merge into a purple-colored piece of matter. After about ninety seconds, what had been a soft egg yolk became a spheroid-shaped mass of purple wax. I removed it from the water; it was the size and firmness of a golf ball, with a gentle pleasant aroma. I now keep it on my desk as a paperweight and constant reminder of my awe.

Rosita interpreted the transmuted wax ball as a symbolic materialization of a piece of cartilage "still in the knee joint." Over the next few days, the pain gradually diminished and I have not worn a knee brace since the healing.

During December 1982 I visited with Rosita again and she invited me to observe several healings. In one of these sessions I saw the egg yolk slowly change form and transmute into a hydralike tubular polyp with a distinguishable head and body. It was four inches in length, a half-inch wide, grayish in color, and felt like a small sardine. The interpretation Rosita offered made sense to the patient. She left the room quite pleased but apparently indifferent about what she had just observed.

Sitter Groups

People living in North America may wonder if these naked mysteries unfold only in distant places like Tibet, Brazil, or Mexico. In 1966, British psychologist Kenneth Batcheldor (1979, 1982) established a "sitter group" in England to investigate "massive psychokinesis (PK) effects (or paranormal physical phenomena)." The members of the group would sit around an ordinary wooden table, hands placed lightly on its upper surface as if at a seance, and then wait for results. There were no assumptions that spirits were involved, only that the table would move purely as the result of mind influencing matter. Sittings with various groups have continued intermittently up to the present. The results have been astonishing. Over the years, various sized tables have moved, bounced, and levitated off the floor. As the group became more confident, they were able to levitate a heavy wooden table several times and, once, a piano, completely without touching.

In order to induce PK, levitations, and the appearance of apports (sudden materializations out of thin air), certain conditions were necessary. The group had to have a strong belief that a table could move. Skepticism inhibited the process. Sometimes the group would engage in laughter, singing, humor, and trivial chatter to prevent negative thinking. When nothing was happening Batcheldor would purposefully create a fake levitation or simulate a movement. Trickery or pretending seems to be very *psi-*conducive and this would usually trigger two or three genuine levitations. It was also important to focus on the end goal (PK) rather than the means by which it occurs. Finally, the development of a group mind or "suggestible whole," without striving or effort, produced the best results. Disconcertingly, whenever the group introduced a test or control, the effect would shyly decline or vanish. Occasional attempts to photograph the levitation resulted in the camera being "knocked over" by some force or it would "develop a mysterious fault."

The work of Batcheldor stimulated other sitter groups. One of the most original and compelling experiments was designed by physicist Dr. George Owen and his wife Iris in Toronto, Canada (1976). His group decided to create a ghost by inventing a complete history for it. They called their character Philip and provided him with specific personal details, names of his contemporaries, wife, and even a mistress. He "lived" during the time of Oliver Cromwell in Didington Manor. (Owens used a house which actually existed and he posted photographs of it to stimulate the sitter group.) Following Batcheldor's model, they developed an atmosphere of levity and humor. Philip made his presence known by rapping once for "Yes," twice for "No." He not only answered questions about his fictitious history but actually corrected the group's erroneous information about one of the principals in the royal court at that time. "Philip" increased his repertoire of paradoxes by producing macropsychokinetic effects. Pictures tilted on the wall or fell to the floor without anyone near them. A table slid across the floor and bounced up a set of stairs. No one touched it during its outlandish display. The "Philip group" permitted drop-in visitors, observation by interested scientists, and the filming of several sessions by the CBC. Four other Canadian groups modeled on the Philip experiment evolved, and one of them also obtained levitations.

SORRAT Experiments

One of the most important yet controversial experiments on semi-controlled psychokinesis began in 1961. The Society for Research on Rapport and Telekinesis (SORRAT) was founded by John G. Neihardt (1982), a widely acclaimed author and poet. There were a dozen founding members of SORRAT and their meetings and experimental sessions were held at Neihardt's farm in Missouri. In 1966, SORRAT instituted one of the longest and most exhaustively documented ongoing series of experiments in the history of psychic research. Dr. Thomas Richards (1961–1981) kept a detailed record of each meeting and observations for eighteen years. Each member was encouraged to be skeptical about the proceedings but they unanimously agreed on the authenticity of the phenomena.

To control possible fraud, they constructed an aquariumlike, mini-lab apparatus and padlocked it. The results included hands-off levitations, sudden materialization of apports, and an earthquakelike vibration of the meeting room. Films taken of the locked mini-lab showed leather rings linking and unlinking, pencils writing by themselves, objects passing through the glass wall of the mini-lab, and balloons inflating on their own. In one of the most contentious and bizarre occurrences, letters left in the mini-lab turned up in different parts of the world. Paradoxically, they had a local postmark but assorted foreign stamps on the envelopes.

The SORRAT experiments differed from Batcheldor's and Owen's work in two ways. Neihardt did not preclude the possibility of spirit intelligences participating in and creating some of the phenomena. As a matter of fact, some of the table raps claimed to be spirit entities; various tests and procedures were established to validate their authenticity. Secondly, the SORRAT phenomena were generally much more powerful and varied. However, all three groups shared the viewpoint that "quantum teleportation" or *psi* results should not be measured in terms of weight or distance but rather by the transformation of the participants' expectancies or belief systems.

The Geller Phenomenon

Just as Batcheldor kindled a series of sitter "PK groups," Israeli psychic Uri Geller ignited a conceptual cataclysm with his worldwide demonstrations of metal-bending and other feats. Neurologist and psychic researcher Puharich (1974) documented his experiences with Geller that ranged from telepathy and metal-bending to Geller's sudden physical transteleportation of a distance of thirty-six miles from New York City to his home in Ossining, New York. However, Geller and Puharich ran into a thicket of scientific skepticism and professional denigrators. For whatever reasons, Geller's displays resulted in accusations of fraud and an even tighter embrace of the mechanistic model of reality. Stanley Krippner (1977) edited a special issue of a scientific journal on international researchers' investigations of Geller's claims. The papers ranged in perspective from the analysis of a metal fracture physicist to a theoretical paper on the structure of images. Cantor (1978) summarized a refreshingly balanced and objective series of papers on research with "Geller children"—children who had heard of or seen Geller performing on television. In a series of controlled experiments they demonstrated metal-bending far more difficult and "artistic" than what Geller had done. Cantor's articles are supported by a remarkable series of photographs and introspective insights on the development of *psi* abilities both by the children and their families.

British experimental physicist Hasted (1981) conducted a series of laboratory tests with Geller, Jean-Pierre Girard, a French psychic, and several "Geller children." He used strain gauge detectors, sealed glassware tubes, electromagnetic signal devices, and other electronic equipment to measure structural changes and the psychokinetic sequel of metal-bending. His results are generally straightforward and impressive in supporting the influences of mind over matter. Somewhat mystifying was the "induction effect" that Geller apparently provoked after visiting Hasted at his home. Both Professor Hasted and his wife experienced a series of transteleportations of objects, apports falling from space, the disappearance and reappearance of objects in their home, and the production of "paranormal clock chimes" in a clock that had no pendulum and had not worked for years.

Induction Effect

Despite the occasional nagging feeling of self-delusion generated by supporters of the mechanistic worldview and stage magicians, Panati (1976), Robinson (1981), Hasted (1981), and others have provided rigorous and convincing evidence of metal-bending. However, what intrigues me is the "induction effect." The induction effect suggests that a particular psychic ability can be induced or "transferred" from one person to another. This gives credence to the idea that *psi* may be latent in all of us as opposed to only a gifted few. Author and psychic Stanford (1974) was traveling in heavy traffic with his wife along Interstate 10 in Texas on September 18, 1973. They were discussing a recent conversation with Uri Geller on transteleportation, joking about how Stanford would like to be transteleported to their destination to avoid the traffic. He then began to experience "an electrical sensation of the brain" and instantaneously they were "thirty-seven miles away, approaching the outskirts of Columbus." There was no sense of scenery passed or time elapsed—just a sudden transteleportation from one reality to another. Following their "materialization" outside Columbus, the electrical system of their station wagon incinerated and was left a tangle of charred wires. Could this be an example of the "induction effect"?

More Metal-Bending Experiments

In May 1980 I was invited to present two workshops at Madrid International University to the Young Presidents Organization. The members, between the ages of thirty and forty, are presidents of corporations grossing five million to several billion dollars a year. Most of the members have an entrepreneurial outlook on life, characterized by healthy skepticism and a fascination of the further reaches of possibility.

Uri Geller had also been invited to Spain to offer a demonstration of his psychic ability. There in Madrid, on a bright and sunny day, I sat in the spacious auditorium with fourteen hundred Y.P.O. members and their wives. Everyone had brought cutlery or broken watches. As Geller led the group, we all held up our spoons and forks and unabashedly shouted, "Bend! Bend!" My spoon did not bend, but shrieks of excitement erupted all around me as stereotyped concepts about mind and matter were annihilated. Several people held up twisted cutlery. A surprising number of persons bent silverware that day. One participant found that his thick hotel key had curled up in his pocket at some point during the two-hour session. More importantly, many experienced the first crack in the consensus trance that determines our culture's ordinary, waking consciousness. Again, this experience is suggestive of the induction effect.

Two years later, I finished reading Hasted's *The Metal Benders* in a Capetown hotel room. Immediately after putting the book down, I took my hotel key and began stroking it lightly and silently thinking, "Bend, go soft," over and over. Suddenly, the key arched into a thirty-five degree curve. I then began to doubt what had happened and speculated with rational explanations, such as "The key was probably bent" and "I am imagining things." I went to the desk, obtained another key, and compared the two. There was no question, my key was shaped like a crescent moon; I could not open my door with it.

Metal-bending has now become so common that large groups of people are learning to do it as easily as they learned to ride a bicycle. Jack Houck (1984), a systems engineer from California, has organized more than two hundred "PK Parties." Participants bring their own cutlery and in less than an hour of practicing simple imagery, coaching, and considerable humor, anywhere from fifty to eighty-five percent of the group manifest "warm-forming" or metal-bending. In 1983, I took part in a PK party with five hundred participants. A significant number of the persons in the room bent their cutlery to varying degrees. One eight-year-old boy sitting next to me held up a fork by its end and shyly exhorted, "*Bend! Bend!*" The fork slowly drooped in his little hand as if it had turned into soft butter. I handed him my soup spoon and in his hands it met the same fate. Interestingly, the most successful metal-benders were children up to age twelve, and senior citizens, who apparently have nothing to lose by appearing silly.

Psychic Ability in Children

The abilities of normal consciousness in normal individuals are being stretched in the most unlikely settings. In December 1982 I was an observer during a filming session in Mexico City. Alan Neuman, a highly respected Los Angeles filmmaker and producer, had been invited to document the curriculum of a rather extraordinary school in one of the suburbs. The teachers are Carlos de Leon and Francises Semital, two men in their early thirties who have a marvelous rapport with their students.

Nine children, ranging from age nine to thirteen, attend class twice a week. They are also enrolled in regular grade school fulltime. The unusual course content was a rich interplay between a child's innocence and the timeless world of the unconscious. For the first demonstration, cotton was taped over their eyes and blindfolds were applied to keep out light. Magazines were provided by the film crew. Dancing their fingers over print and photographs, the children were able to identify what was on the randomly chosen pages without using normal retinal vision. They were also able to spell out, letter by letter, English language words. Each child was asked to select a piece of cutlery brought to the school by our group. One by one, the children began lightly stroking the metal and within minutes, spoons and forks bended and curled. At the end of this demonstration, fourteen pieces of cutlery were bent, ranging from a slight arc to significant distortions and loops. Finally, each child was presented with a fresh, tightly closed rosebud. Clutching the stems with one hand, the children began beaming energy at the rosebud with the palm of the other hand. As if time had been persuaded to move to "fast forward," the closed buds began to yawn, awaken, and open to fully bloomed flowers.

For children, an open mind is not equivalent to gullibility. Perhaps their ingenuousness allows nature to proceed simply, unhampered by rules and preconceptions.

Jacobo Grinberg-Zylberbaum, a psychology professor at National University of Mexico, has provided further evidence of extraocular vision from Mexico City's experimental schools (1983). Nineteen children, eleven girls and eight boys ranging in age from five to thirteen years, were included in a major study. Each child was taught simple, alternate nostril breathing, visualization, and meditation exercises. Swimming goggles filled with cotton were placed over their eyes. Slowly, the children were encouraged to "see" without sight until they could walk around a park and accurately describe the scenery and other things commonly found in a park. Then they were asked to "go inside" the bodies of selected individuals and describe what they saw. They were unusually accurate in perceiving old surgery scars, healed bone fractures, and infections. In one case of an ear infection, the child "fixed it" by changing the color of the pus and sending energy to the area from his hands. Peer success seemed to influence some of the more reticent children, and an "induction effect" improved their skills. With practice, more children acquired the ability to "go inside" people's bodies and heal.

The final phase of Grinberg-Zylberbaum's program added a new dimension to the trellis of ideas he was investigating. One young girl was having difficulty in "seeing" a television program while blindfolded. Based on previous experience, she was given a quartz crystal and held it in her right hand. The "fuzziness" in her mind's eye-screen disappeared and she described in complete detail the scenes and Spanish subtitles on the screen. Two of the other girls took crystals in their hands and reported that what they were viewing suddenly became tri-dimensional, as if they were inside the landscape and could see all around them. The quartz crystals apparently acted as amplifiers or step-up transducers and significantly deepened and enriched their capacity for "extraocular vision." The children's experiences were very similar to Thomaz's descriptions during his demonstrations of

"X-ray vision." Some of the most moving consequences of the children's participation in the program were their increasing questions—"Who am I? Is there a deeper self?"—and their motivation to investigate and gain greater contact with their "true being."

Recent studies in China report that children have dematerialized objects in space and rematerialized them later in different locations. These experiments were conducted under the most strict laboratory conditions. Shuhuang (1983) describes one test in which Shuen, a twelve-year-old girl, was able to mentally move a watch's hands from several minutes to five hours. In another experiment, a micro-wireless transmitter dematerialized from one part of the laboratory with a corresponding loss of signal. It then "re-emerged" in another part of the room, still in operation. In fifteen subsequent experiments, it took between twenty-four seconds and sixty-one minutes to "disappear" and "reappear." Shuhuang reported that it went through a process of "existence" to "nonexistence" (though the latter does not necessarily imply the total disintegration of matter but perhaps location in another kind of space or simply an inability to be detected by human sense organs or electronic sensors).

In other experiments, children were able to apport a light-sensitive paper from one lightproof bag to another across the room. The paper was examined and there was no evidence that it had been exposed to light. Another child was able mentally to cause a screw to pass through a hole much smaller than itself. The purpose was to prove they could paranormally penetrate solid barriers with physical objects. One child, Ping, was then able to transteleport the screw to different locations in the laboratory as requested by the experimenters. Another child, a sender, was able to transteleport a strip of aluminum and a wristwatch from one sealed bag to the sealed bag of a receiver across the room. Somehow, the objects made the trip without crossing the intervening space. In a final experiment, four live fruitflies, inside a small glass bottle within a matchbox, were apported from the pocket of Ping, one of the more adept subjects, to the trouser pocket of his friend Chang, on the other side of the laboratory. The fruitflies survived their paranormal journey unharmed.

Lyall Watson (1979) describes a stunning experience with space and matter, a mental arabesque with a different arrangement. A five-year-old girl named Claudia, from Venice, was provided with a new, fuzzy tennis ball from a container that had just been opened. She cradled the ball gently in one hand and stroked it lightly with the other. Suddenly, there was a "short implosive sound . . . like a cork being drawn" from a bottle. What had been a fuzzy tennis ball was now a "smooth, dark, rubbery globe." Watson held the transformed ball; it was still pressurized and bouncy. He cut the ball in two and discovered that the inside was lined with the fuzzy pile that had previously been outside only moments before. The ball somehow inverted, inside out, without loss of pressure and with no other visible manifestations during its fleeting transition. Claudia successfully repeated her demonstration later in the evening. Again, the guileless little five-year-old unwittingly sent another banner of conventional belief fluttering to the ground.

Italian Psychics

Besides Brazil, which has been described as a culture with an endless mindscape of psychic richness, Italy is emerging with its own galaxy of miracles. During the fall of 1982, I spent almost a month traveling throughout northern Italy, interviewing and observing five well-known psychics. Paul House, a freelance journalist based in Rome, had written extensive articles about four of these men. He agreed to travel with me and help me gather background information, make the necessary introductions, and serve as an interpreter.

Gustav Rol

Our first stop was at the home of Gustav Adolfo Rol in Turin. Rol is a tall, well-educated man in his late seventies. His aristocratic background is reflected in his bearing and in the art objects and stately furnishings of his home. He made a fortune in antiques but has recently donated much of his money to various charities. Rol is an accomplished painter and pianist, but he is best known for his abilities as a seer, a materializing medium, and a healer. He still receives as many as four hundred letters a week from persons all over Italy requesting absent healing. In his youth he knew Lenin, and Einstein visited him while he was living in Zurich. Rol, in a reflective and moving moment, recalled how Einstein had told him that "light is the shadow of God." Perhaps of interest, just over thirty years later, physicist Bohm was quoted as saying that "all matter is frozen—or condensed light—light is energy, information, content, form, and structure. It is the potential of everything." (Bohm, 1983)

With us the first evening were Dr. Luigi Giordono, a Turin surgeon, and his wife, Maria Louisa. Shortly after we were seated around a coffee table, Rol began glancing above my head and to either side of where I was seated. He then began to cite accurate details of my personal life and health history known only to me. He stated that the information was "coming" to him from the energy field around my body. He then agreed to demonstrate some "experiments."

I produced two new decks of cards bought in anticipation of Rol's working style. I broke the seals and shuffled the decks; at no time did Rol touch them. I selected a card and placed it in the center of the deck. Rol concentrated for thirty seconds or so; I was then asked to turn over the top card. The card I placed in the center of the deck was now on top. In a series of carefully monitored "experiments," Rol, by quietly focusing his concentration, was apparently able to move cards psychokinetically through a deck, and twice mentally influenced the target card to pop out of the deck and flip over. At all times the cards were out of his reach.

Later, I was asked to take four sheets of paper from my notepad, fold them, and place them in my briefcase. Again, Rol became intensely absorbed and said that something would be written on the inside page. Upon unfolding the page, we saw written in pencil, "Gail, age 24, Lee age 42," the respective ages of my ex-wife and me at the time of our marriage. There were other experiments of "psychic writing" and, one time, of a coded card being transteleported from a sealed container to another part of the room.

In a subsequent interview, Mrs. Giordano related her personal experiences with Rol. Dr. Giordano was initially a skeptic, but after observing a number of "experiments," she became convinced that Rol could be one of the most powerful mediums in the world. On one occasion, both Giordanos were in the sunroom and were startled by the curious fluctuations of Rol's paintbrush next to the easel. The brush then levitated and began moving in quick strokes perpendicular to and touching the canvas. Rol was called from the kitchen where he had gone to make tea. The brush, suspended in midair, was scandalously disregarding gravity. He smiled and quietly stated that the brush's outlandish antics were a "sign" for him to return to his painting.

On another occasion, the Giordanos were participating in a session with Rol, an engineer from Milan, and the engineer's wife. Following the usual period of intense meditation, several envelopes suddenly materialized in midair and fell to the table below. They had a musty odor and the paper was brittle and moldy. They later were authenticated as the love letters written by the engineer's grandfather and sealed in his casket in a tomb in Milan. Rol explained that he simply allowed himself to "bilocate" and was guided unconsciously "to the burial chamber." Later that same evening, Rol appeared to "grow to a great height . . . almost to the ceiling . . . he became very luminous and then shrunk to about one foot . . . and then returned to his normal size." This occurred in a lighted room and was attested to by four reliable witnesses. Reason lends illusive sense to such incidents. However, Rol's luminosity and body expansion sound persuasively similar to Thomaz's body enlargement and contraction in front of several witnesses. Rol is a somewhat private and retiring person, but he has permitted psychologist Giovetti (1982) and noted parapsychologist Hans Bender (1982) to conduct extensive and successful tests with him under controlled conditions.

Paolo Paris

Although they live within one mile of each other, Paolo Paris has never met Gustav Rol. Paris is a thirty-nine-year-old psychologist and psychotherapist who practices in Turin. He is a shy, gentle, unpretentious man who could easily pass for a Hasidic scholar. He is an authority on hermetic and mystical literature and is a high-order Rosicrucian. Paul House met him in 1981 and through mutual friends was invited to participate in an evening of "experiments." The evening began in "mind-stopping" style. A friend of Paul's stopped to admire an orchid painted on a lampshade in the hallway. Suddenly, a beautiful fresh orchid with dewdrops on it materialized at the base of the lamp. Paul, who was the only other person in the hallway, actually saw the transition of "non-form becoming form." Paris had not intended the materialization but saw it as an omen of the presence of "harmonious energy." Later that evening, another woman began talking about a recent holiday in the South Pacific. She was describing swimming in a freshwater lagoon, teeming with underwater life. Without warning, "a small terrapin" (a freshwater turtle) was seen crawling across a paper on the table before her. Paris, sitting six feet away, was just as surprised as the other observers.

Then, in what has become Paris' personal trademark, he asked Paul to go to the bookshelf, select a book, open it randomly, and read aloud the first line of the page. The passage had to do with "kitchen decorations." He then followed the same procedure with three other randomly chosen books. The themes of the first lines on these pages were cooking, the spread of "Red Communist Chinese ideology," and the "agitation of a football game," respectively. Suddenly, as if an invisible connection dramatized into a tangible metaphor, four red-hot peppers silently materialized on a plate in front of the group. What happened next, however, was just as startling as the appearance of the peppers. The plate that they were sitting on got progressively warmer until it was too hot to touch without being burned.

Paris was born in Italy in normal family circumstances. At the age of eleven, he experienced a severe electrical shock. This was followed by a rather high fever that lasted almost a year. Following his recovery, the family noticed the emergence of his powers and "strange things began to happen" around the household. Paris spoke very articulately about harmony and how important it was to resonate with and not destroy any living creature. He also acknowledged the importance of all the forces of nature and that one could unconsciously harmonize with and utilize any level of air, water, earth, or fire.

Our first "experimental session" was attended by friends and admirers of Paris. The group included a journalist, industrialist, engineer, and several artistic friends of his wife. We sat around a dining room table in full light. At Paul's suggestion, I had brought two new sealed decks of cards. Before the session began, I was asked to wrap one of the decks in tinfoil, immerse it in a bowl of water, and place it in the freezer in the kitchen. I also added my own touch by placing a small metal object on top of the sealed deck in the water and positioning it in such a way that I could tell if someone tampered with it. I was then requested to break the seal on the second deck, select one card, and place it inside my jacket. No one saw the card and I chose not to look at it.

Over the next two hours, Paris conducted several experiments with cards similar to the demonstrations performed by Rol. With the deck of cards beyond Paris' reach, several cards were psychokinetically moved from the middle to the top of a deck. We also observed a target card "drawn out" of a deck psychokinetically and flipping over without touch. Another time a card was selected by Paul, placed under a container with his hand on top, and transteleported "through" the table to the other end of the room. During the several rest periods Paris spoke in greater detail on the importance of harmony in mobilizing his powers. He prefers working in warm rooms since heat is a better conductor of energy for him. He also acknowledged "tapping into the subconscious of observers" and using their energy to create the experiments. People frequently complain of being drained after Paris finishes "working." Feelings of "low energy . . . no vitality" were expressed by several members in our group at the end of the evening.

Two hours after I placed the sealed deck of cards in a bowl of water in the freezer, I was asked to retrieve the bowl. By then a crust of ice had formed over the cards and around the metal weight on top of the deck. I placed the bowl in the center of the table and Paris asked for a candle to be set in front of him. He went into a deep respiratory trance and then held his finger just above the flame. I sat next to him, carefully observing his finger.

Suddenly, in a fraction of a second, a small triangular-shaped fragment of paper materialized on his fingertip. I took it; it felt like a corner of a playing card. One edge was slightly scorched. Then, at Paris' request, I broke the ice, took the deck out, and unwrapped the tinfoil. I broke the seal and fanned the cards out in my hand. All of the cards, as expected, were quite cold, except one. The king of clubs felt very warm. Most astonishing, however, was that one corner of the king of clubs was missing and the jagged edge was scorched. I then took the piece that had materialized on Paris' fingertip and placed it on the corner. A perfect fit! The group then asked me to remove the card from my inside jacket pocket. It was the king of clubs.

Paris was beginning to tire but he offered one more demonstration to "celebrate" my visit to Italy on a more personal level. I was asked to describe a scene that was "very dear" to me. I immediately thought of my farm in the country and related the most memorable scenes of the grassy fields, two trout streams, two resident blue herons, and other animals on the property. A journalist at the table was asked to "continue the free association" for me and not concern herself with accuracy. She described two roads, rows of flowers, a barn, and a pile of gravel. I was then asked what my "dominant color" was (red) and the remainder of the group was asked to name something red. Such things as red maple, red door, and "lots of red flowers" were mentioned. Two others also referred to red flowers. I was then asked to select a card (nine of hearts) and told that I should come up with a final number by either dividing, adding, or subtracting any number to or from the nine. I chose to divide by three, and at that precise moment three red flowers "apported" out of thin air and fell onto the middle of the table. A dozen or so red petals identical to the petals on the flowers also materialized and were scattered around the table. The flowers and petals were camellias; there are two camellia (japonica) bushes in front of my house in the country. What I did not mention at the time was that when the first person in the chain of associations said "red flowers," I had seen the camellia bushes in my mind's eye.

It might be tempting for some to muffle the experiences with Paris by attributing them to a clever sort of conjury, but I tend to agree with Paris that it was quite likely our energy that fulminated the phenomena. His function was that of a maestro orchestrating mind-over-matter potentials where they probably originated—at the levels of the psyche where introspection is not possible.

Claudio Cabianca

Baldagno, a small picture postcard town in northeast Italy, is the home of Claudio Cabianca, a most unlikely-looking psychic. He is a tall, charismatic, handsome man who could easily pass as a professional soccer player. He is married and very devoted to his wife and two children. Curiously, Claudio, like Thomaz, suffered a severe electrical shock at the age of twelve that threw him across the room. A short while later, he fell from a ladder, struck his head, and was unconscious for several hours. Following these two incidents he began to develop "strange powers," which initially manifested as the ability to heal by laying on hands.

Claudio runs a pizza shop in Baldagno but had not been to work for the ten days before our first visit as he was grieving the recent death of his mother. Paul had visited with Claudio on two previous occasions. He had witnessed a number of experiments in which, again under carefully controlled conditions, coded playing cards were transteleported from sealed containers to locations inside and outside the house of Professor Urbani Camillo, a physics instructor at the University of Padua. Camillo (1982) has conducted more than a hundred well-designed psychokinesis experiments with Claudio. These have ranged from the transteleportation of a wooden shoe thirty yards into the front seat of a locked car to the familiar "card experiments." In one experiment in his physics laboratory, he placed an equal number of playing cards on two balance scales. Claudio was then asked to exchange the cards on top of each stack of cards mentally. Following a period of intense concentration, he stated that it had been accomplished. Camillo had been watching the two sensitive sensors indicating activity on either balance. Nothing had moved. Upon examination, the two cards had silently and instantaneously exchanged positions without even a jiggle of motion.

Claudio demonstrated his ability to "psychically relocate a card from the top of a deck to somewhere in the middle without touching the cards. One day, during a laboratory class in physics, Camillo gathered several of his students around him, set up a deck of cards, and explained how Claudio transteleported matter without any apparent distortion of density or form. He stated that this was "probably a normal human ability" and asked for volunteers to attempt the experiment. Two students stepped forward. Taking turns, each stood with one hand palm down above the deck. Their instructions were simply "make the top card move to some other position in the deck." One of the young men was unable to do it, but the other mentally moved the card three out of six times. Somehow, the thought of Claudio's ability had induced the same skill in a psychically naive subject. The student who failed in his attempt went home and told his father of his classmate's success. The father said, "I think I can do that," and proceeded to mentally "push" the top card through until it became the eleventh card down in the deck. The father was able to demonstrate this feat on one other occasion for his co-workers at the factory (Camillo, 1982).

In our final interview with Claudio, he explained his internal mental processes during his transteleportation experiments. Whether using a playing card or some other experimental object, he creates an "intense concentration and visualization." This step is followed by "seeing the molecules disintegrate . . . coming apart . . . like falling snow . . . then moving like a swarm of bees and reconstituting" at the target site. If the visualization is "dead clear," he knows it will happen. If it is "out of focus . . . in a grey phase," he may have difficulty and the results are unpredictable. Claudio has successfully utilized his visualization technique to reduce a brain embolism, disintegrate tumors, and heal a man suffering from the paralyzing effects of a rare virus fever.

Luciano Muti

As mentioned before, a history of electrical shock or physical trauma is a mysteriously recurring theme among gifted psychics. Forty-one-year-old Luciano Muti was an electronics components technician in Bergamo, a charming small town in northern Italy. At the age of twenty, he was critically injured in a motorcycle accident and remained in a coma for three weeks. Muti (1982) later stated that upon recovery, "I wasn't the same person . . . something had changed deep within me." He had been severely beaten and abused as a child and the prolonged coma "somehow loosened up bottled energy which now becomes my psychic powers." For the next several years, his unchanneled energy would erupt into unpredictable poltergeist activity. Twice, while having dinner with his wife in a restaurant, an adjacent table began bouncing, then "floated" several feet away and tipped over. No one was near it. As if expressing a mindless excitement, the side leaves on their dining room table would frequently "flap up and down" until Mrs. Muti secured them. Two years later, Muti began to channel his powers into healing and the spontaneous poltergeist detonations stopped abruptly.

His abilities eventually came to the attention of Arnaldo Zanatto, a physician from Milan. Zanatto (1982) conducted a number of experiments with Muti. One of his trials included a twenty-two-year-old woman who was sitting on a chair. From a distance of six feet, Muti "projected an invisible force" and dragged the woman, still seated, across the room. At one point, she attempted to hold onto a table but the "energy overcame her strength."

On two subsequent occasions, Muti appeared in front of national audiences on Italian and French television. I obtained videotapes of both programs for review purposes and for my records. They were the most intense and compelling demonstrations of psychokinesis I have ever observed. A four-hundred-pound wooden table was placed in front of the studio audience. Skeptical Nino Lango, station manager of "Tele Nord Italia," recruited four friends for the demonstration. They positioned themselves so that they could put all their weight along one edge of the table. Their task was to keep Muti from levitating the table and tipping it over on its side. Muti was positioned eight feet from the edge of the table. Muti told me later, "I entered the table with my mind. I sent my bioplasma (energy) into the floor and into the people's bodies—I used their energy to create the levitation." During the demonstration, Muti became almost frenzied, shouting over and over, "I am the table, I am the table." His arms waved in the air as if he were a puppeteer with invisible strings. The table could not be contained. It lurched, levitated, then flipped over on its side, yanking two of the men over the table and tumbling them onto the floor.

Immediately following these demanding psychic displays, Muti develops a gelatinous crust on certain parts of his body. He refers to it as "bioplasma" and it "sweats through my pores—especially on my legs and upper body." He then has to "peel it off, like stale chewing gum."

Psychiatrist Antonio Calogero of Bergamo has functioned as an adviser to Muti's practice and development as a healer. According to Calogero, Muti has demonstrated the capacity for "mentally entering people's bodies—he can actually see the atoms and molecules of a tumor and dissolves them" (1982). His psychic diagnoses are consistent with the medical records of other physicians from whom he has taken referrals.

Luciano Muti offered to do a healing on me. He claimed to enter my body and could "mentally see" specific problems. He accurately described the anatomy of chronic physical difficulties and of a more recent athletic injury. He then made "passes" over my body without touching me. I experienced shifting sensations of warmth and cold simultaneously in different parts of my body. This was followed by sensations of weightlessness and that my limbs were disconnected from my body. Inexplicably, my arms and legs were thrown into a series of random, involuntary spasms. In the following month, I experienced considerable relief from both the chronic and acute physical problems troubling me.

During our last evening together over dinner, Muti explained that his body's "electromagnetic field is the conductor of all energy." He attempts to resonate his electrical field with that of his patient or subject. His eyes twinkled as he said, "Once harmony is achieved, there is nothing that can stop our cosmic dance." As he was talking, a part of me disassociated and I silently mused about the fusing of our body fields since we were sitting so close to each other. In a dreamy manner, I directed the energy playfully to a rather large sterling silver fork on the opposite side of the table. Moments later, I was startled out of my twilight reverie by seeing the fork arched in the middle and now shaped like a half circle. I was exhilarated. I mused that perhaps the best way to confound the common sense world is not to hold our waking consciousness in such tight rein.

Erickson (1979), Harner (1980), and others have suggested that the temporary masking or distraction of conscious activity can awaken the "slumbering giant" that is our subconscious. This can be achieved through hypnosis, shamanic ecstasy, trance dancing, or religious conviction and prayer.

Faith Healing

In the spring of 1968, an eleven-year-old girl named Cheryl was riding in the passenger seat of an automobile traveling thirty-five miles an hour. It was on a two-lane country road in Choctaw

County, Mississippi. In order to avoid a parked car, the driver crossed the midline and collided head-on with a car coming in the opposite direction. Bodies flew everywhere. Cheryl was pinned between the firewall and the engine. She was in great pain, but as she glanced at her left leg she tried to pretend she was dreaming. From her left hip to her knee, there appeared to be no bone. The flesh surrounding her thigh had become slack, jelly-like, and collapsed, offering no support to the shattered bones. Her X-rays looked as if "someone had taken a hammer to her thighbone . . . and the bone looked like bitty pieces of shattered glass" (1981).

Following extensive surgery, Cheryl was placed in a cast. Three months later the cast was removed. The left leg, extended to its fullest, was two inches shorter than the right. She was told that she might never walk properly again.

Three years later, at age fourteen, she had grown considerably, but she still limped because of the two-inch difference in the length of her left leg. One memorable evening, friends invited Cheryl to a prayer meeting thirty-five miles away in Jackson, Mississippi. A large audience had gathered to pray and evoke energy for healing. Cheryl shyly joined members of the congregation who wanted to "receive the Holy Spirit." As the pastor walked down the line with his hands outstretched, he rousingly prayed and urged the devotees to "focus your thoughts toward Jesus." As he passed in front of Cheryl, she suddenly began speaking in another, more beautiful and graceful language that "seemed to flow from the depths of my spirit." Some people might refer to it as "speaking in tongues." Slowly, Cheryl lost track of time and slipped into another reality, "a bright shining place." She slowly sank to the floor, her legs extended straight out, as though in deep sleep.

There was a buzz of bioelectricity in the air. When she sat up, her "left leg had extended until my two heels, like two perfectly matched bookends" were equal in length. In a matter of seconds, her left leg "grew" just over two inches and returned to a pre-accident, normal state. Of course, to many it is biologically impossible and intellectually scandalous. It would be much easier to attribute the so-called "miracle" to the preternatural drivel of an irrational, mesmerized fourteen-year-old. But can we?

Eight years later, Cheryl Prewitt won the 1980 Miss America pageant. In a later appearance on national television her orthopedic surgeon described the biologically impossible healing that had indeed occurred. He then displayed the before-and-after X-rays as visual evidence of the "magic of belief." Cheryl Prewitt's autobiography describes in detail her inspiring transfiguration. Cheryl now makes her home in Tennessee but travels and lectures extensively on the power of faith and positive attitude.

Beyond Science

Returning to our original questions and speculations about Thomaz, there can be little argument that our knowledge of nature's laws is incomplete. Rationalism and skepticism have succeeded in cutting off access to the source of miracles in our deeper psychic and spiritual dimensions. Somewhere in the seamless universe there are allegories of the mind that can materialize objects out of quantum realms and transteleport matter into and out of "hyperspace."

The psychic fault-line is shifting and becoming more restless. What mechanistic science has self-righteously chosen to outlaw as a tangle of religious or occult superstition is surfacing irrepressibly. Mental snapshots of internal landscapes are slowly illuminating the DNA of the spirit.

As humans, we constantly seek meaning, but a large portion of our being is starving in the shadow of our ignorance. I suspect that individuals like Thomaz, Gustav Rol, the Geller children, Claudia, Cheryl, participants in PK parties, Rosita, and all the others represent a new evolutionary image. This image is emerging from and drawing us into the future. It appears to be species-wide and portends a much broader definition of what it means to be human.

CHAPTER TWELVE

Conceptualizations and Implications

Theory does not prevent facts from existing.
Jean Charcot

Psychic Phenomena and Physics

As creatures in search of meaning, where do we turn in order to make sense of the incomprehensible areas of our being? Are they indeed what Koestler (1979) referred to as a "festival of absurdities" that totally violate common sense? One typical solution to the intangible is to retreat gracefully and subscribe to the rationalist's illusion: "What I cannot explain cannot exist." The history of science is littered with the debris of unexplained events that simply do not fit within our consensus version of reality. Yet, it would be misleading and irresponsible to ignore the sporadic surfacings of other levels of our psyche.

Science is at a crossroads. It has historically dealt with only the part of our experience that can be objectively measured and quantified. Subjective experience and the gradations and metaphors of the unconscious have generally been ignored or denied by mainstream scientific theorists. Paranormal phenomena may represent the greatest challenge to revisioning the current mechanistic world view. I am convinced that the deepest wisdom of our psyche, the unconscious knowledge of ourselves, and perhaps even our ultimate purpose in being, is camouflaged in the outer fringes of the paranormal. Psychic phenomena exemplify a metaphorical bridge from the old to the new, and a potential vehicle for rediscovering our sense of the divine and our importance in the cosmos.

Unfortunately, these same psychic phenomena represent a collage of the logically empty and intellectually unnavigable, a Pandora's box of romanticized madness. We have not yet been able to construct a theory capable of accommodating the disparate phenomena of parapsychology. I have examined the scientific literature, explored philosophical models of reality, and considered several metaphysical treatises. Speculations on *psi* have ranged from the from the pedantic and ponderously scientific to the "ooh-ahh" reactions of those with blind faith. Indeed, no current theory adequately explains even the most basic of psychic anomalies.

Part of the difficulty in developing models has been that scientists and theoreticians cannot be persuaded to pay attention to facts that defy belief. Discussions among psychic naturalists and laboratory researchers resemble an argument between an astronaut and an advocate of the flat-earth theory: The astronaut has returned from space with pictures proving that the earth is round; the flat-earth advocate simply dismisses the photographs as fakes.

Based on the principles of physical science, the earliest attempts to decipher psychic phenomena invoked a physical explanation. Jahn (1982), in a thoughtful review, described the first efforts to prove that psychic effects are the products of the wavelike qualities of electromagnetism. Radio became the metaphor of communication during that period, with telepathic experiments frequently referring to "senders," "receivers," and "mental static" that would interfere with successful telepathic transmission.

The distinguished Russian physiologist Vasiliev (1963) conducted a series of experiments that ultimately provided evidence contrary to his electromagnetic theories of "action at a distance." He hypothesized that hypnosis could be induced telepathically. The subjects and hypnotist were placed in metal cabinets in different rooms. Using a copper-insulated Faraday cage, he shielded them from the effects of electromagnetic waves within the ultrashort, short, and medium wavelengths. He found that shielding the subjects in this way did not interfere with the telepathic transmission of instructions. In a subsequent study, Vasiliev doubled the copper and metal shielding and separated the subject and the experimenter by a thousand miles. The extra shielding and distance had no effect on the successful telepathic induction of hypnosis and accompanying suggestions.

Other wave-model theories, such as electrostatic fields of the atmosphere, infrasonic waves, geoseismic waves, and barometric fluctuations have been suggested (Jahn, 1982) with discouraging results. Parapsychologist Rao (1977) examined in great detail how various theorists explored quite different regions of the electromagnetic spectrum. However, over one hundred years ago the narrow realism and the Victorian crust of science were simply unable to go beyond physical models of *psi*.

Developments in twentieth-century physics contributed greatly to a radical redefinition of the "basic stuff" of the universe. The central dogma of Newtonian and mechanistic models was that matter was solid and indestructible. Atoms, the fundamental building blocks of the cosmos, were thought to be as dense as billiard balls. Not so according to recent discoveries. Bubble chambers and the collision process of high-energy physics forced the revision of the myth of indestructible matter to include protons, neutrons, and electrons. These particles in turn were differentiated into a pantheon of hundreds of even smaller particles. Even this subatomic panorama dissolves into waves, processes, patterns, and a quasi-undecided universe of increasing or decreasing densities of occurrences. Stanislav Grof (1986), one of our foremost cartographers of consciousness, reports that many prominent physicists believe that "mind, intelligence, and possible consciousness are woven into the fabric of the universe."

The next important milestone in the revisionary perceptions about psychic events was the understanding of consciousness as an important interaction variable. Based on the concept of the hidden variable in quantum mechanics, Walker (1974) proposed a theory that would account for telepathy and psychokinesis. The "certain" cause and effect of classical physics gave way to a system with probabilistic qualities. Walker suggests that any system or situation contains several subsequent states of responses. When an observation or decision is made within a system, the quantum probability collapses into one real outcome. In other words, "All the potential states become the single physical state of the brain. The process continues at such a rapid state as to present a continuous stream of consciousness." Walker goes on to propose that "will," one's conscious experience of control, effects changes within the brain. For example, by "willing" or selecting one stream of consciousness from the aggregate of possibilities, the probability distribution or "wave packet" is collapsed into one choice or response.

Walker contends that consciousness psychokinetically moves electrons from one nerve cell to another. This determines the collapse of the electron wave packets. If one electron can be influenced psychokinetically, why not hundreds or thousands, or more? Walker also raises this question: If electrons can be moved from one nerve cell to another within the brain, why can't "will" influence electrons outside the brain?

Krippner and Villoldo (1976) view Walker's theory as an explanation for healing and psychokinesis. They report that Walker calculated Russian psychic Nina Kulagina's ability "to mentally move a small object across a table would require 10^4 bits of information per second—a feat within the range of the will's capacity." Extrapolating to the case of psychic surgery, a healer in an altered state could mobilize "the full 'conscious data rate' of

10^8 bits of information per second." Theoretically, this would be sufficient to alter the molecular bonds in the body's cells so that the skin could be "separated" and then "rejoined."

Walker's theory is a courageous attempt to explain psychic phenomena within the conceptual framework of modern physics. Though its logic and mathematics are complex, it is the most testable theory available at present. The major weakness in Walker's proposals is that he provides neither specific data nor the psychological factors needed for identifying and amplifying the "will."

Several efforts have been made to explain paranormal phenomena by expanding the basic laws of physics. The hyperspace hypothesis proposes additional dimensions to the known time and space coordinates. Physicist William Tiller (1978) suggests a lattice model of space in which spaces of higher dimensions exist, one vastly more complex than the commonly accepted three-dimensional model of physical space plus the added dimension of time. Tiller's mathematics and description of the mechanisms for interaction between the new dimensions involve propagation velocities much faster than the speed of light. The remarkable potential of this theory for our purposes is that simply the addition of another dimension could explain the materialization and dematerialization of objects.

Other tantalizing possibilities include the interaction of mind and spirit with the physical world. Tiller also proposes different kinds of energy, energies that modulate and amplify in three-, four-, five-, or six-dimensional space. These different "energy bands" interact synergistically and coherently. Thus, a modulation in an individual's consciousness would increase the spectrum of energy available, with a corresponding increase in the dimensionality of the energy. Tiller's provocative hypotheses appear imaginatively valid in that they suggest psychic warps connecting different universes of experience. Almost the entire realm of paranormal phenomena could be accounted for and interpreted within Tiller's hyperspace theory.

LeShan (1976), in a similar vein, proposes that reality takes on

Conceptualizations and Implications

different forms, depending on how we interact with it. Our everyday way of perceiving provides us with a "sensory reality." It is the common sense way of looking at the world, in which objects and events are separated by space and time, and information is interpreted by the senses. By changing consciousness, we can shift into "clairvoyant reality," where we can experience directly the oneness of being and the more profound patterns of the universe. The "transpsychic" and "mythic" modes of being provide even wider world views of time, space, and dimensionality. LeShan's examination of the four levels of reality blends the mystical, physical, and paranormal world views to account for psychic events.

Jung (1955), in a startling endeavor to explain *psi*, began by dissolving the glue of causality. He was convinced that any cause-and-effect explanation of paranormal phenomena was "unthinkable." Since causal interaction involves the expenditure of "energy and is bound by time and space," paranormal phenomena, he suggests, belong to another system of the universe. In his rejection of cause-and-effect explanations of the paranormal, Jung postulated that the unconscious possesses "absolute knowledge" of all that is. He introduced the concept of archetypes, the activating echoes of past civilizations. Archetypes mediate unconscious knowledge to the conscious level of the psyche where that knowledge can sometimes influence and create paranormal experiences.

Arthur Koestler (1979), however, suggests that Jung's reasoning is flawed and contradictory. On the one hand, he says, Jung argues against causality but then ascribes a causative action to archetypes and symbols in producing psychic occurrences. Koestler suggests that paranormal phenomena represent the highest order of nature's integrative affinity. There is a seamless unity in which everything is connected. All matter, all objects, macrocosmically and microcosmically reflect, complement, and contain each other in a surrealistic yet fundamental way.

Our medium-sized world is constrained by notions of time, space, and causality. The macrocosmic world, however, is characterized by curved space, time that can speed up or slow down, black holes in which gravitational collapse and trapped light are catapulted through white holes into superspace, and parallel universes where time is reversed or multidimensional.

The microcosmic world is even more mystifying and iconoclastic. The laws of nature as we know them simply do not hold up on this level. As LeShan points out, what is perfectly normal on a subatomic level (for example, an electron jumping from one "orbit" to another without crossing the intervening space) is teleportation in our everyday world and definitely paranormal. In what Nobel Laureate Richard Feynman (1967) described as the most fundamental experiment in physics, the two-slit experiment established that a single electron can pass through two separate holes of a plate at the same time without splitting. On a quantum level this is perfectly normal. In our common sense world, that would be bilocation, an "impossible" paranormal event.

Bell's theorem, which developed out of the "Einstein-Podorsky-Rosen" paradox, poses an even greater challenge to our tight mechanistic grasp of the everyday world. His theorem states that when two subatomic particles interact and then disperse in opposite directions, interference with one particle will instantly affect the other particle, regardless of the distance between them. This implies some sort of connection or telepathy between the particles. Again, the notion of quantum interconnectedness reinforces the idea of "unbroken wholeness" and harmony in the order of things. As Koestler (1972) suggests, the "baffling paradoxes of physics make the baffling phenomena of parapsychology appear a little less preposterous."

Holograms

One of the most recent theories to address the interaction of consciousness with time, space, and matter is the "holographic" or "transform" model. Holography is a method of lensless photography. The wave fields of two light sources are scattered on a photographic plate as an interference pattern. This is analogous to dropping two pebbles simultaneously into a small, still pool of water. As the ripples made by the pebbles spread out, interfere, and overlap, they would suddenly be "frozen." That "frozen state" is what the photographic plate registers. Since there is no focusing lens, the plate appears as a meaningless pattern of swirls. If a coherent light source such as a laser, however, is projected through the plate, a three-dimensional or holographic image of the "photographed" object is created. The unique feature of a hologram is that the plate could be cut into hundreds of pieces and any single piece could be used to reproduce the complete original image. The part of any hologram contains the whole. Neurosurgeon Karl Pribham (1969) has proposed the hologram as a model for memory storage in the brain.

Physicist David Bohm (1983) frequently refers to the hologram as a metaphor for a new description of reality, suggesting that the universe is constructed on the same principles as the hologram. The world as perceived by our senses appears on the surface as composed of isolated, separate parts. He refers to this as the "explicate or unfolded order of things." The basic order, wholeness, and unity of the universe, however, is enfolded into the "implicate order." The undivided totality of the implicate order is an "energy sea" of electromagnetic waves, electron beams, sound waves, and other energies and resonances, including human consciousness. The brain "lifts" data or mathematically constructs "concrete" reality by interpreting frequencies from that energy sea, a realm beyond time and space.

Bohm's "holoverse" might be compared to our current world communication network. We are all enveloped by the frequencies and resonances of AM and FM radio stations, ultra-high-frequency channels, a spectrum of television and cable stations, short waves, microwaves, ultraviolet rays, and cosmic rays. We are not aware of this vibratory energy field until we tune a receiver into one of millions of frequencies and retrieve the ongoing flow of sound, visual patterns, color, and possibly kinetic stimulation. In other words, the implicate or basic order of the universe is arrayed, not in terms of spatial position and time as we generally perceive it, but rather as frequency and amplitude information. The human brain or consciousness interprets this invisible matrix and translates it into our everyday sensory world. Thus, the explicate or physical universe is only a ripple on the surface of consciousness. In essence, the brain functions as a hologram, interpreting a holographic universe. Neurosurgeon Pribham assumes that the brain could not operate as a hologram unless it were part of a larger hologram. If individual beings are part of the whole, our individual brain-mind holograms contain all the information of all that is or was—past, present, and future.

What are the implications of this theory for parapsychology? If one had access to the primary realm, or the "holoverse," this could account for accessing such abilities as telepathy, clairvoyance, and precognition. As one alters one's consciousness and becomes more coherent with the vibratory rate of the molecular structure of, say, a spoon, might it be possible to change the resonance field of the molecules? This could cause the molecules to loosen up and the metal to soften. Conceivably, an increased synchrony with the sea of holographic frequency might allow matter or objects to move from one spatial dimension into and through the invisible flux of vibrations and then back out into another spatial location. Dematerialization? Materialization? Transteleportation? The sudden appearance and disappearance of particles from a seeming nothingness points to the idea of a fundamental energy matrix existing behind the universe of known matter. After all, the various practices of traditional magic in so-called primitive societies underscore the application of resonance or synchrony as the interconnecting communality of all things.

Invisible Fields Theory

The most recent serious challenge to the old way of looking at reality is the theory of British biologist and biochemist Rupert Sheldrake (1981). His "hypothesis of formative causation" proposes that the universe functions not so much by laws as by habits. The habits are created by repetition of events or learning over time. In a striking echo of Jung's theory of archetypes, Sheldrake theorizes that all living systems are regulated not only by known energy and physical factors but by invisible organizing fields. These morphogenetic fields, or "M-fields," are without mass or energy and act across space and time, serving as energy blueprints for all form and behavior. Thus, whenever an atom, cell, organism, or any other "morphic unit" comes into being, it creates an M-field that in turn becomes a nuclear energy matrix. For example, newly synthesized chemicals do not have M-fields for their crystals. Initially, they are very difficult to crystallize. However, it has been found that if one laboratory succeeds in crystallizing a particular compound, laboratories in different parts of the world very soon find it much easier to crystallize the same compound. In other words, once an M-field has been created, it becomes easier for an event to happen a second time.

Further support for Sheldrake's hypothesis emerged from animal studies conducted by Harvard psychologist William McDougall (1938), who trained rats to maneuver through a water maze and found that subsequent generations of rats learned the maze more quickly than their predecessors. This effect persisted even when McDougall bred only the slowest-learning rats in each generation. Some of the rats learned immediately, without making a single error!

According to Sheldrake, the first generation of rats established the M-field for the specific learned behavior. That field became the energy blueprint for, and guided the learning behavior of, all subsequent generations through the process of morphic resonance. These experiments suggest that the influence of past forms is cumulative and that each animal contributed to and participated in the incremental information field.

Sheldrake uses a simple but intriguing analogy to explain morphic resonance. If a man from the early 1900s were shown a television set for the first time, he might assume that the set contained little people whose images were seen on the screen. After inspecting the set and finding only wires, transistors, and condensers, he might think that the images were created from complex interactions among the electronic components inside the set. Any changes such as tuning, damaging wires, or removing certain transistors would support the conclusion that only the components were involved in the TV screen images. However, if it were suggested that the images were dependent on invisible influences entering the set from a distant source, he would most likely reject the idea.

That person would be in much the same position as conventional biology today. Biologists assume that genes and DNA—the "wires and transistors"—account entirely for heredity. Sheldrake, on the other hand, suggests that heredity also involves M-fields from similar past forms (the television broadcast station).

The idea that invisible fields influence physical form dates as far back as Plato's "ideal forms" and Aristotle's "eternal forms." More recently, in the nineteenth century, experimental biologist Hans Driesch (1914) concluded from his work with sea urchins that all living organisms are regulated by a invisible force called "entelechy." Brazilian parapsychologist Hernani Andrade (1976) first hypothesized morphic resonance and organizing fields in 1949. In a number of personal discussions with Andrade during 1976 and 1977, the authors found his theory to be remarkably similar to Sheldrake's recent proposals. During a brief conversation with Sheldrake in England in 1982, he stated that he had only heard of Andrade's work the week before. It is tantalizing to think of the M-field hypothesis reinforcing itself by the "tuning in" of ideas between the two men. We must remember, however, that it was Sheldrake and not Andrade who provided a more conceptually consistent, inclusive, and testable synthesis of ideas. The first two experiments testing Sheldrake's theory have verified it (Sheldrake, 1983).

The implications of Sheldrake's elegant, far-reaching theory are staggering. Among the phenomena that could be accommodated and explained by it are: accelerated learning and the breaking of past records by calling on the cumulative experience of everyone who ever attempted a task, physical or mental; parallel inventions; phantom limb pain; limb regeneration; the storage of memory; acupuncture meridians; and a model of inheritance—the transmission of acquired characteristics. Sheldrake's theory also adds credibility to the resonant effects of group meditations and memory of prior lifetimes. The "energy blueprints" of such paranormal phenomena as psychokinesis, metal-bending, telepathy, and related psychic skills are growing in number and becoming increasingly accessible to more people. The explosion of metal-bending and transteleportation demonstrations by children all over the world certainly supports both the social and personal implications of Sheldrake's hypothesis.

Bioelectric Fields

While M-fields are postulated as being invisible and without energy, yet causative, the organizing life-fields or L-fields described by Harold Saxton Burr (1972) have been measured and mapped with electronic instruments. Burr, a Yale neurophysiologist, spent his career attempting to establish that all living systems are surrounded by a vital, changing electrodynamic matrix. As one changes the content of one's consciousness, there is a corresponding shift in the voltage gradient of the cocoonlike energy field. In addition, the field also reflects physical milestones such as the precise moment of ovulation, the first signs of an impending illness, ongoing metabolic processes, and healing potential at a wound site.

Of particular interest, however, is that fluctuations in one's consciousness profoundly change the voltage gradient and bioelectric potentials of the field around a living body. Hypnosis, anger, joy, meditation, or any change in one's imaginative state is reflected electrodynamically in the field potentials surrounding a human organism. This suggests that consciousness and will indisputably influence the bioelectrical organization and integrity of the body. My work with body fields has induced profound trance phenomena, total body analgesia, and a number of unexpected paranormal and parasensory experiences in human subjects (Pulos, 1980).

Robert O. Becker (1982), an orthopedic surgeon, has investigated direct-current (DC) stimulation and its effects on biomagnetic fields for more than twenty years. Through his work he has identified a primitive electronic communication system in all living things. This system, he suggests, is part of a web of electromagnetic energy and a useful tool in explaining both "paranormal" phenomena and "normal" phenomena that have resisted a rational biological explanation. For example, Becker proposes that a "healer" could generate "supportive" electrical currents and voltages and convey them to a patient. The patient's internal DC field would engage and step up like a transducer the patient's own bioelectrical healing potential.

But where do all these theories and tests leave us? We still have no logically compelling reason for accepting one theory over another. Theories in parapsychology seem to remain little more than explanatory fictions; they tell only part of the story and tend to compress experiences into narrow concepts to accommodate our limited contemporaneous understanding. It is almost as if dreary old dogmas are rehashed and cloaked again in worn stereotypical images. The new physics is at least beginning to acknowledge domains that are nonmaterial, real, and possibly infused with consciousness. As the tectonic plates of our old view rumble and shift, new readouts on the possible nature of our psyche are surfacing.

While there is still no imperative or commanding model to accommodate the nexus of links in the paranormal world, we can at least look at the phenomena that trigger or liberate psychic abilities. Somehow, I keep being attracted to and am fascinated with the role of electricity and its effects on human energies. The personal histories of Thomaz and several other "world-class" psychics include the experience of a strong electrical shock to the body. It was after this staggering insult to their systems that they were able to demonstrate an array of provocative psychic skills. An intense electrical stimulus, somehow, at some level, seems to serve as a galvanizing midwife that releases previously untapped energies from an embryonic slumber.

Biasing and Psychic Ability

But how? A metaphor from electronics may provide a hypothesis. A term commonly used among electronic and sound engineers is "biasing." As discussed in Chapter Nine, through the introduction of electrical pulsations, an environment can be rearranged, or biased, so that it behaves differently and its functional range is extended. For example, linemen will bias their bodies when working with high-tension wires to prevent electrocution. By working well above ground level, they attach themselves so their bodies are both carrying and "floating" at hundreds of thousands of volts above the normal baseline level. Thus, when they touch a potentially lethal hot wire, there is no voltage difference. They have disconnected themselves from a return source, the electricity has nowhere to go, and they avoid being electrocuted.

A magnetic sound tape can be biased by introducing a low-voltage electrical current through the plastic. This increased "excitement" causes the molecules on the tape to vibrate at a higher rate and to polarize. In other words, they align in a less random, more coherent fashion. Since the magnetic field is now more organized, there is less noise or "confusion" and the signals and information on the tape are much clearer. Because the vibration rate of molecules has been increased, it would take a correspondingly weaker signal to cause them to move even faster. Biasing in this way stretches the information on the tape—it now takes less energy to obtain a larger energy output.

To continue with the metaphor: Once an audiotape has been stimulated and biased electrically, it retrieves high frequencies with much less effort. Thus, the sound of two cymbals crashing together can be lifted from the now organized field of molecules on the tape with less energy. Or, if just the right resonant note, usually in the bass range, projects out of a stereo speaker, it can set up a sympathy resonance with an object in the room, such as a picture hanging on the wall that starts vibrating only when a note with corresponding resonance is played. The cone of the speaker is being vibrated at, say, one volt of energy. The picture, however, may be vibrating at ten volts of energy because it is in perfect attunement with the one note of the speakers. It has less resistance and can vibrate much more easily than the speaker, which is tuned to all frequencies.

Similar kinds of biasing have been reported in the vicinity of microwave and broadcast tower sites. Persons who live near these sites have reported an increase in clairvoyance or telepathy, auditory hallucinations (hearing mysterious voices), and the presence of peculiar tastes emanating from the dental work in their teeth (Becker, 1982). An explanation for these phenomena may be found in the fact that a great deal of stray energy surrounds an antenna site because the transmitter has to beam excess energy to overcome the natural resistance in the atmosphere. Thus, the envelope of energy floating in that area is acutely vibrant because of "beat frequencies"—some signals bounce off each other while others blend to create new frequencies. These new, unexpected frequencies may tune into and bias an individual's body in the immediate environment. This could account for increased psychic sensitivity reported by these persons.

A word of caution for anyone considering an "energy shower" under a microwave tower. Becker reported a number of epidemiological studies and surveys of persons who live or work in the vicinity of high-frequency electromagnetic fields. The death rate from leukemia, lymphomas, and tumors of the nervous system was twice that where simple high-current electricity was present. Other groups investigated showed significant increase in tiredness, headaches, irritability, and cardiovascular disorders. The conditions were greatly reduced or reversible with removal from the source of exposure.

Early in my career I conducted group therapy programs for teenagers with epilepsy. Several patients at different times reported that they preferred to sit in a particular section of a room simply because "it feels better here." In retrospect, I believe that different voltage gradients were present in different parts of the room. There is less voltage in a fluorescent tube, and the patients were probably responding to the different intensities of vibration

Conceptualizations and Implications 231

in different parts of the building or in their homes. There were reports of "fewer seizures" in the parts of the room or building where "it feels better." Unfortunately, this interpretation of their experiences was unavailable at that time.

Thus, the electrical properties of high-frequency electromagnetic fields, it would appear, have at least two effects. They can potentiate or liberate latent powers by biasing one's being into high vibrations and they can activate various maladies and physical disorders. The ranges, distances, and power densities of health risks are being charted by a number of researchers, but at this time the effects of biasing on psychic abilities remain unpredictable. The incidence of biasing among psychics, however, is persuasive.

Fred Lichota (1985), a sound engineer, reported that he received a number of severe electrical shocks over several years while working with high-voltage electronic equipment. It was an occupational hazard, but he slowly built up a tolerance. Now it takes a much larger shock or voltage to affect him. Often he has entered an equipment room to repair malfunctioning electronic apparatus and has found that his mere presence is sufficient for the apparatus to "repair itself." Lichota also discovered that he could repair a broken tape recorder merely by taking it apart and putting it together again. No replacement of parts. No tinkering or adjustments. His presence alone corrected the problem.

Lichota has bent spoons and forks simply by holding the cutlery loosely by the stem and willing the metal to go soft. I witnessed one demonstration in which the tines of a fork bent into a grotesque shape, similar to the metal arabesques created by Thomaz. Lichota believes that his gradient field has been biased by the electrical shocks he has received. He also suggests that if one person's energy, because of biasing, is significantly different from another's, this energy can be transferred and affect the other person's gradient field. This is analogous to radiation from a microwave tower influencing or biasing persons in that environment.

This deceptively simple phenomenon may offer an explanation

for the induction effect. Uri Geller, who received a severe electrical shock as a three-year-old in Israel, has been able to "induce" in normal people the ability to bend metal, repair broken watches, and to transmit and receive telepathically. It could be assumed that because of the early shock to his system, a variant or higher gradient field surrounds his body: In other words, the higher the energy level, the further it can "transmit" and the greater the field of effect. (This would certainly be worthwhile as a test for psychic ability.) Thus, some persons, after being influenced by Geller's force field, retain Geller's original frequency but to a lesser degree. This is similar to a magnet magnetizing an iron nail. Once inducted, the iron nail can pick up metal filings on its own.

These experiences suggest the existence of an underlying connectedness among living organisms. If we can bias each other's fields in an "upward" fashion, might it be possible for the opposite to occur? Could someone with a negative gradient draw energy down and reduce one's force field? A few years ago, I assisted Felician Omiles, a Philippine healer, over a one-week period, observing how he worked and documenting his results. At the end of each day, I was fatigued to a point of weakness. We saw thirty to forty patients a day, each afflicted with a severe and frequently chronic illness. I can now speculate that their negative gradient fields were enfeebling to other fields and drained my energy. Fortunately, a good night's sleep replenished my energy.

Biasing may also account for the so-called "bare-handed openings" of the Philippine healers. If healers can somehow "vibrate" their own bodies at a multiple of the vibratory frequency of a patient, they could conceivably slip in between the crests and waves of the target object. In other words, through prayer, fasting, or channeling of a "higher energy source," a healer could increase the vibratory rate of his hands at a multiple (say, one-tenth faster) of the patient's rate and slip in between the crest and troughs of the vibrating wave form of the cells. As the healer increases his or her healing vibrations, the wave forms may become more coherent and move together. Their action would be additive, going up and down at the same time in synchrony. As all the patient's cells vibrate in an upward node, the healer could possibly "get out of phase 180 degrees" and go down, thus separating the skin. The cells remain bipolar but are synchronous and vibrating in the same direction in unison. The process might be compared to the reverse play in American football. The offense moves as a unit to the right, bringing the defensive unit with it to stop the play. The running back takes advantage of this deception and runs left, away from the pack, presumably into an open field.

Thomaz, of course, was also struck by lightning—a powerful lightning bolt that caused him to lose consciousness for more than twelve hours. This intense electrical charge caused the molecules in his body to vibrate at a much higher rate than normal. In other words, the lightning spread over his entire body and the voltage potential was raised instantaneously to a much faster level. Had there been a differential in the flow of current between, say, his head and body, he would have been electrocuted. Instead, there was a sudden biasing throughout his whole being. Compared to other human bodies, his was (and probably still is) vibrating at much higher frequencies.

Neurophysiologist Burr (1972) has measured the difference in voltage between two points on the surface of living systems. He used a vacuum-tube voltmeter for his experiments because it required a minimum of current for its operation. Burr discovered that the voltage gradients and field characteristics of a human organism would shift as the content of one's consciousness changed. Sadness, joy, hypnosis, alcohol intoxication, and rage all elicited different voltage gradients and electromagnetic field effects around the subject's body. With our consciousness we are all constantly biasing the electrical fields of our bodies. The biasing effect of hypnosis has been particularly effective in creating healing imagery (Simonton, 1978) and to facilitating telepathy in parapsychology laboratories (Ryzl, 1962; Honorton, 1969).

At the lower end of the vibration scale, more energy would be required to bias or expand the "window of information." Deep hypnotic trance, prolonged meditation, or devotion and prayer can produce remarkable physical and psychological transformations (Burr, 1972). In Thomaz's case, since he presumably vibrates at a significantly higher rate due to his lightning experience, less "signal" or energy input is required to produce a much broader spectrum of change. Nevertheless, Thomaz still biases himself by concentrating intensely on a goal or phenomenon. During his focusing there is almost an exponential increase in the final outcome. He seemingly catapults himself into the spaceless areas of dimensional and psychological warps. His window of possibilities is much more magical, miraculous, and unfathomable.

Source of Thomaz's Powers

What does Thomaz think of the biasing/electricity hypothesis? I don't know. We have never discussed it with him. He has gone through an "interpretation crisis" several times about the source of his powers. Initially, he ascribed them to the bolt of lightning. Then his psychic boundaries changed and he felt the lightning was really an astonishingly brilliant ray from a spaceship. As his friends and spheres of influence shifted, the spaceship ray took on more divine and cosmic significance, becoming the celestial and alchemical light of Jesus. He rarely speculates about the sources of his powers anymore.

Recently, Thomaz has been describing a curious physical excitement that presages or announces the arrival of his powers. He experiences the gathering of an "electrical buzz" in the base of his spine. It then feels like "electricity creeping—sometimes shooting up my spine." As the energy unleashes itself, it travels to the crown of his head and "exits through my brow—more energy then comes up my spine and goes through my shoulders, down my arms, and the hairs on my arms become electrified and stand straight up . . . then I know the power is strong." A physical consequence of the frequent electrical rushes in his body is that Thomaz now has an almost permanent burn mark on his forehead where the energy exits. The mark is circular, reddish in color, about the size of a silver dollar, and could be diagnosed as a second-degree burn. A second reddish, circular burn has begun to develop on his solar plexus.

The surge of electrical energy experienced by Thomaz sounds remarkably similar to what is referred to in the mystical literature as the rising of the Kundalini. Scott (1983), Sannella (1976), and Pearce (1981) have described the Kundalini as the dormant creative energy located in the subtle or etheric body at the base of the spine. The awakening of this "coiled" energy can be accomplished through long and arduous training, it can happen spontaneously, or an evolved "master" can liberate it suddenly in certain devotees (a form of induction effect?). Once unleashed, this "fire of the gods" or basic energy of the universe can animate latent paranormal abilities. A creative coherence of mind and brain may emerge, and in some individuals this can be accompanied by spiritual enlightenment.

But where does this all leave us? A stretching of our mental horizons perhaps, but no final theoretical formulations on the origins of Thomaz's psychic powers.

I feel quite content in leaving things as they are. Seeking neat definitions or tidy solutions is not the answer because the explanations will always be too small and limiting. After all, no scientific theory seems to be endowed with immortality. I doubt that the mystique of scientific expertise can ever really understand the basic forces of human nature. What is most important for me is the impact that Thomaz has had on my life, on Gary's life, and hopefully, in the changes that might come about in the consciousness of our readers.

Thomaz has created a fissure in my belief systems about reality. The astonishing eruptions of his spontaneous magic and miracles have made me question my own inventory of unfulfilled potentials. When one begins to realize that other realities and experiences of consciousness are possible, it activates or ignites our hidden, untapped potentials.

Initially, we developed a shameful appetite for more phenomena, more miracles. The more Thomaz could produce, the better. We were very disappointed in him if he could not produce a "magical fix" or if his energy simply was not available. Then, I began to *listen* to Thomaz. Repeatedly, he emphasized the importance of harmony, of being at one with nature, and that we are all connected. But what does this mean?

My prosaic mind wanted logical explanations—labeled and sorted in easy-to-handle packages. Then I realized that I was trying to know with my intellect alone and ignoring what I already knew intuitively and in my heart. In some instinctive way, we all know that everything is alive, interrelated, and connected. When shamans invoke certain powers or when a medicine man does a rain dance, they are inviting nature to respond in a participatory, celebrative dance. Nature may not always be in the mood to respond, but at least the shaman recognizes that nature cannot be taken by force. Berman (1984), in a balanced critique of western science, points out that most scientists seek to conquer, dissolve, or overcome nature. He also poses the thoughtful question, "Who knows more about nature, the person who caresses it or the one who takes it by force?"

Perhaps we have all been taken in by the tunnel vision of our western "shamans," our scientists. Modern science has drifted into difficulties by claiming to be the only true description of reality. This is very similar to the Catholic world view during the medieval era. We do not want to repeat that error.

Apparently, there are huge gaps in the official versions of reality. We may never find the subterranean currents which animate our deepest roots. But because we are limited in our vision, let us try not to level things out into linear expression alone. Nor should we try to squeeze our experiences into a framework much too small to contain them.

Thomaz, in his own way, is suggesting that we can transcend our usual limitations, that we can learn to caress nature. It is a blessing that the Uri Gellers, PK children, mystics, and Gustav Rols refused to wait for the official light of recognition to shine forth. I am convinced that psychic abilities are human qualities that are latent in all of us, wizards and fools alike. Miraculous healings are simply instances of nature being permitted to function unhampered in any way. By separating ourselves from what is natural, we are severing our roots from the deepest sources of our biological and spiritual wisdom.

But I have digressed. Enough intellectual etiquette. How has Thomaz affected my life? I have begun to pay more attention to the inner landscapes of my dreams, fantasies, and the nonlogical aspects of my thoughts. I have stopped trying to engineer or force changes in my life. I have begun to experience a series of remarkable synchronicities—meaningful coincidences—that have reinforced my instinctive conviction about connectedness. The synchronicities started when I began assuming that my ego was a highly specialized but very limited portion of my self. I began to explore various levels of trance and was able to access more of the uniqueness of the metaphoric language of my subconscious. I discovered that the imagery and metaphors differed in expression and meaning through the various levels of trance. This led to the suspicion that possibly one of the reasons I am having difficulty in translating psychic data into absolute terms is that I have not yet learned to distinguish gradations of consciousness which serve as the wellspring for *psi* phenomena. Different levels of trance seem to have a different language represented by a condensed richness in metaphors and symbols. I am still on uncertain ground. It is difficult for me to deal with the soft and subtle information of the unconscious rather than the sharp, clear data and facts of my everyday conscious mind.

Finally, I have come to a greater appreciation of the possible real meaning of miracles. I am convinced that much of our society is starved for spiritual nourishment. Many persons, nonetheless, substitute shallow and frivolous technologies of consciousness for authentic myth, magic, and mystery. For me, miracles represent the opportunity for a personal reenchantment. They can lead us to our roots and nourish a rediscovery and renewal of our basic beings and spirituality.

Although Thomaz and his phenomena cannot be easily explained at this point, he serves as a prophecy for the true potential of the human psyche. Thomaz is a living illustration of the stern limits we have imposed on the definition of self. We seem to go through life acquainted only with the thin surface membrane of our being.

The miracles in the Bible were intended to enlighten, not amaze; to remind us, perhaps, of a much higher spiritual heritage. I am convinced that present-day miracles have a similar purpose. They are meant to restore and heal the mind's basic plan or design and to heal the wounds which come from forgetting that design. To rediscover a state of grace. To rediscover the path leading us to a sense of oneness and harmony with All that is.

Epilogue

Sufficient time has elapsed since the completion of the manuscript to warrant an update on Thomaz and the unfolding drama of his development. His powers, if anything, have become stronger, and he seems to be continually opening new skylights of consciousness.

Thomaz has also experienced an enormous surge of popularity. Throughout Brazil he is known as "O Homen do Ra!" (The Ra! man). He was the subject of the cover story of the October 1983 issue of *Isto E*, the Brazilian version of *Newsweek* or *Time*. The November 1986 Brazilian equivalent of *Playboy* headlined Thomaz as its interviewee of the month and the issue sold out within days.

Along with his increased popularity and the general public's awareness of his powers, Thomaz has gained a very special social standing and prestige among the elite of Brazilian artists, statesmen, and corporate leaders. The gossip columns of Rio's leading newspapers reported his attending the opening night of a new play with the president of Brazil's Federal Reserve Bank. Thomaz's name is linked with many actors and musicians who apparently adore him.

Two of Brazil's best known musician-singers, the husband-wife team of Baby Consuelo and Pepeu Gomez, asked Thomaz to use his powers to reduce the suffering and pain of one of their closest friends who was terminally ill. Using his transmutational powers, Thomaz "energized" various substances into a powerful analgesic. In the course of his "treatments" they saw Thomaz put on a staggering display of phenomena tempered by a special kind of caring for their dying friend.

Baby and Pepeu began sharing their experiences with their colleagues in the entertainment world. Soon after, a small town became a regular gathering place for some of Brazil's most popular humorists, stage and screen stars, fashion designers, and musicians. There Thomaz encouraged his friends to periodically abandon the trappings and glitz of their roles, to walk barefoot on the soil so they could reconnect themselves with nature, and to begin resonating with the presence of a divine essence in all things—especially themselves. Everyone participated in the daily 6:00 P.M. meditation, Thomaz's inspirational ritual that continues to "encourage the transmission of positive energy and love between all people."

Baby and Pepeu began mentioning Thomaz during their TV performances and the audience would respond with a series of "Ra's!" During one program that attracted over thirty million viewers, they encouraged the audience to meditate at 6:00 P.M. and "generate a force field of peace and goodwill." Thomaz's fame continued to grow even though he personally has never appeared before a television audience.

When rock stars were interviewed during a ten-day music festival, "Rock in Rio," in January 1985, many spoke animatedly about "O Homen do Ra." Several of the artists asked for "energy applications" from Thomaz before their performances. Two of the better known entertainers opened their act by asking everyone in the crowd of three hundred thousand to shout "Ra!" over and over.

In Rio's elite Baxo Lebion cafe, the traditional greeting, "Oi! Tudo bem?" (Hi! How is everything?"), has been replaced by exclamations of "Ra!" Nearby, the Real Astoria, another of Rio's "in" habitats, has been renamed the "Ra!" After Thomaz dined there one evening, not one piece of cutlery was left unbent or physically sculpted.

Despite his being labeled the "guru of the stars" by one Rio tabloid, Thomaz actively rejects that portrayal. Instead, he finds a greater kinship with artists and musicians because "we are all mystics . . . trying to tap in as deeply as we can to the depths of reality . . . to the sources of our consciousness . . . and power. . . ." He feels they know what he means when he discusses the forces of nature, the flight of a bird, or the power in a lightning bolt because their visions and creations are inspired by those same forces. During a conversation with Jose Carlos Guerro, the cinematographer and author applauded Thomaz for "pulling down the scientists' philosophical comfort blankets." Others have similarly appreciated Thomaz's irreverence for the logical mind that confines itself to a much too narrow spectrum of reality.

In another interview, a fashion designer described Thomaz as a "new age alchemist . . . but he is also a human being with the right to have off-days . . . defects . . . and mortal sensitivities. . . ." These artists and intellectuals have taken Thomaz's signature "Ra!" from a closely guarded secret to a Brazilian household word that signifies "Positive Energy!"

In March 1985, Thomaz made headlines again—this time on the political pages of Brazil's newspapers. Tancredo Neves, Brazil's first elected president in over twenty years, became seriously ill the night before his inauguration on March 15, 1985. The seventy-two-year-old statesman was rushed to the intensive care ward and over the next six weeks was operated on seven times. Thomaz was approached by Neves' grandson to provide "energy transfusions." Though his involvement was supported by the Neves family, the team of specialists treating the president would not allow Thomaz to see him. Neves died on April 21 without knowing that Thomaz had been meditating for him two rooms down the hall from his hospital suite.

Gary and I returned to Pouso Alegre in January 1988. As we reached the outskirts of the small town, we saw a large "Ra! Energia Positiva" painted on the wall. We looked at each other and joked about crossing the "frontiers of logic" without any special visas. Thomaz was in the hotel lounge surrounded by a group of friends. Following the initial excitement, hugs, and greetings, Thomaz introduced us to the family and friends of a thirty-eight-year-old woman who he was "treating" during the terminal stages of her illness. We spent some time talking with the widow of Henfil, Brazil's best-known political cartoonist. She was there offering emotional support to the patient's family. A hemophiliac, Henfil had died three weeks before of AIDS, the result of a contaminated blood transfusion. Henfil spent his last four months with Thomaz receiving "energy infusions" and ingesting transmuted substances that "completely took away his pain and suffering."

Thomaz's focus was changing. According to one of his friends, "Thomaz is still walking the supernatural path but with practical feet." He is now spending most of his time working with terminal patients, ". . . helping them overcome pain . . . and to die with dignity."

During the next five days we worked closely with Thomaz. He scandalized our intellects with his curious healing rituals, skirting the boundaries between pharmacology and his own unique brand of spiritual shamanism. We also saw a Thomaz with a very special kind of compassion. He spent between three and fourteen hours a day with his patient, very preoccupied to the point of obsession.

Alvaro Delacoste Torres, the patient's father, provided us with the background of her illness. He is a retired president of a large multinational pharmaceutical company and described himself as "initially, very skeptical" about Thomaz. His daughter began having severe headaches in March 1985. A CAT scan revealed an intracranial tumor inside the fourth ventricle. She chose to have surgery in the United States, and the operation was a success. Six months later she developed a brain stem tumor and a series of smaller tumors along her spinal column. Nothing further could be done medically.

Her condition deteriorated, she was unable to walk and had a great deal of pain. Thomaz began by "energizing and transmuting" sugar into a powerful analgesic. This allowed her to be totally pain-free for periods of twenty-four to forty-eight hours.

On the second day of our visit, the patient's kidneys failed. She endured extreme discomfort from being unable to void. Thomaz took her into the special "energizing room" on his property and invited his "energy friends" to assist. Flashes of light—very much like lightning—exploded in the room, creating an almost blinding, dazzling brilliance. The "lights" formed an aura around the cottage that could be seen over two hundred yards away. This continued for a half hour.

During this storm of "cosmic energy," Tomaz injected six 20 milligram ampules of Sinaxial (a muscle relaxant) intravenously into the patient. A physician later told us that one intravenous ampule of Sinaxial could kill a person. Thomaz, however, had "energized and transmuted" the substance. She felt immediate relief and her kidney functions were restored to normal.

For the remainder of our visit, she seemed very tranquil. She also had greater control of body functions and did not complain of any pain. Torres and the family were satisfied with the unorthodox treatments and movingly spoke of the increased emotional bonding of the family that transpired during this period. Torres also pointed out to us that Thomaz never once mentioned a fee or asked for any payment, although he offered Thomaz a gift, as have many other "patients."

During our dinners with Thomaz we saw the usual metal-bending; it has become such a "normal" phenomena around Thomaz we hardly gave it a second thought. He has added a new effect, however. Thomaz gives many of his friends demitasse spoons that are twisted. The spoons are worn as necklaces that signify his psychic signature. As Thomaz presents the spoon, the person's name is instantaneously "engraved" on it. While we were there, he presented a visiting French author whom he had met only minutes before with this talisman. Excitedly, she took it and noticed that her name, Lynette, was engraved on the bottom of the bowl of the spoon. I examined the spoon, noticed engraving on only one surface, and handed it back to her. Suddenly, she shrieked again and shouted that her middle name, Evelyne, was now engraved on the inside of the bowl. "No one," she exclaimed, "except my parents know my middle name!" Thomaz did not touch the spoon during this process and he seemed very pleased with her exuberance. He said, "Wait, I have not finished." He squinted his eyes and said, "Ra!" Beneath the name Evelyne was now engraved "Ra! T.G.M." (for Thomaz Green Morton).

Later that day, Thomaz "energized" Lynette. She began to perspire profusely, and the moisture smelled like mint. The essence oozed through her pores, drenching her red-striped blouse until the colors ran. Her blouse turned into a blur of pink, and a mint-like perfume permeated the whole room. We could smell it on her for days afterwards.

Her clamorous curiosity prompted a deceptively simple response from Thomaz. "It is easy," he said, extending his arm. "Right now, my hand is totally dry. All I do is look at my arm, 'mentalize' the circulation increasing, and feel the energy running down to my fingertips." Just as he said that, small beads of liquid began to slowly drip from each finger and thumb. Gary tasted and smelled each odor, which ranged from sweet peppermint, eucalyptus, camphor, and lilac to other sweet, flowery essences. Days later we could smell the fragrance, both in the hotel and on ourselves.

Thomaz's kaleidoscope of powers continues to grow. A visiting São Paulo lawyer was presented with a bent, rippled Las Vegas dollar token as a souvenir for her son. Thomaz held the bent coin in his hand and said, "A hole will now appear in the coin for the chain. Ra!" We were all gathered around Thomaz and most of us were within three feet of the solid metal token. Suddenly, a circular hole, large enough to fit the end of a small chain, appeared, as if penetrated by an invisible laser.

It is difficult to maintain rigid assumptions around Thomaz. Transmutation continues to be his most baffling phenomena. Once Thomaz placed a piece of ice on a table. In a few moments,

Epilogue

a tiny puddle of water had formed. Thomaz squinted his eyes and concentrated. In twenty to twenty-five seconds the ice transmuted into a hard, granular piece of crystal with a mint taste. Thomaz asked Lynette to lick it as a remedy for her sore throat.

Thomaz was able to transmute ice into variously shaped crystals. While Gary held a piece of ice, Thomaz transformed it into a rough-shaped crystal with a coarse texture. We surrounded Thomaz as he placed the crystal on the table and with his index finger began to deftly sculpt it into a rectangular, faceted and polished quartz crystal. Engraved on one side of the stone was "Ra!" and on the other, "Gary." He handed it to Gary and as we all examined it closely, Thomaz suddenly said, "I forgot to sign it ... Ra!" Again, under the "Ra" appeared the initials "T.G.M." We also watched carefully as he psychically cut another chip of crystal into a beautifully shaped heart, complete with signature.

During dinner one evening, Thomaz asked for several pieces of soft cardboard, the kind used to keep pizza warm. With a pair of scissors he carefully cut out several small circular and rectangular shapes and asked Lynette to hold them between the palms of her hands. "I 'mentalize' that these transmute into gold jewelry, Ra!" She spread her hands and two golden-metallic bracelets and a necklace fell onto the table. A graceful design of dancing figures was etched on the bracelet and, of course, "Ra! T.G.M." For the São Paulo lawyer, he psychically transmuted a silvery wraparound bracelet with a delicate gridwork design etched into the metal. Each psychic creation took about fifty seconds.

Thomaz's phenomena continue to be like cosmic meteors shooting through our smug, logical reality. For some, Thomaz stimulates a closer examination of spiritual and biological directives. Others are driven to rely on reason alone, which unfortunately leads to a true/false kind of world.

Despite his flamboyant presence and innocent mocking of the absurd patchiness of our sensory world, Thomaz has changed. He rarely drinks anymore and seems much more committed to Lygia and his son Raphael. Before we left Pouso Alegre we visited

Thomaz at his home and asked him to reflect on the past five years.

Pensively, he explained that the "circus phase" of his life as a metal-bending entertainer was behind him. He feels he has matured considerably and now has "absolute control" over his energies. He gives top priority to channeling the energies so that people can utilize his phenomena to open up spiritually and "discover their connection to the Divine."

Thomaz also wants to put more effort into helping people die in peace and dignity rather than playing the role of "miracle man." He feels that by illuminating a path of light and energy for his patients, he can help them "ignite and open their hearts and minds to other planes of reality," thereby offering hope on their final journey.

He calls transmutation his most important phenomenon. He feels that the transmutation of tinfoil into a powerful analgesic like "gold" or sugar is merely symbolic of inner mental, psychological, and spiritual transformations. He now spends more time in his "laboratory," sometimes up to three days without leaving. He goes into deep meditative states, opening himself to the guidance of his "energy friends."

Once more, Thomaz has revised his understanding of the source of his powers. The lightning bolt that struck him on his twelfth birthday was "not electrical energy as we know it" but instead emanated from his friends in the parallel universe, Aphron-V. He considers Aphron-V "my energetic home" and feels a much greater connection with the sources of information and orientation from that dimension. Thomaz still dematerializes into a ball of light and transteleports to Aphron-V periodically. The silver dollar-size area that looks like a second-degree burn is now a permanent emblem on Thomaz's forehead.

Thomaz referred to Uri Geller in our conversation and said that he considers Geller "a master." He identifies with the negative abuse and criticism that Geller has had to endure. He is convinced that "Geller is capable of much, much more than he

Epilogue

gives himself credit for." He feels a silent connection with Geller and implies that each in his own way has a similar quest.

As we were leaving, Thomaz returned to the question of his power source. He said that the ultimate source of his powers and all human energies is love. "Only by attuning to the ultimate energy of love can we transmute ourselves inwardly . . . then biological transformation . . . and then, harmony and peace . . . there is nothing else of greater value. . . ."

Thomaz has changed, and it was refreshing to see the transformation. He still gushes exuberantly and is maddeningly impulsive at times but these traits are now tempered by maturity and alloyed with a deeper spiritual awakening.

For us, Thomaz still symbolizes the silent urgings of the collective unconscious that seek new thresholds of reality and ways of being. Just as dreams loosen the reasoning mind's hold on perception, Thomaz reminds us that the five senses provide only a flat view of the surface of reality.

We know skeptics will ridicule our theories; some people have built careers around the rigid focus of reason alone. Yet when reasoning is relied on exclusively, it can limit the practical use of the intellect's faculties. Belief in nothing is the most confining belief of all. We choose to believe that Thomaz in his own way is a kind of underground fissure of our consciousness—he awakens in all whom he touches an exhilarating sense of how deep the roots of the self can reach and what strange and mysterious powers they contain.

Lee Pulos, Ph.D.
Gary Richman
June 1988

References

Abrams, Stanley. 1983. The multiple personality: A legal defense. *American Journal of Clinical Hypnosis.* 25:225–31.
Andrade, Hernani G. 1976. *The psi matter.* The Brazilian Institute for Psychobiophysical Research, Monograph No. 2. São Paulo, Brazil.
Barber, T. X. 1982. The fantasy-prone personality: Implications for understanding imagery, hypnosis, and parapsychological phenomena. *Psi Research.* 1:94–116.
Barker, D. R. 1979. Psi-phenomena in Tibetan culture. In W. G. Roll (ed.) *Research in Parapsychology, 1978.* Metuchen, N.J.: Scarecrow Press.
Batcheldor, K. J. 1979. PK in sitter groups, *Psychoenergetic Systems.* 3:77–93.
———. 1982. Contributions to the theory of PK induction from sitter-group work. *Proceedings Society for Psychical Research and Parapsychology Association.* Centenary Conference, Trinity College, Cambridge.
Bearden, Thomas E. 1980. *Excalibur Briefing.* San Francisco: Walnut Hill.
Becker, Robert O. 1977. An application of direct current neural systems to psychic phenomena. *Psychoenergetic Systems.* 2:189–96.
Becker, Robert O., and Andrew A. Marino. 1982. *Electromagnetism and Life.* Albany State University of New York Press.
Beloff, John. 1983. Three open questions. *Parapsychology Review.* 14:1–6.
Bender, Hans. 1982. Personal communication.
Berman, Morris. 1984. The re-enchantment of the world. New York: Bantam Books.
Bersani, F., and A. Martelli. 1983. Observations on selected Italian mini-Gellers. *Psychoenergetic Systems.* 5:99–128.
Bogoras, V. 1904. Memoirs of the American museum of natural history. *The Chukchee.* New York.
Bohm, David, and Renee Weber. 1983. Of matter and meaning: The super-implicate order. A conversation between David Bohm and Renee Weber. 6:34–44.
Braud, William. 1975. Psi-conducive states. *Journal of Communication.* 25:142–152.

Browning, Norma Lee. 1970. *The psychic world of Peter Hurkos.* New York: Doubleday and Co.
Burr, Harold Saxton. 1972. *Blueprint for immortality.* London: Neville Spearman.
Calogero, Antonio. 1982. Personal communication.
Camillo, Urbani. 1982. Personal communication.
Cantor, Robert M. D. 1978. The psychokinetic world of tomorrow's children today. *Human Dimensions.*
Capra, Fritjof. 1975. *The tao of psychics.* Berkeley: Shambhala Publications.
Carrington, Hereward. 1935. *Loaves and fishes.* New York: Charles Scribner's Sons.
Castaneda, Carlos. 1968. *The teachings of Don Juan.* Berkeley: University of California Press.
Collins, Robert. 1982. Personal communication.
Cousins, Norman. 1977. The mysterious placebo. *Saturday Review.* (October) pp. 9–16.
Culbertson, James. 1977. The spacetime structure of mental images. Part I, *Psychoenergetic Systems.* 2:45–78.
David-Neel, Alexandra. 1931. *Magic and mystery in Tibet.* London: Souvenir.
Dossey, Larry. 1982. *Space, time and medicine.* Boulder: Shambhalm.
Dougherty, J. 1982. Hot-feat-fire walkers of world. *Science Digest.* (August) pp. 67–71.
Driesch, Hans. 1914. *History and theory of vitalisms.* London: MacMillan.
Edmunds, S. 1961. *Hypnotism and the supernormal.* London: Aquarian Press.
Eisenbud, J. 1968. *The world of Ted Serios.* London: Jonathan Cape.
Erickson, Milton, and Ernest Rossi. 1979. *Hypnotherapy.* New York: Irvington Publishers.
Esdaile, James. 1846. *Mesmerism in India and its practical application in surgery and medicine.* London: Silus Andrus and Sons.
Estabrooks, G. H. 1957. *Hypnotism.* New York: Dutton.
Feynman, Richard. 1967. *The character of physical law.* Cambridge: M.I.T. Press.
Franklin, Wilbur. 1977. Metal fracture physics using scanning electron microscopy and the theory of teleneural interactions. *Psychoenergetic Systems.* 2:13–29.
Frazer, James. 1929. *The golden bough.* New York: Book League of America.
Fukurai, T. 1931. *Clairvoyance and thoughtography.* London: Rider.
Fuller, John G. 1974. *Arigo: Surgeon of the rusty knife.* New York: Thos. Y. Crowell Company.
Geller, Uri. 1975. *My story.* New York: Praegen Publishers.
Giovetti, Paola. 1982. The physical mediumship of Gustav Adolfo Rol. Paper presented at *Society for Psychical Research and Parapsychology Association*, Centenary Conference. (August) Cambridge: Trinity College.
Grinberg-Zylberbaum, Jacobo. 1983. Extraocular vision. *Psychoenergetics.* 5:141–158.
Grof, Stanislav. 1986. *Beyond the brain.* New York: State University of New York.
Halifax, Joan. 1979. *Shamanic voices.* New York: Dutton.

Harner, Michael. 1980. *The way of the shaman.* New York: Harper and Row Ltd.
Hasted, John. 1981. *The metal benders.* London: Routledge and Kegan Paul Ltd.
Heard, Gerald. 1963. *The five ages of man.* New York: The Julian Press.
Honorton, C. and S. Krippner. 1969. 1963. Hypnosis and ESP performance: A review of the experimental literature. *Journal of American Society Psychical Research.* pp. 214–52.
Houck, Jack. 1984. Surface change during warm-forming. *Archaeus.* 2:27–50.
Hynek, J. Allen, and Jacques Vallee. 1975. *The edge of reality.* Chicago: Henry Regnery Company.
Jahn, Robert G. 1982. The persistent paradox of psychic phenomena: an engineering perspective. *Proceedings of the Institute of Electrical and Electronics Engineering.* 70:136–70.
Jung, Carl. 1973. *Alchemy: The secret art.* New York: Avon Books.
Jung, C. G., and W. Pauli. 1955. *The interpretation and nature of the psyche: Synchronicity and the influence of archetypal ideas on the scientific theories of Kepler.* New York: Pantheon.
Koestler, Arthur. 1972. *The roots of coincidence.* New York: Random House.
———. 1979. *Janus.* New York: Vintage Books.
Krippner, S., and A. Villoldo. 1976. *The realms of healing.* Millbrae, California: Celestial Arts.
Krippner, Stanley, ed. 1977. *Psychoenergetic systems.* 2:1–185.
Lapponi, Joseph. 1974. In *Encyclopedia of Psychics Science.* New York: University Books.
———. 1907. *Hypnotism and spiritism.* New York: Longmans, Green & Co.
Leshan, L. 1976. *Alternate realities.* New York: M. Evans & Co.
———. 1978. Psi and altered states of consciousness: Necessary methods in physics and parapsychology. *Parapsychology Review.* 9:13–17.
Lichota, Fred. 1985. Personal communication (January–June).
McDougall, W. 1938. Fourth report on a Lamarckian experiment. *Journal of Psychology.* 28:321–45.
Manning, Mathew. 1974. *The link.* New York: Holt, Rinehart, and Winston.
Masters, Robert, and Jean Houston. 1966. *The varieties of psychedelic experience.* New York: Holt, Rinehart, and Winston.
Mauss, Marcel. 1972. A general theory of magic. New York: Norton.
Meek, George, ed. 1977. *Healers and the healing process.* Wheaton, Illinois: The Theosophical Publishing House.
Montagno, Elson de A. 1982. Informal observations from the symposium "Thomaz G. M. Coutinho: Three perspectives," *Centenary Conference of the Society of Psychical Research and the Parapsychology Association.* England: Cambridge University.
Morgan, Beverly. 1982. Personal communication.
Morton, Thomaz Green. 1982. Personal communication (September).
Motoyama, H. 1975. The ejection of energy from the chakra of yoga and the meridian points of acupuncture. Proceedings II *International Congress on Psychotronic Research.* Monte Carlo. pp. 375–386.
Muti, Luciano. 1982. Personal communication (October).

Opler, M. 1983. Some points of comparison and contrast between the treatment of functional disorders by Apache shamans and modern psychiatric practise. *American Journal of Psychiatry.* 92:1371–87.
Ovendon, Michael. 1984. Personal communication (August).
Owen, Iris. 1976. Continuation of the Philip experiment. *New Horizons.* 2: 3–6.
Owen, Iris M., and Margaret Sparrow. 1976. *Conjuring up Philip.* Toronto, Canada: Fitzhenry and Whiteside.
Owen, Iris M. 1982. This house is haunted. Book review. *Theta.* 10:46–47.
Palmer, John. 1971. Scoring on ESP tests as a function of belief in ESP 1. The sheep-goat effect. *Journal American Society of Psychical Research.* 65:373–408.
Panati, Charles. 1976. *The Geller Papers.* New York: Houghton Mifflin.
Pearce, Joseph C. 1981. *The bond of power.* New York: E. P. Dutton.
Playfair, Guy Lyon. 1976. *The indefinite boundary.* London: Souvenir Press.
———. 1980. *This house is haunted.* New York: Stein and Day.
Prewitt, Cheryl. 1981. *A bright shining place. The story of a miracle.* New York: Doubleday and Company.
Pribham, Karl H. 1969. The neurophysiology of remembering. *Scientific American* (January).
Pribham, Karl. 1986. The cognitive revolution and mind/brain issues. *American Psychologist.* 41:507–520.
Puharich, Andrija. *Uri.* New York, Doubleday & Company, 1974.
Pulos, Lee. 1980. Mesmerism revisited: The effectiveness of Esdaile's techniques in the production of deep hypnosis and total body hypnoanaesthesia. *American Journal Clinical Hypnosis.* 22:206–211.
Rao, K. R. 1973. An autobiographical note. *Parapsychology Review.* 4:13–15.
———. 1977. On the nature of psi. *Journal of Parapsychology.* 41:294–351.
Rhine, J. B. 1974. A new case of experimenter unreliability. *Journal of Parapsychology.* 38:2:215–25.
Richards, John Thomas. 1961–1981. *SORRAT: A history of the Neihardt psychokinesis experiments.* Metuchen, N.J.: Scarecrow Press.
Roberts, Jane. 1981. *The God of Jane.* New Jersey: Prentice-Hall Inc.
Robinson, Diana. 1981. *To stretch a plank.* Chicago: Nelson-Hall.
Rogo, D. Scott. 1982. *Miracles: A parascientific inquiry into wondrous phenomena.* New York: The Dial Press.
Roll, William G. 1982. *Centenary Conference of the Society of Psychical Research and the Parapsychology Association.* England: Cambridge University.
Roszak, Theodore. 1975. *Unfinished animal.* New York: Harper and Row.
Ryzl, M. 1962. Training the psi faculty by hypnosis. *Journal Society Psychical Research.* 41:234–52.
Sannella, Lee. 1976. *Kundalini—psychosis or transcendence?* San Francisco, 3101 Washington Street (Published Privately).
Schatzman, Morton. 1980. *The story of Ruth.* New York: Putnam.
Scott, Mary. 1983. *Kundalini in the physical world.* Boston: Routledge and Kegan Paul.

Sheldrake, Rupert. 1981. *A new science of life: The hypothesis of formative causation.* Los Angeles: J. P. Tarcher.
Sheldrake, Rupert. 1983. Tests support Sheldrake theory. *Brain/Mind Bulletin.* 8: (September 12).
Shuhuang, Lin, et al. 1983. Some experiments with the moving of objects through exceptional functions of the human body. *Psi Research.* 2:4–24.
Simonton, O. Carl, S. Mathews-Simonton, and James Creigton. 1978. *Getting well again.* Los Angeles: J. P. Tarcher, Inc.
Stanford, Ray. 1974. Interview, psychic. 5:6–11.
Tart, Charles. 1964. A comparison of suggested dreams occurring in hypnosis and sleep. *International Journal of Clinical Experimental Hypnosis.* 12:263–89.
Tiller, William A. 1978. *A lattice model of space.* Phoenix. 2:27–48.
Vasiliev, L. I. 1976. *Experiments in distant influence.* New York: E. P. Dutton & Co., 1976 (originally published as *Experiments in mental suggestions,* 1963).
Walker, E. H. 1974. *Consciousness and quantum theory, in psychic exploration: A challenge for science,* edited by John White. New York: Putnam.
———. 1975. Foundations of paraphysical and parapsychological phenomena in L. Oteri (Ed). *Quantum Physics and Parapsychology.* New York: Parapsychology Foundation.
Watson, Lyall. 1979. *Lifetide.* London: Hodder and Strougton Ltd.
White, Rhea A. 1982. An analysis of ESP phenomena in the saints. *Parapsychology Review.* 13:15–18.
Wilson, Colin. 1978. *Mysteries.* New York: G. P. Putnam's Sons.
Winkelman, Michael. 1982. Magic: A theoretical reassessment. *Current Anthropology.* 23:37–66.
Zanatto, Arnaldo. 1982. Personal communication (October).